David Bell...y's

Mountains & Moorlands

IN WATERCOLOUR

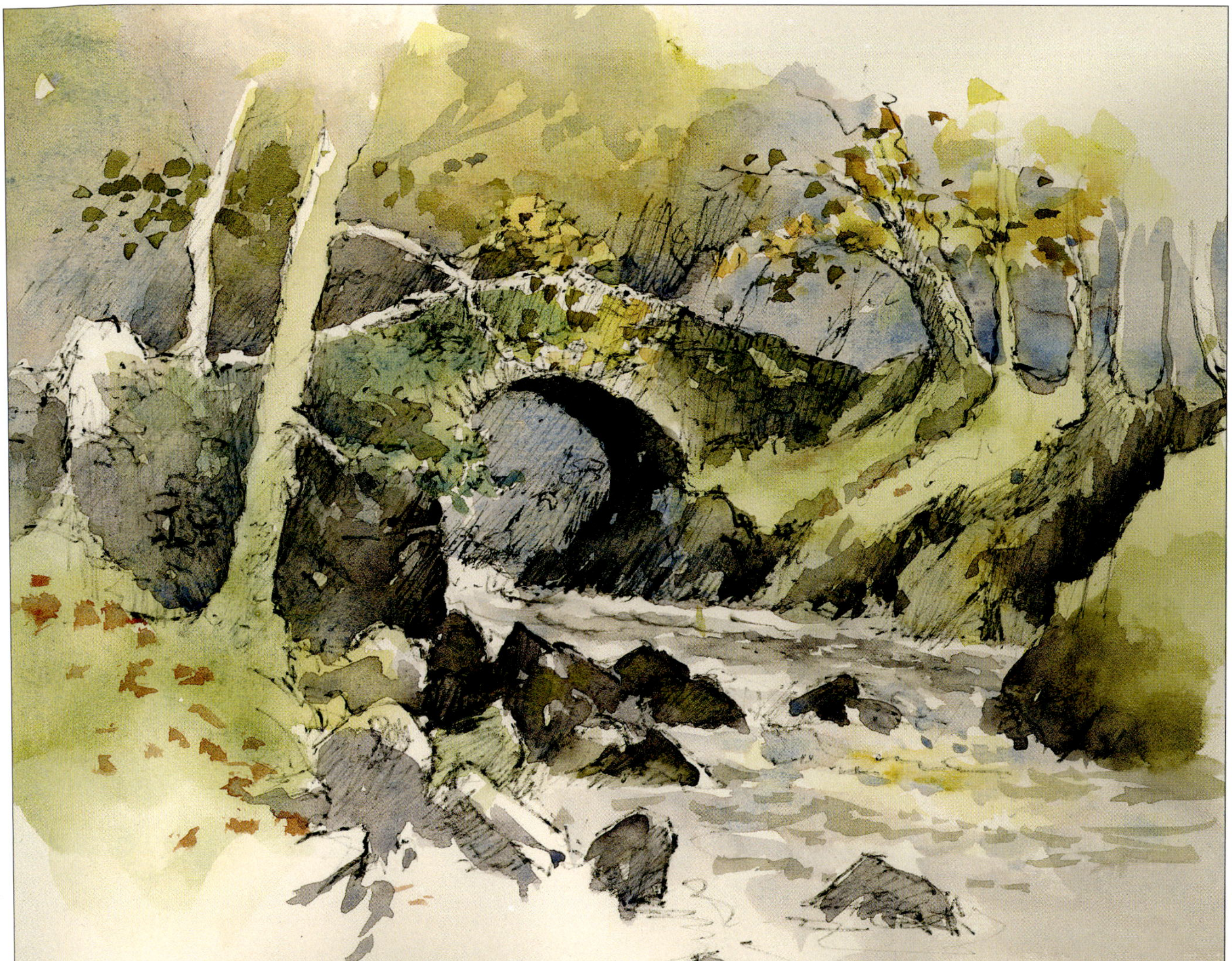

Dedication

To Carrie, who loves the mountains but hates going up them.

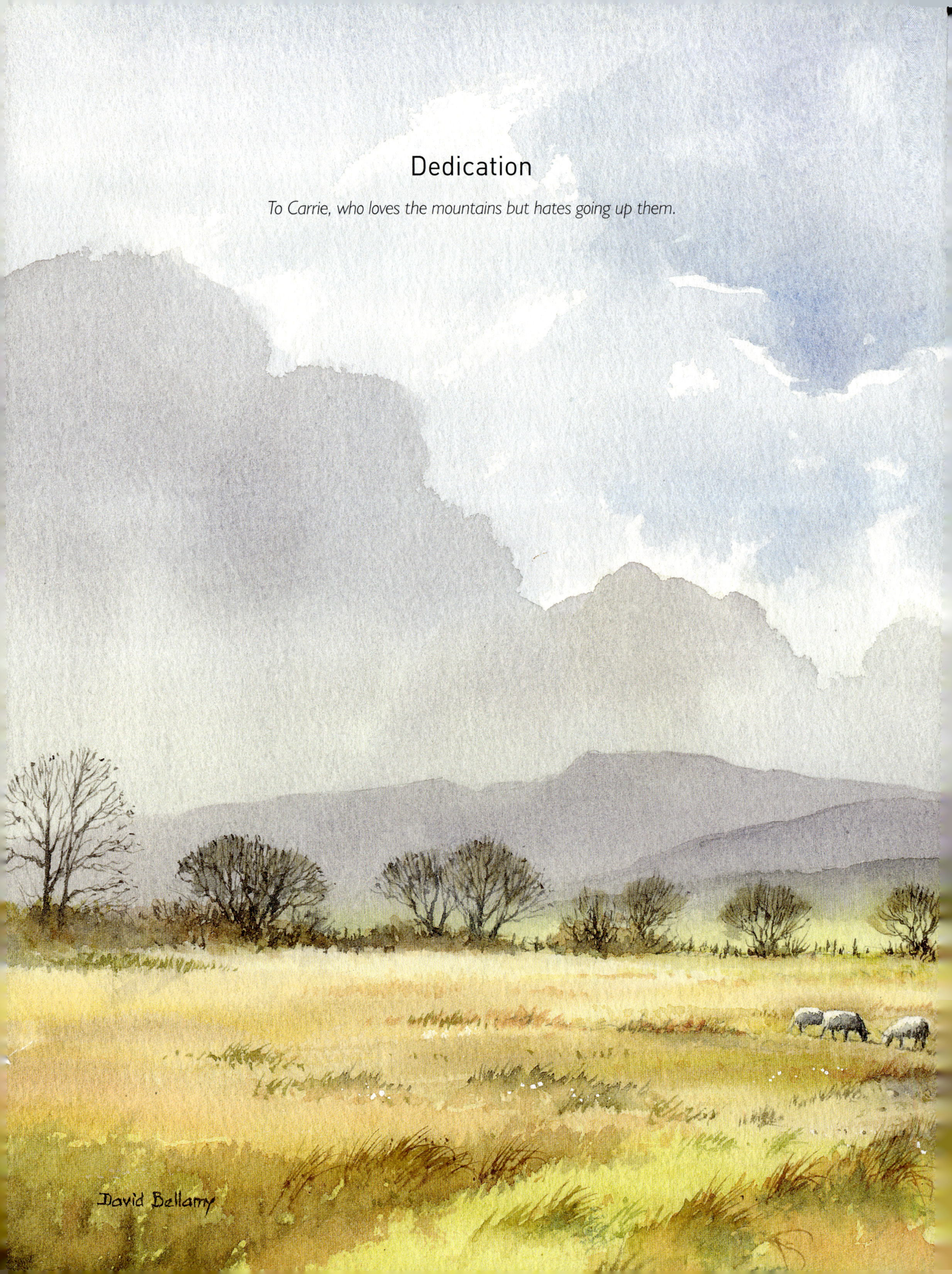

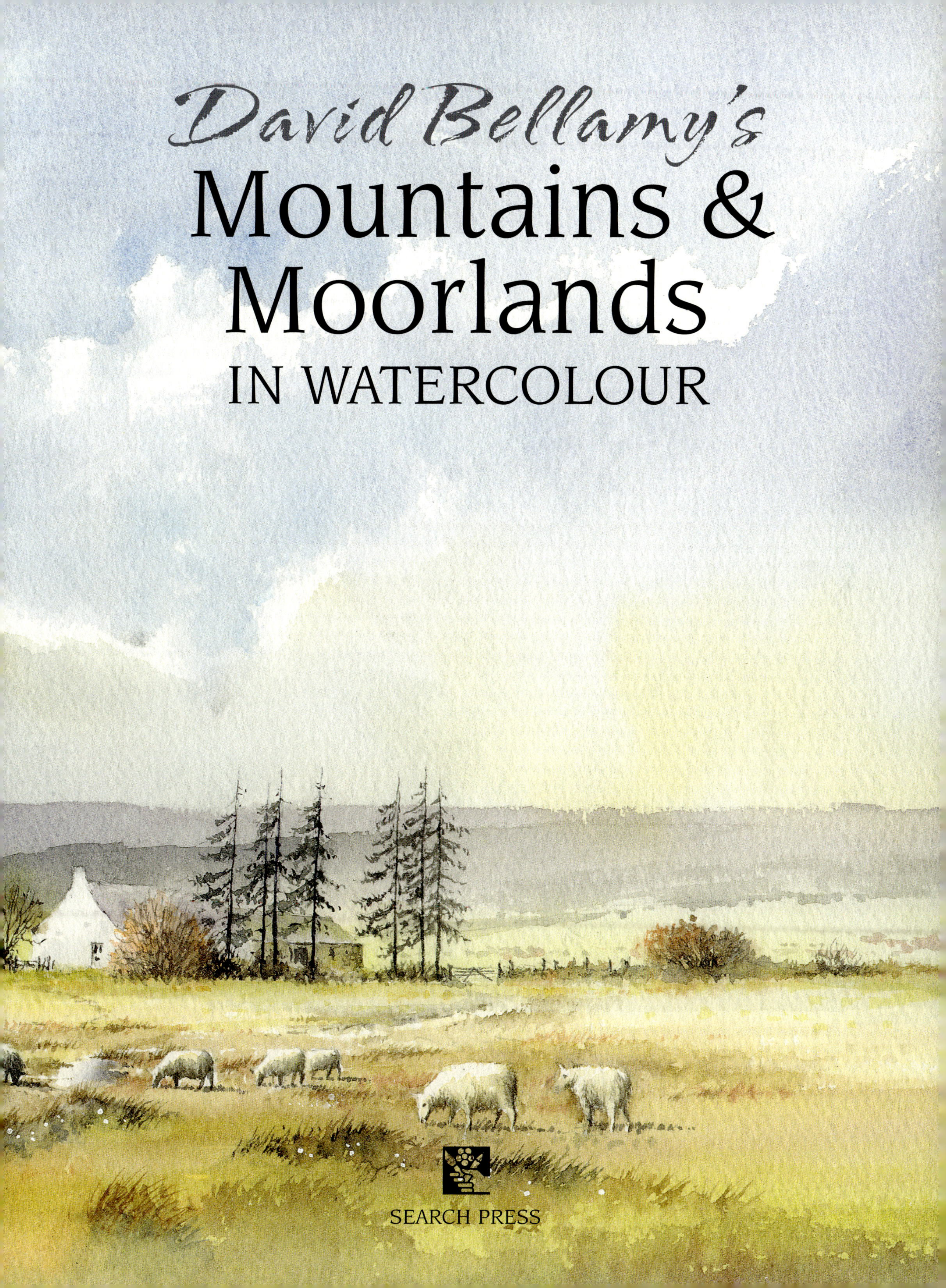

David Bellamy's

Mountains & Moorlands

IN WATERCOLOUR

SEARCH PRESS

First published in Great Britain 2010

Search Press Limited
Wellwood, North Farm Road,
Tunbridge Wells, Kent TN2 3DR

Reprinted 2011, 2012, 2016

Photographs by Roddy Paine Photographic Studios

ISBN: 978-1-84448-583-3

The Publishers and author can accept no responsibility for any consequences arising from the information, advice or instructions given in this publication.

Suppliers
If you have difficulty in obtaining any of the materials and equipment mentioned in this book, then please visit the Search Press website for details of suppliers: www.searchpress.com

Publisher's note
All the step-by-step photographs in this book feature the author, David Bellamy, demonstrating his watercolour painting techniques. No models have been used.

You are invited to visit the author's website: www.davidbellamy.co.uk

Printed in Malaysia

Acknowledgements

I am indebted to Jenny Keal and also to Roz Dace and Sophie Kersey at Search Press for all their help and encouragement.

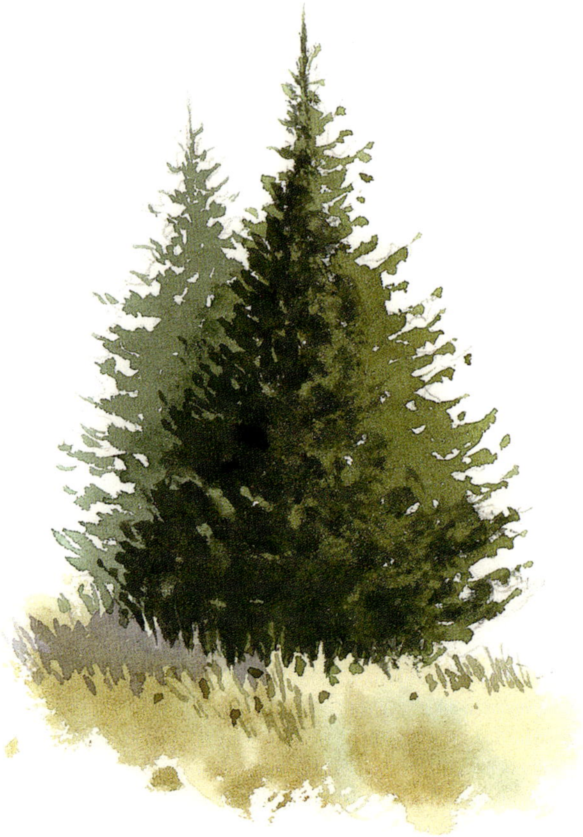

Front cover
Stream in the Dolomites
22.8 x 16.5cm (9 x 6½in)
Also shown on page 25.

Page 1
Bridge on the River Artro

Pages 2–3
Moorland Farm
28 x 43.2cm (11 x 17in)
Also shown on page 44.

Contents

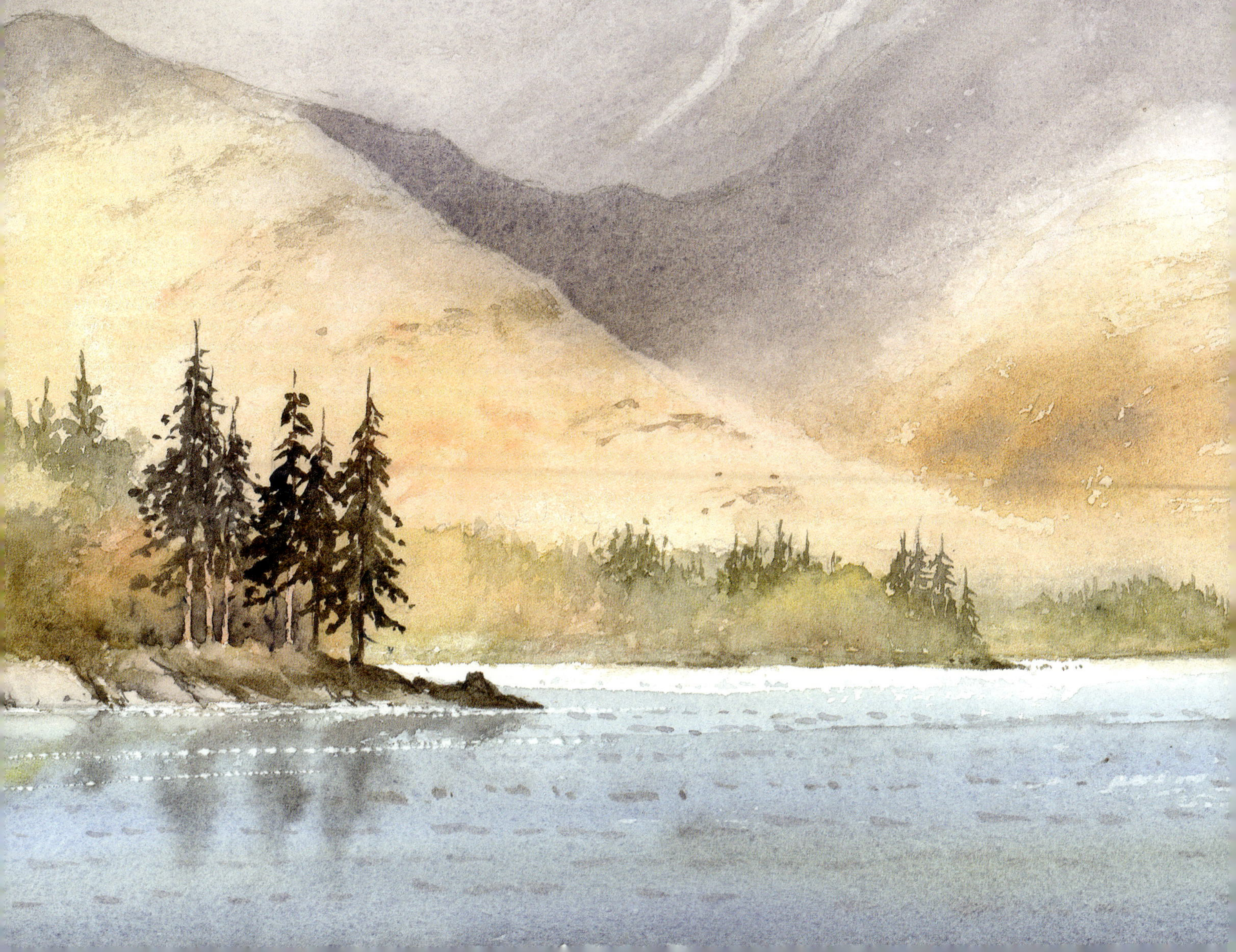

Introduction

The more uncultivated landscapes of mountain and moor have held great fascination down the years as subject matter for landscape painters. In the early days they were seen as places of terror and mystery, the haunts of bandits and the like, and attracted dramatic descriptions such as 'the horrid graces of wilderness' as Lord Shaftesbury put it in 1709. He was actually eulogising the beauty of raw nature.

In this book we are not just concerned with the savage places, but chiefly the outstanding scenery encompassed within the mountain and moorland environment. Many of the techniques and examples are applicable to lowland landscapes, of course, but in the mountains you are far more likely to find rustic subjects such as ancient dwellings, rutted cart tracks (yes, even ruts can have tremendous visual appeal) and colourful characters, and where better to find waterfalls and tumbling, rocky streams that are delightful companions as you seek that ideal subject? They are also great places to get away from people who look

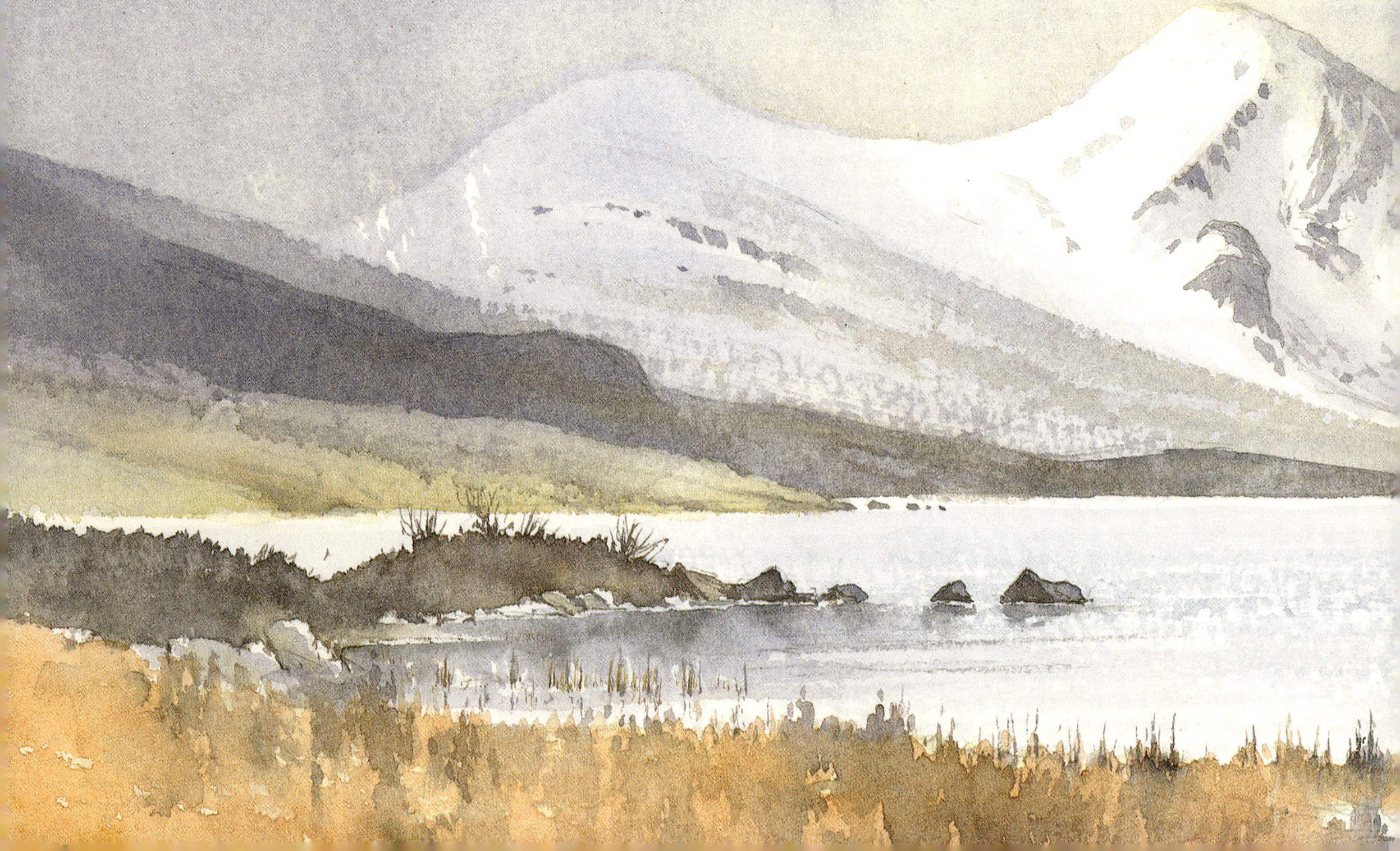

over your shoulder and comment on how beautiful your painting is, even when you've only drawn a couple of lines.

Whether you enjoy painting mountains as a backdrop to a floral extravaganza in some Alpine meadow, or perhaps recording the 'horrid graces' with pencil in one hand whilst clinging to a precipitous crag with the other, this book is aimed at helping your work along. Being amidst nature, well away from the noise and bustle of those frightful cities, gives me the most pleasure, and to be able to record these moments and places is sheer joy. I hope that while you may get great satisfaction out of painting from the ideas in this book, you will also feel the utter peace and tranquillity of being away from the stresses of modern life. Enjoy your painting.

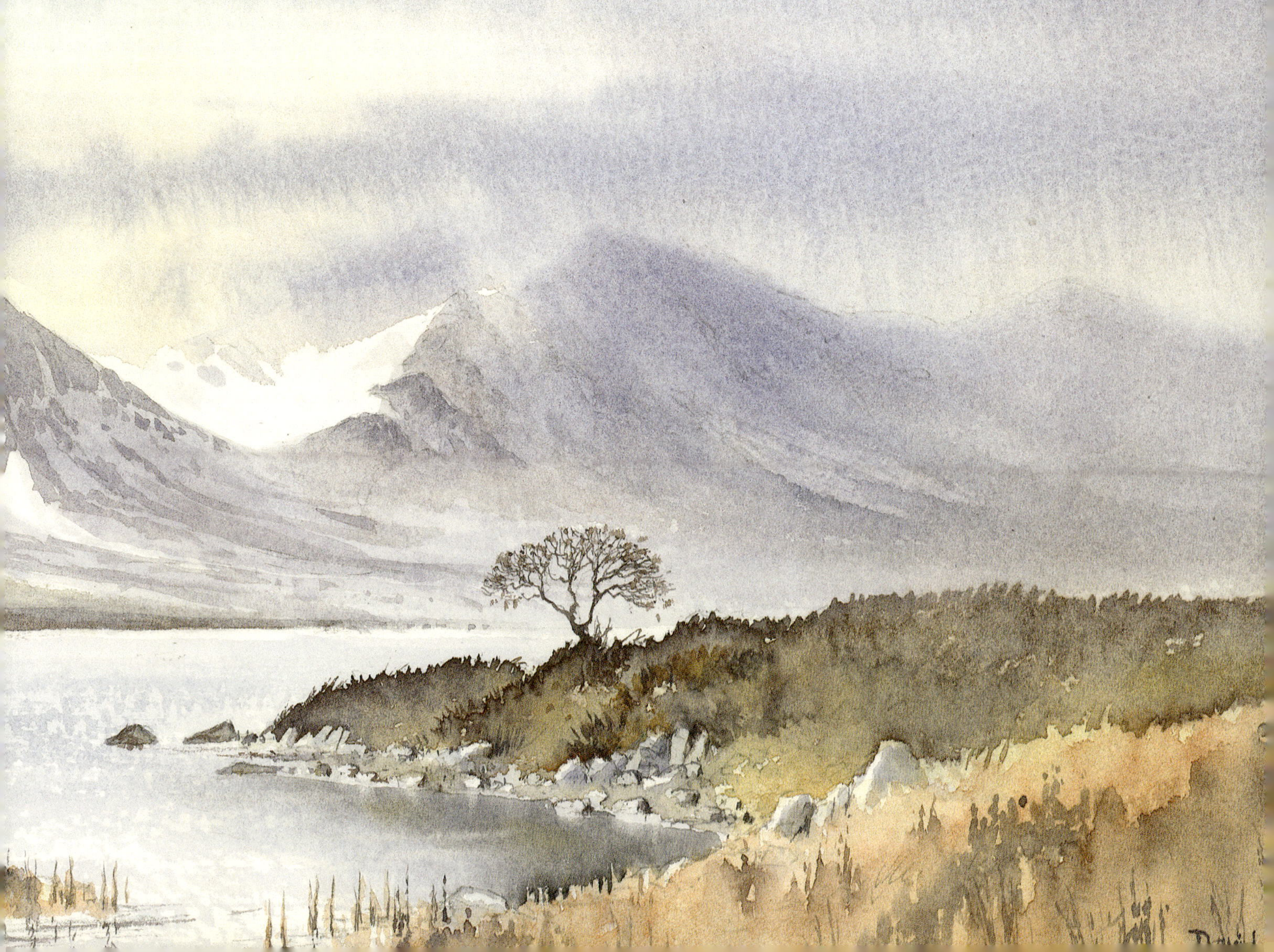

Blackmount
28 x 45.7cm (11 x 18in)

The water of the loch has been kept simple with just faint dry brushing horizontally across the central band, and only a hint of reflections in the more sheltered waters in the foreground. The dry brush technique has also been used over the gently sloping left-hand mountainside. The small tree not only forms the focal point, but is important in breaking up the strong horizontal nature of the composition.

Materials

I always try to use the best quality materials available, but for someone who is inexperienced or simply painting as a hobby, there are excellent less expensive alternatives. In this section we will briefly cover the necessities for watercolour painting.

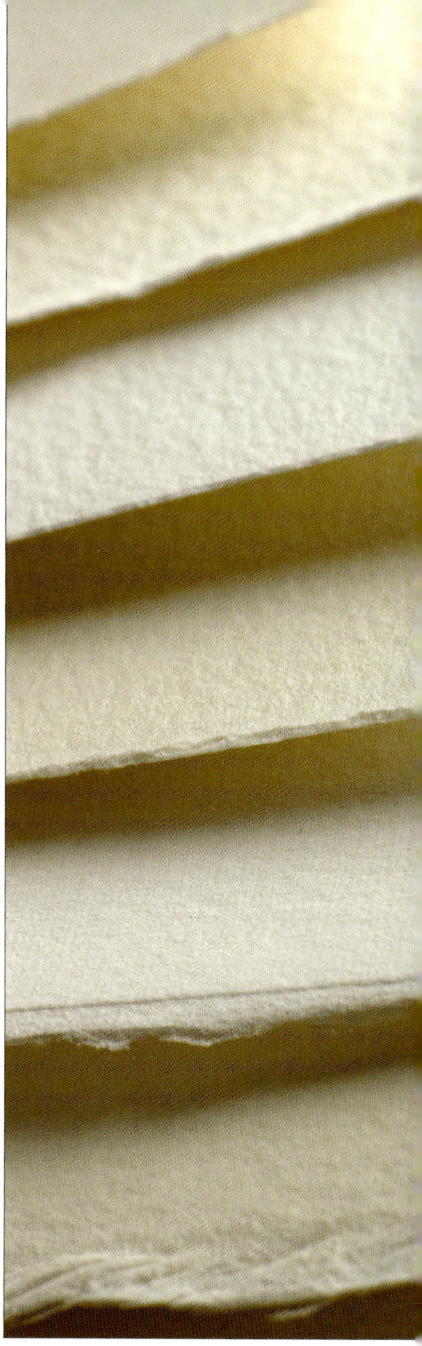

Paints

The finest paints are artists' quality, though they tend to be more expensive than the students' variety which are less finely ground and not so powerful. Inexperienced artists may well find students' colours perfectly fine until they become more proficient. In the studio I prefer to use tube colours because I can squeeze out as much paint as I need for mixing, but outdoors, a small box of half-pan watercolours is usually more convenient, especially when working to a smaller size. Uncapping several tubes in icy conditions on a windswept mountain ridge is no fun.

Each individual has a preference for colours, and the list I recommend should be changed and added to according to your taste as you gain experience. If you add one or two new colours at a time, you can gradually get to know their characteristics without feeling overwhelmed by a mass of colours. Avoid fugitive colours as these will fade with time and then your painting may well take on a strange appearance. Some artists only use transparent colours, avoiding the more opaque ones, but most transparent colours are difficult to lift out. Many prefer raw sienna to yellow ochre, for example, but I love the more opaque yellow ochre as it is such a good colour for dropping into a wet wash to create a variegated effect.

My basic colours are: French ultramarine, burnt umber, cadmium yellow pale, cadmium red, cobalt blue, new gamboge, light red, Winsor blue or phthalo blue, yellow ochre or raw sienna and alizarin crimson or quinacridone red. Other useful colours are: aureolin, burnt sienna, cadmium orange, cerulean blue, indigo, Naples yellow, perylene maroon, vermilion hue and viridian.

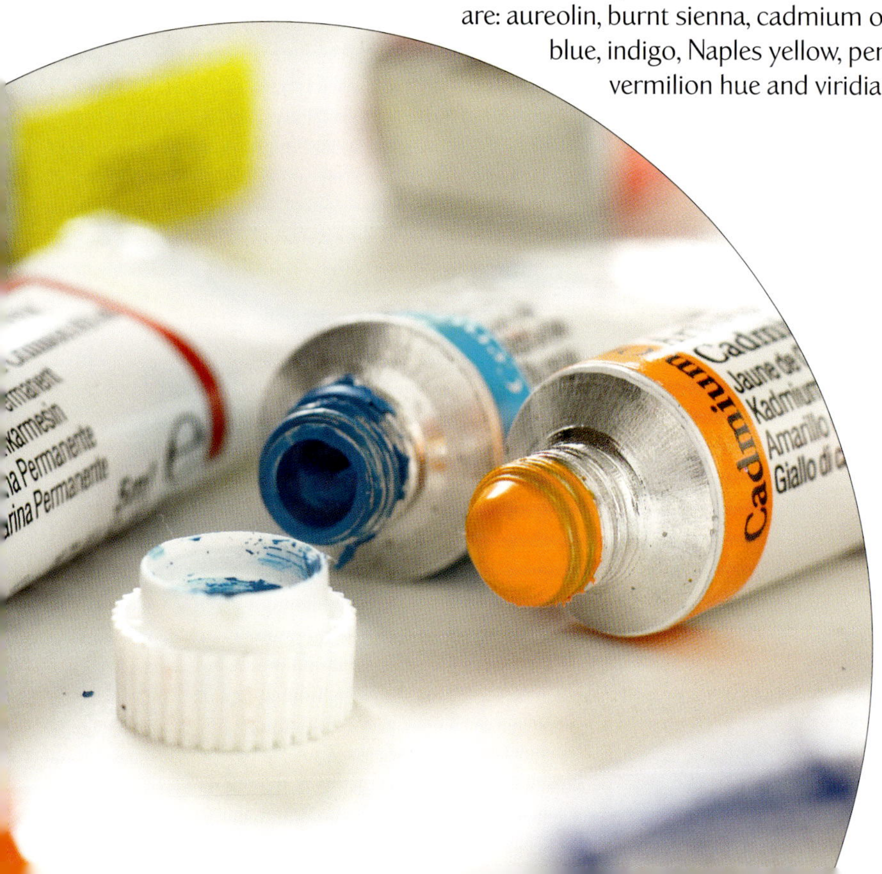

Paper

Watercolour paper normally comes in three types of surface: Rough, Not or Cold Pressed, and Hot Pressed. A Rough surface is excellent for creating textures, ragged edges to a wash or broken colour, so for subjects such as wind-torn clouds, rough mountain slopes or sparkling water it makes life easier for the artist. It is slightly less effective when you are describing fine detail. For really fine detail, the Hot Pressed surface is superb, but as it dries quicker than the other types, it can be a challenge for the less experienced artist. The most popular and versatile surface is the Not (short for not hot pressed), or as it is sometimes known, Cold Pressed. While not so good at rough edges as the Rough surface, it is better for a more detailed subject.

The papers are available in several weights, usually ranging from the rather flimsy 190gsm (90lb) which definitely needs to be stretched on a board, to the 300gsm (140lb) which is best stretched first, to 425gsm (200lb) which can be painted on without stretching unless you work large and use copious amounts of water, and the 640gsm (300lb) which is like thick cardboard and does not need stretching.

To stretch watercolour paper, I cut strips of gummed tape to the length of the four edges, immerse the sheet in water for a few seconds and then hold it up to drip off until the paper is just damp. The damp paper is then placed over the drawing board and stuck down with the gummed strips which have been wetted. The board then needs to be laid flat and allowed to dry. Most of the paintings in this book have been done on Saunders Waterford or Bockingford papers. Waterford, a robust paper that stands up well to harsh techniques such as vigorous sponging and scratching, has always had a slightly off-white tint, but is now available in brilliant High White.

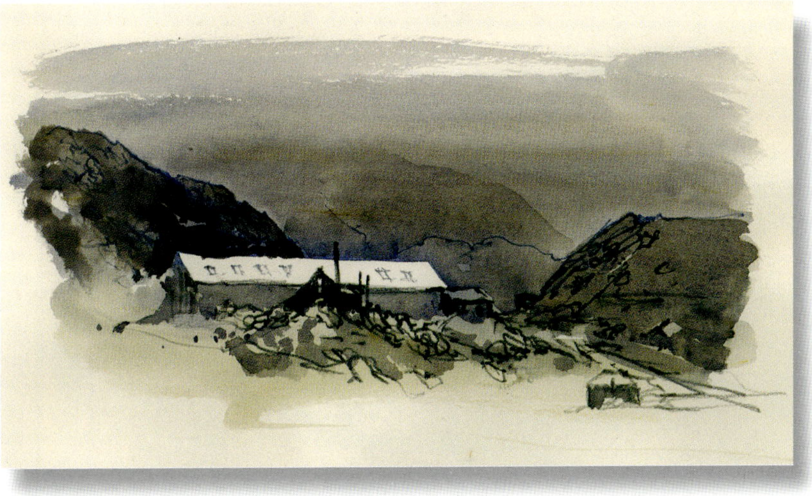

This watercolour sketch of quarry buildings shows the crisp, sharp edges that can be achieved using Hot Pressed (smooth) watercolour paper.

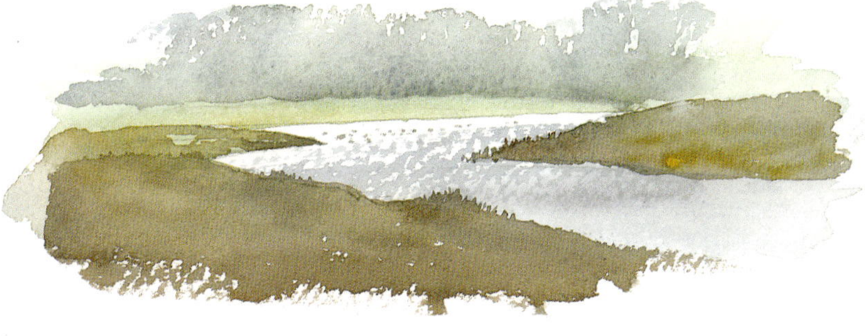

Rough watercolour paper is ideal for creating sparkle and interest on water and other surfaces, as well as ragged edges to objects. The effect is achieved with the dry brush technique, which means dragging a damp (not wet) brush across the paper surface. Experiment with different paper surfaces using reasonably large brushes.

Brushes and pencils

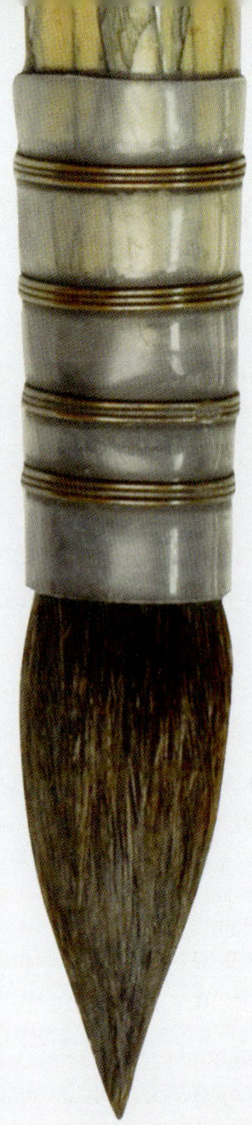

The sable is the finest watercolour brush because of its holding capacity and ability to instantly spring back into shape , but there are many synthetic brushes and some with a mixture of sable and synthetic which work well. It is better to have a few good-quality brushes than to buy a whole range of cheaper ones. You will need a mop brush for the large washes – squirrel-hair mops hold a lot of paint although they do lose their hairs from time to time. A number 10 or 12 round brush with a fine point, a number 6 and a 3 or 4 will give you a good range to start with, together with a number 1 rigger for fine detail. A 13mm (½in) flat can be useful for certain techniques and I often use a 6mm (¼in) flat for correcting mistakes as will be seen later in the book.

Use a range of pencils from 2B to 4B at least. The 2B is excellent for very detailed drawing and the softer ones not only show up better when laying and over-laying washes, but can be erased easily.

The brushes used for the demonstrations in this book: large squirrel mop, vital for laying washes; sable brushes in no. 10, no. 7, no. 4 and no. 1 round, no. 1 rigger, 6mm (¼in) flat and 13mm (½in) flat, a fan brush and a Series 7 finest sable no. 8 round. The 6mm (¼in) flat brush is excellent for correcting minor errors, such as when a wash has slightly strayed too far. It is worth treating yourself to a really good sable, such as the no. 8 in the Series 7 Winsor & Newton range, which will show you how superior these brushes are. You could put it on your Christmas list! The pencils used were a 2B, 3B and 4B.

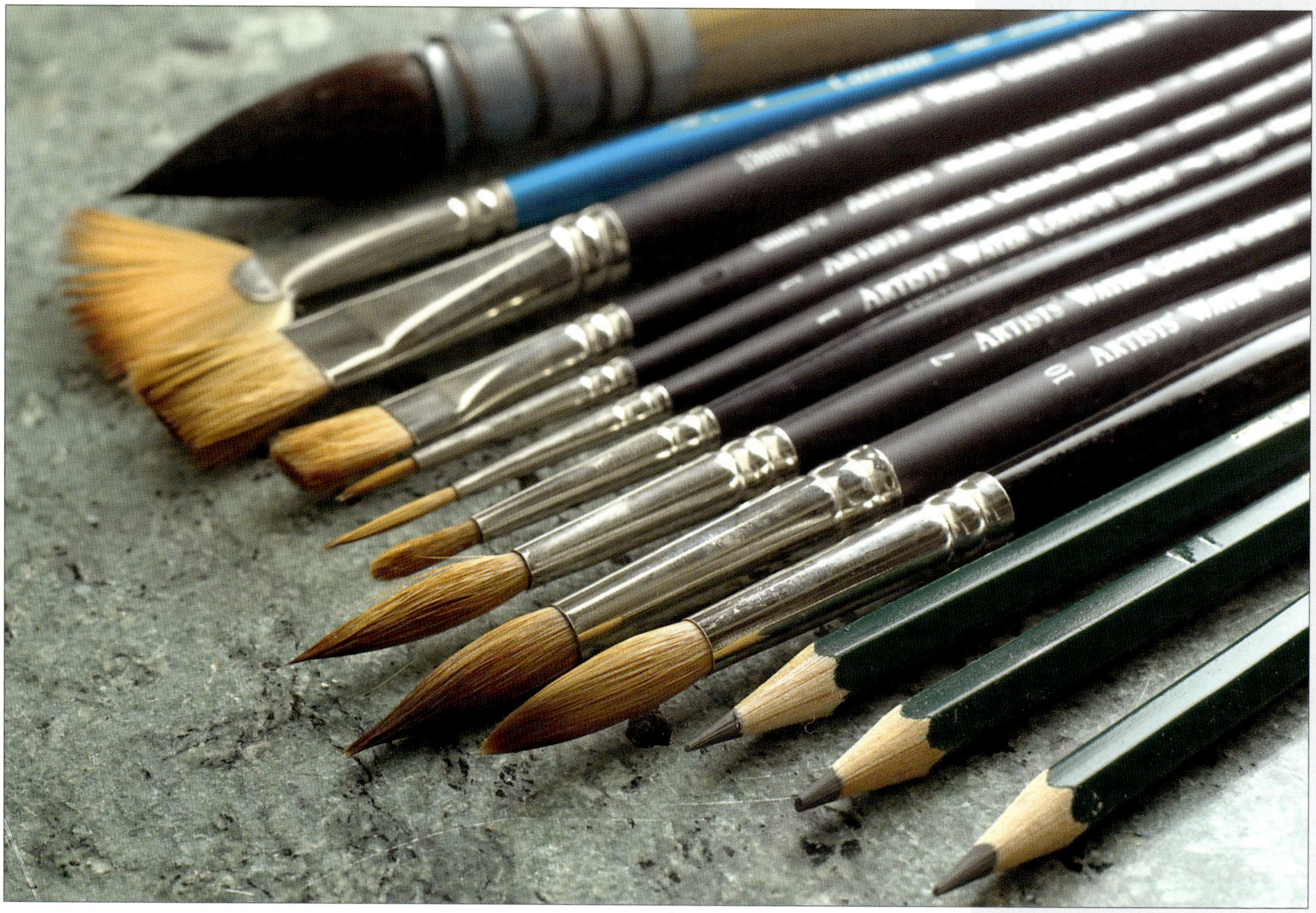

Other materials

The choice of palettes is wide to suit all tastes. One with deep wells for mixing large washes is vital and even saucers and dinner plates can work well, so long as they are white to allow you to clearly see the colours being mixed. Use a large water pot. A soft putty eraser is best for getting rid of unwanted pencil lines. A scalpel is useful for scratching thin lines, rags for wiping excess fluid off brushes, a natural sponge for softening areas of dried paint and bulldog clips for securing unstretched paper to the drawing board. A water spray can be excellent for suggesting texture and masking fluid for reserving white paper in places. Fibre-tipped and draughtsmens' pens and gummed tape for stretching paper complete the studio set-up.

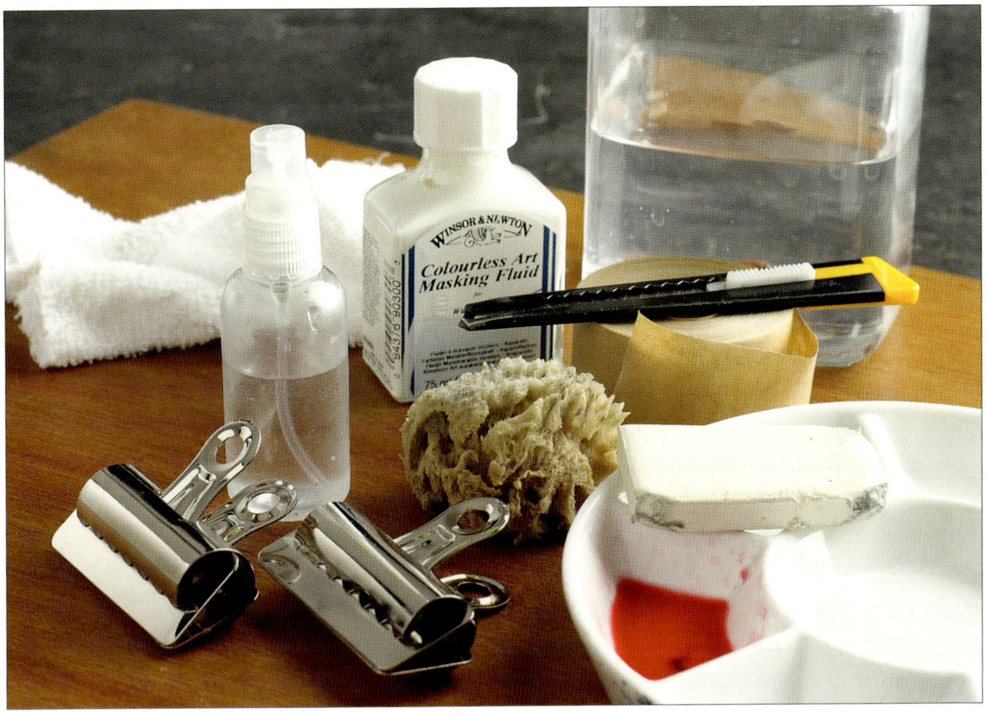

For working outdoors your kit will depend on how you work. Keep materials as few as possible so that it's easier and quicker to set up, especially if the weather is not too good. A lightweight easel can be a pain, as it blows over in any strong gusts. I prefer a heavier metal one which is more stable with less of an area to resist the wind. Cords and tent-pegs can anchor it down on the wilder days.

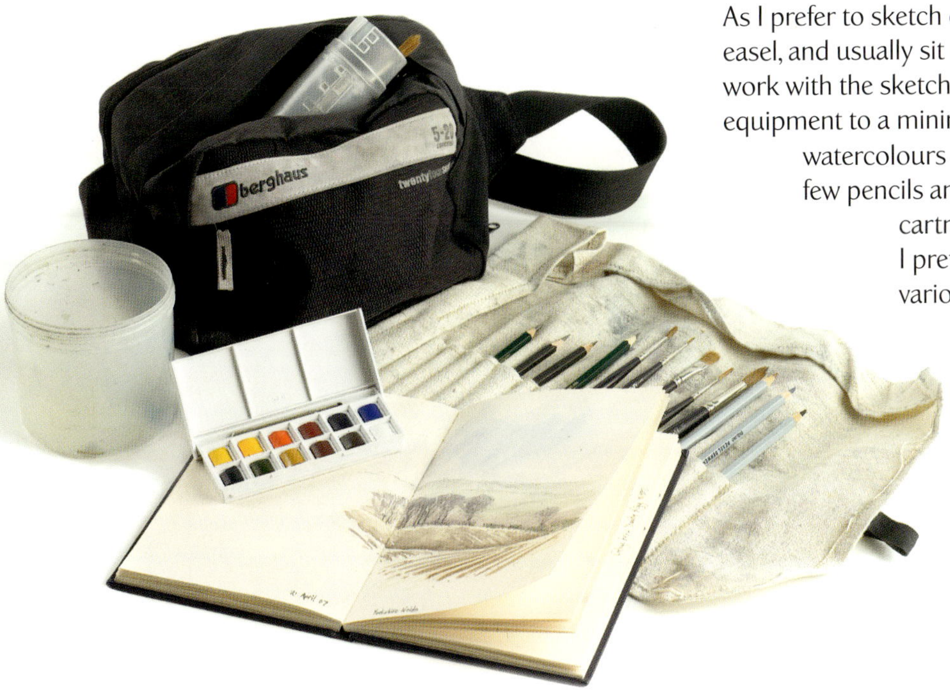

As I prefer to sketch out of doors, I rarely take the easel, and usually sit on a closed-cell foam pad while I work with the sketchbook on my knee. Keep sketching equipment to a minimum. A small box of half-pan watercolours is ideal for outdoors, plus a few pencils and brushes, and sketchbooks of cartridge and watercolour papers. I prefer hardback sketchbooks of various sizes in mainly portrait format, as these make it easy to work over double pages when I need more space. I also take watercolour and water soluble graphite pencils and a plastic water pot. I carry everything in a belt bag.

Finding subjects

Finding subjects to paint can be one of the chief joys of being an artist. Many people are reluctant to go out and sketch and it warms the heart to see the enthusiastic reaction of many coming on a course for the first time and discovering this way of working. Going out and seeking what you especially want to paint is rewarding, whether it's your mum's cottage, friends climbing a mountain, or maybe some favourite old moorland boulder. Believe me, there are distinctive rocks and crags all over the country which I regard as old friends, and have painted many times, with some appearing in paintings from Killarney to Kathmandu.

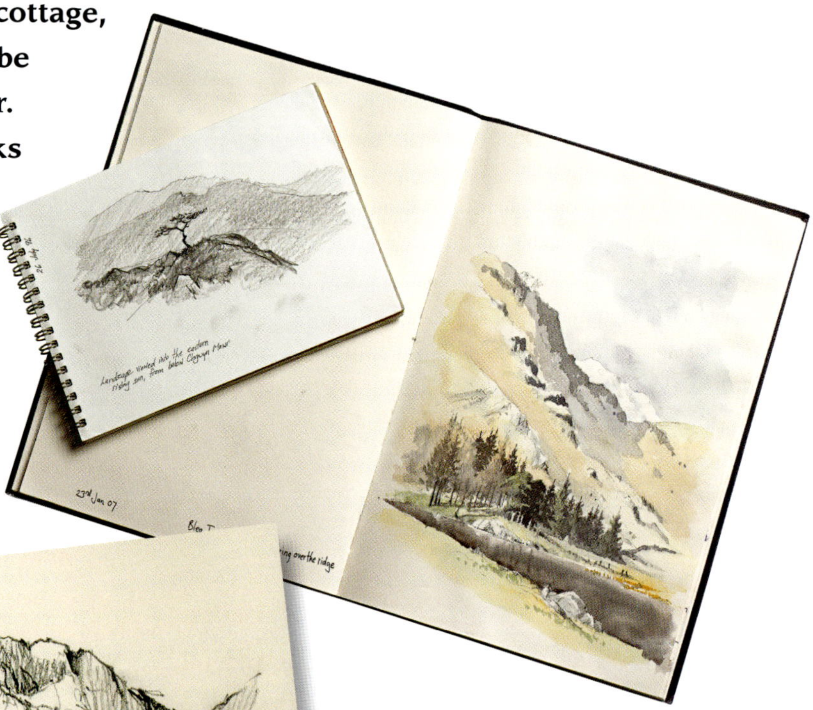

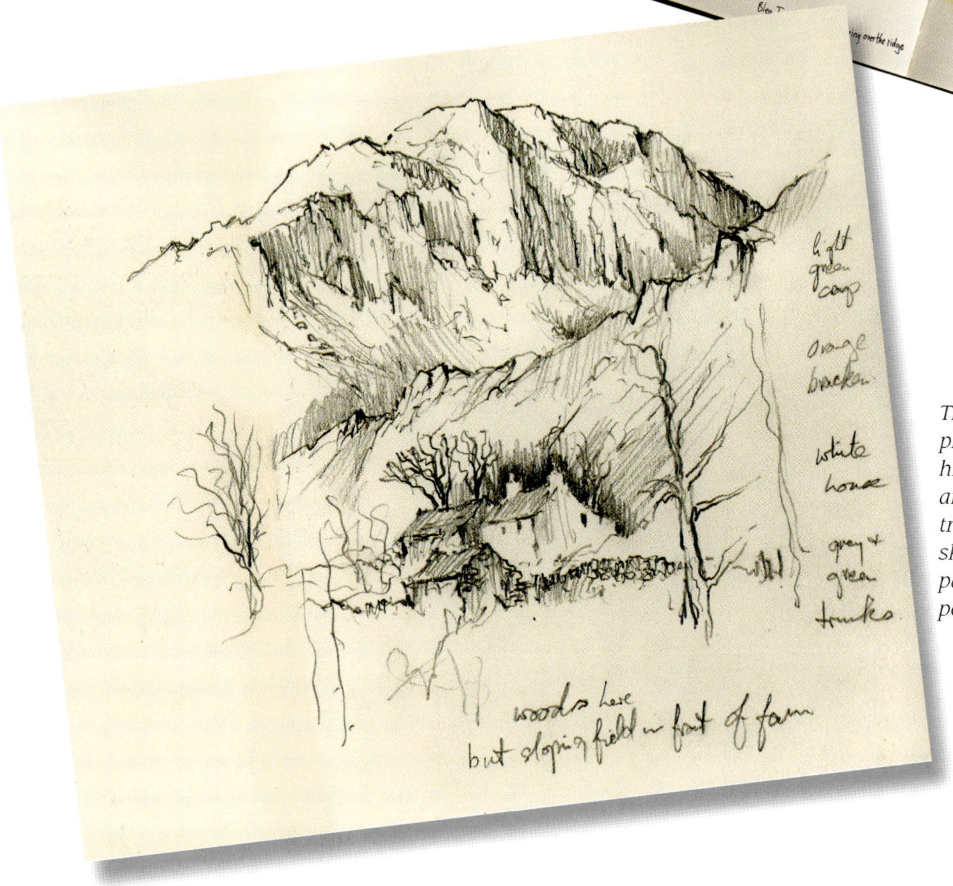

This subject was impossible to photograph properly because it was hidden by trees. However, by moving around I could easily see between the trunks of the trees and created a pencil sketch of the farm without difficulty. It pays to have a sketchbook and a few pencils with you all the time.

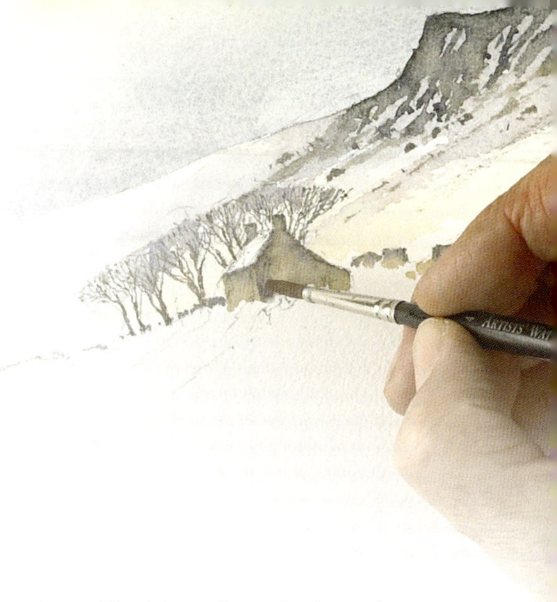

Sketching from a car

Many subjects worth sketching can easily be seen from the car, although finding a parking space can at times be difficult. I sometimes stop in a field gateway for a short while to carry out a quick sketch, but make sure I stay with the car and am ready to move on if someone wants to get through. Often the road itself can act as an excellent lead-in to a composition, and many is the time I have turned a major road into a dirt track. Whatever you do, safety and consideration for other people are paramount and I have never had any problems in this respect. Some maps indicate unfenced roads with dotted lines on each side, and this will give you a fair idea of roadside parking possibilities.

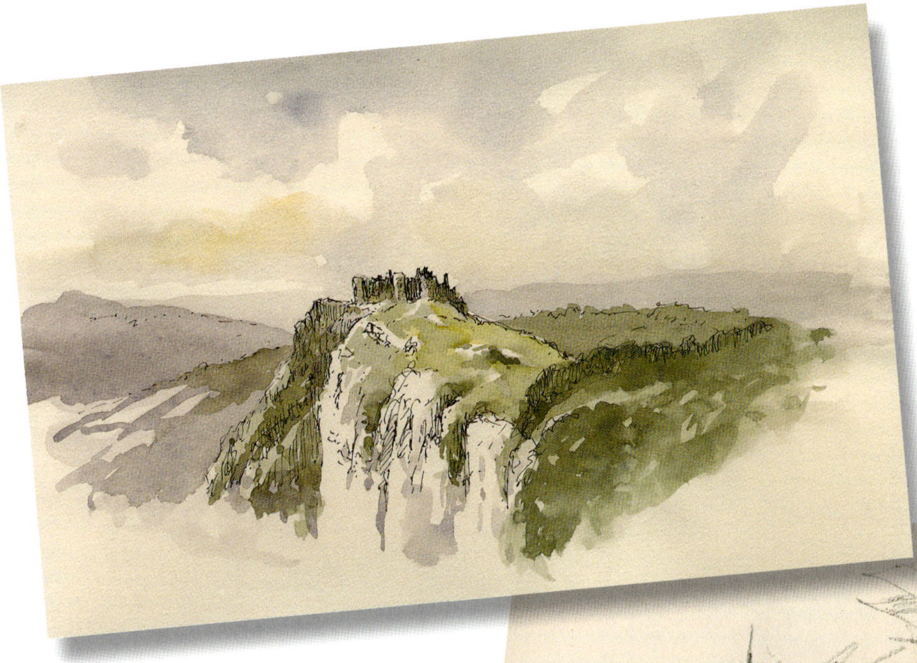

Subjects like this castle, set in dramatic moorland that seems to attract the most glorious atmospheric conditions, can be seen for miles from many directions, and are easily sketchable from a car.

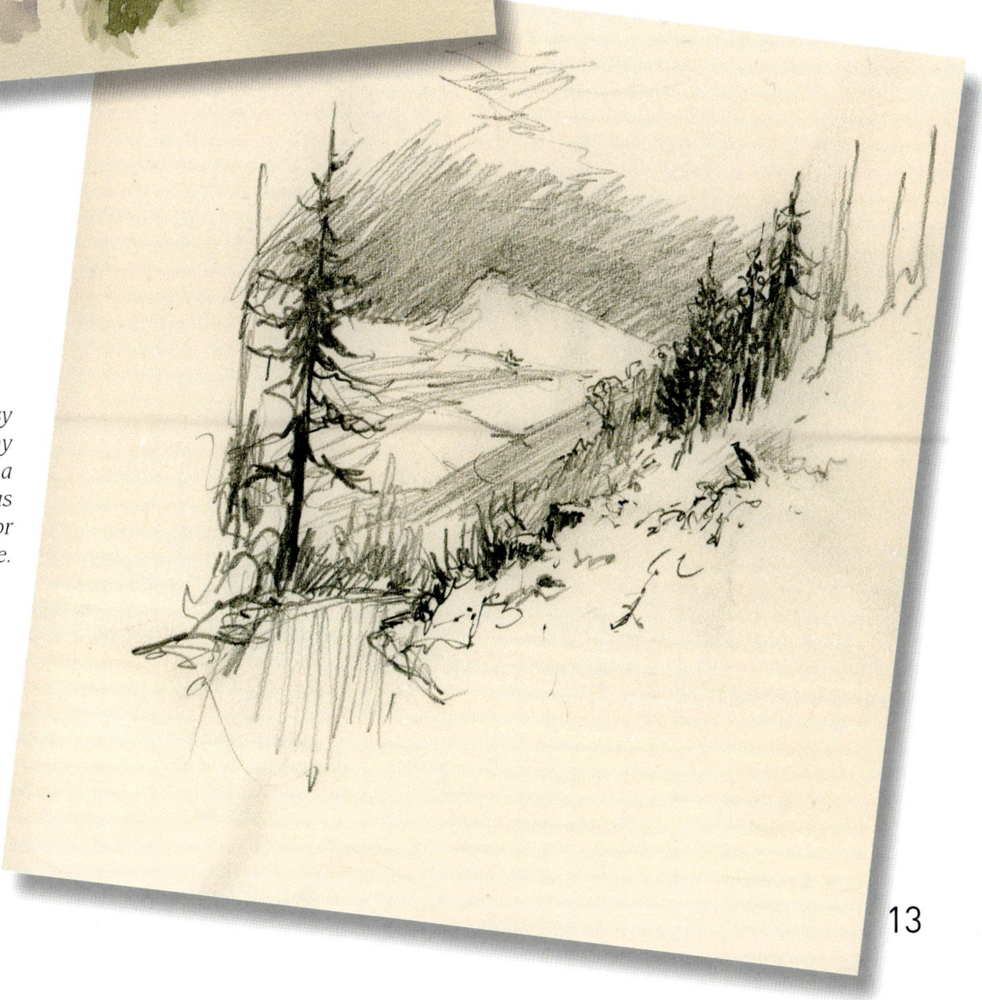

How often we see scenes from a busy main highway while driving along. Many of these can be captured safely from a lay-by, using the road as a lead-in, as in this case. Often I downgrade a major highway to a rustic old lane.

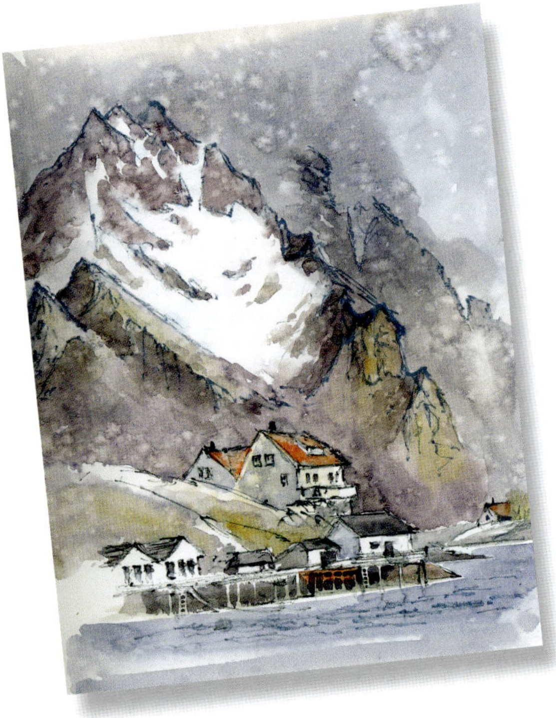

This watercolour sketch of Festvagtinden in Norway's Lofoten Islands was carried out with light rain falling on the paper, so I used watercolour pencils to strongly define the detail. Don't let the weather deter you when you're in front of a good subject – rain can often add a sense of spontaneity to an alfresco watercolour that cannot be achieved any other way.

Sketching in bad weather

While sketching inside a vehicle can make you feel safer and insulated from people who want to see what you are up to, there is nothing like getting out and wandering around for the optimum viewpoint. While it is good to go out in fine weather, don't always pick the sunny days: heavy rain gives waterfalls a much greater appeal and you may be able to sketch in between showers. Distant rain squalls can create a strong sense of mood and lose unwanted features. If a few rain spots spatter your sketch, it is no cause for alarm, and often it helps to suggest a spontaneous response to the scene. I sometimes draw into wet washes with a dark watercolour pencil (black, dark grey, indigo or sepia) to capture detail, and this works when the sketchbook is being spattered with rain.

Many waterfalls stand close to a road and make ready-made subjects needing little alteration in a great many cases. Study the maps to find them.

For the house-bound, acquiring subjects is not so easy. Friends and relatives might be cajoled into taking photographs of scenes for you, but this depends on how resourceful they are. Copying from books, calendars, magazines, etc, is an alternative, but lacks personal input. Maybe you have old photographs, or even memories that can be evoked. In each of these cases it pays to do some studio sketches to rough out the composition and make changes before deciding on the final design.

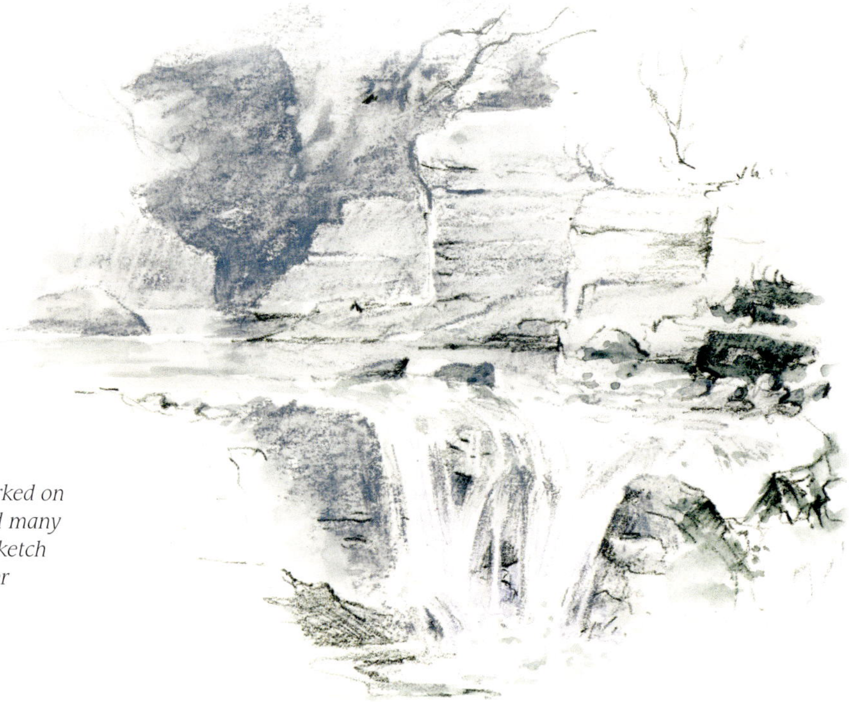

Waterfalls are normally marked on maps of 1:50,000 scale, and many are easily accessible. This sketch was carried out with a water soluble pencil.

Sketching figures

Some places, such as villages, call out for figures, while at other times you may wish to show the immense scale of a mountain by including tiny figures. Where you position them is critical: too close to the foreground and the figures may well dwarf the rest of the composition; too distant and they may become lost in the mass of scenery. A lone figure in a vast panorama is an excellent way of suggesting a sense of loneliness. If you are nervous about adding figures, keep a jar of clean water nearby so that if you make a mistake you can immediately wash it out with a large round brush. Dab the area with a tissue, wait for it to dry and have another go. It helps if you do not have any strong detail beside the figure. Be aware that if you include figures, they will instantly become the centre of interest.

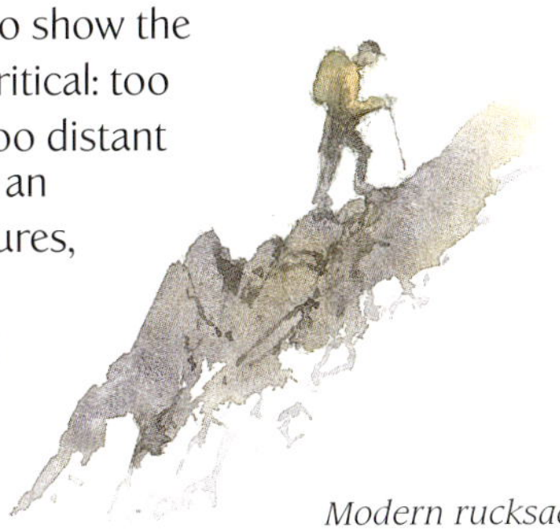

Modern rucksacks should sit fairly high up on the back

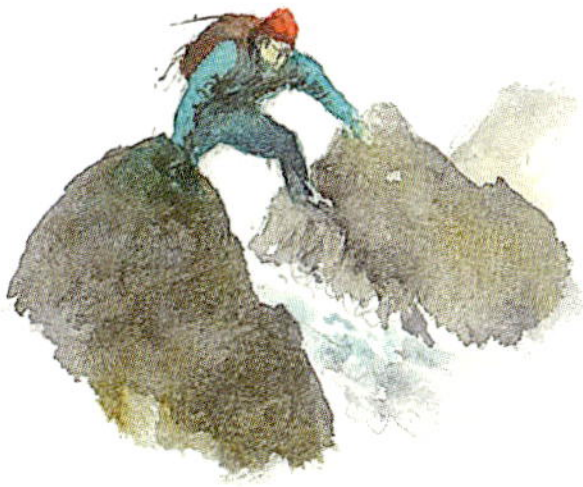

Figures are at their most convincing when seen doing something rather than standing dummy-like. Try to include some action if you can.

It took me some time to work out what this Ladakhi woman, from the northernmost state of India, was doing, as she was wrapped up in furs while weeding crops. Capturing poses like this is a delight.

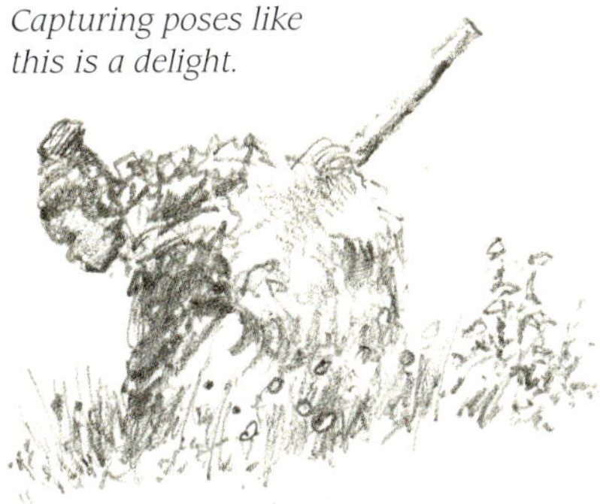

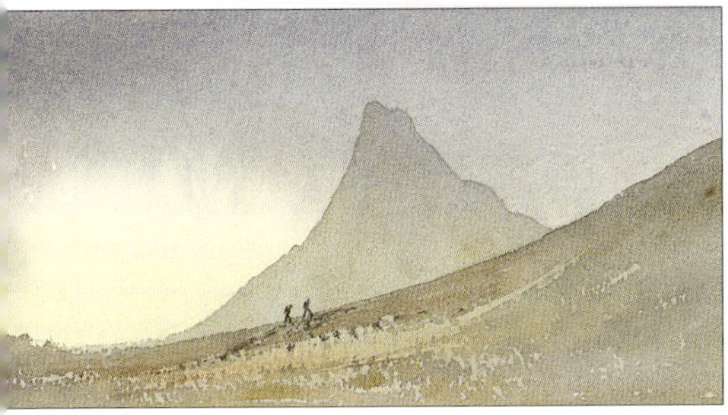

Placing tiny figures in a mountain landscape dramatically emphasises the massive scale of a peak, and at this range figures should present no difficulty.

Troller's Gill, Yorkshire
22.8 x 17.7cm (9 x 7in)

Sometimes a landscape calls out for figures, and this was one such scene. As I had included a ladder stile, the picture seemed empty without someone climbing it, or about to do so as in this case.

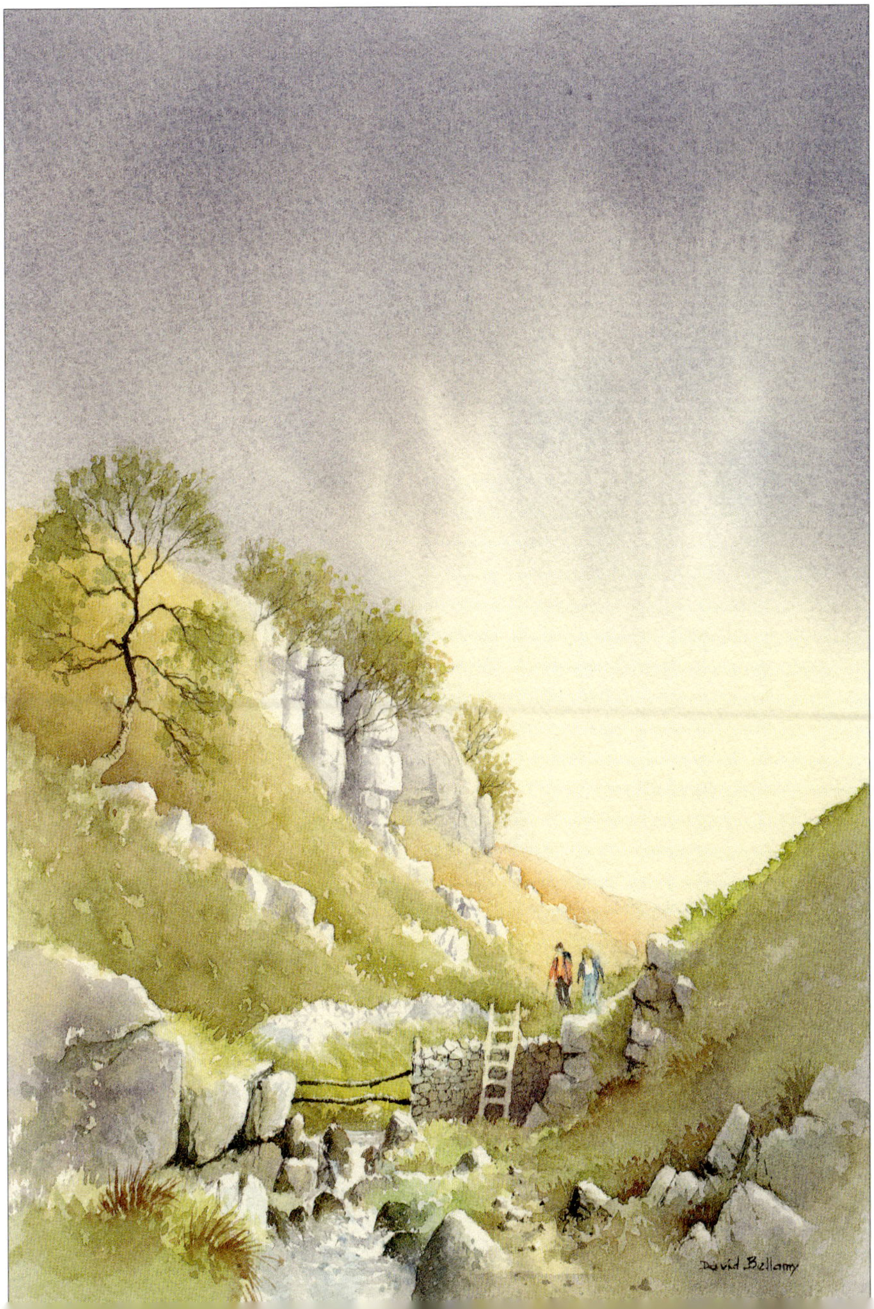

Animals

Like figures, animals will add life, scale and interest to your landscapes and it is worth building up a library of animal images in sketches and photographs to include in your scenes. If you position them against a fairly bland, uncluttered hillside, or perhaps mist, they will stand out. By altering the light and shadow you can turn them into a silhouette or light them up. When out capturing images of wild animals, I like to sketch as much as I can, but also take many photographs. Once, while stalking musk-oxen in Greenland, all my photographs turned out to be under-exposed rubbish, but my sketches, done through binoculars mounted on a tripod, saved the day. The biggest danger of painting animals from photographs is that of making the beasts appear like wooden carvings.

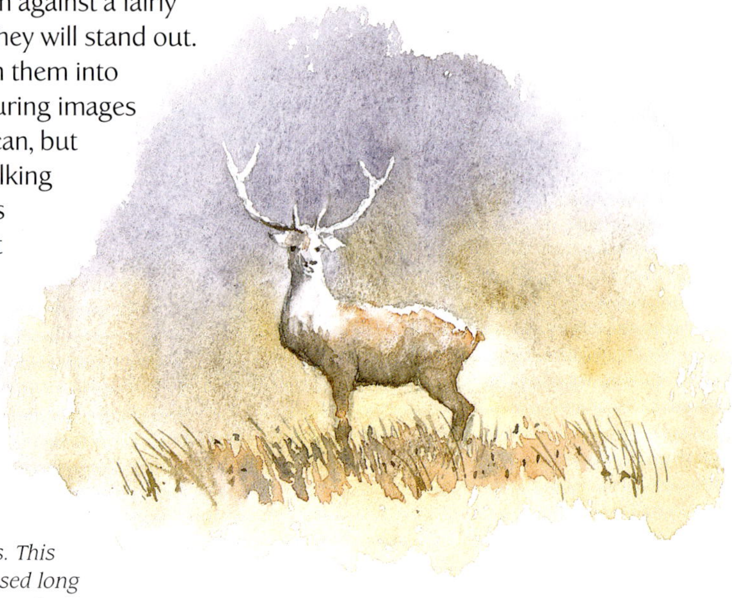

Animals can enhance a scene, or act as the centre of interest, so I take every opportunity to do studies of all manner of wildlife when the opportunity arises. This stag appeared from behind vegetation and boldly posed long enough for me to carry out a sketch and take photographs.

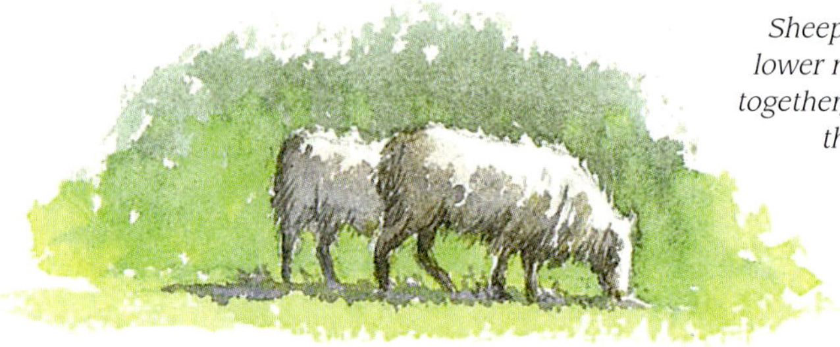

Sheep add life and interest to scenes on the lower mountain slopes. Bunch some of them together, overlapping them as in this study, as they are extremely gregarious creatures.

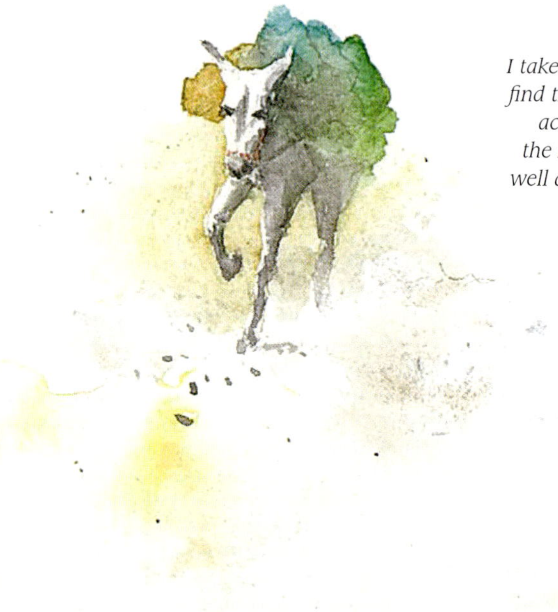

I take many photographs of moving animals but I find there is nothing like sketching to capture the actual sense of movement. A slight blurring of the legs or wings will suggest a moving limb, as well as creating a pose that shows the beast with its legs in a moving position, as in this case.

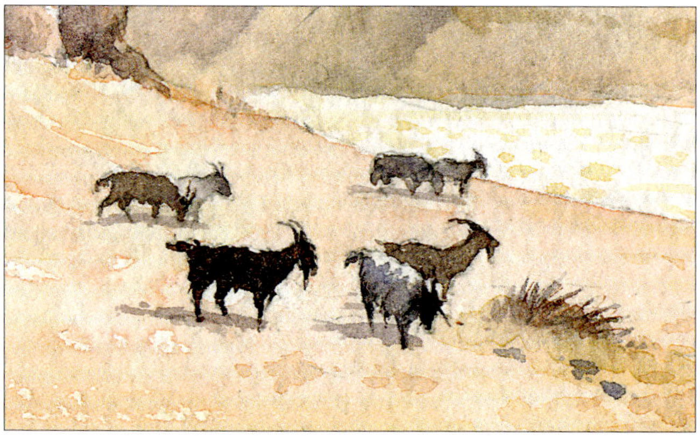

Goats

Working from photographs

The ease with which we can photograph a scene now makes the camera a versatile tool for the landscape artist. Even my small compact camera has a powerful zoom lens which can bring distant images close-up. Make good use of this facility and take a number of photographs of the scene from different ranges and angles. If the lighting is tricky, then take several shots with different settings to over- and under-expose the image, as this technique will doubtless make one part of the image much better exposed.

When working from photographs back at home, it helps to do a studio sketch from the photograph first. This will help you work out the composition, as you will see in the example. In this way you can change emphasis or tones, rearrange the image and add and subtract features before you do the final drawing. Try to avoid slavishly following the detail when working directly from a photograph.

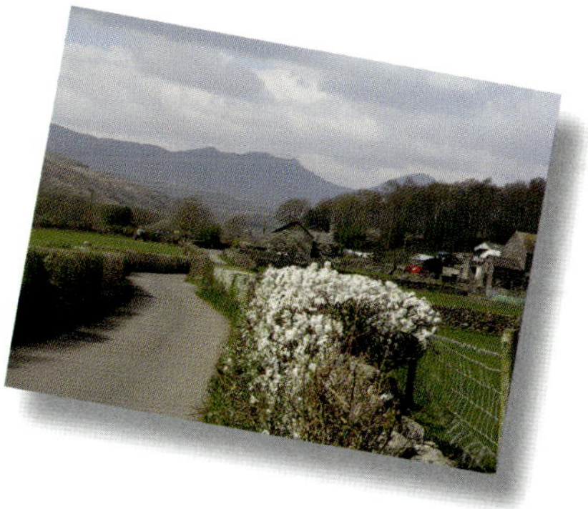

The reference photographs for the painting. Above: the overall scene.

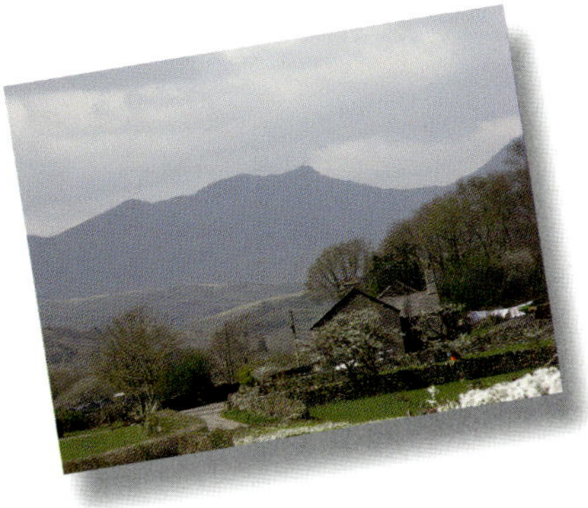

Right: a close-up of the building. Close-up shots, like small detailed sketches of part of a scene, can provide useful information for the finished work. Take some from a slightly different angle to gain a better understanding of complicated features.

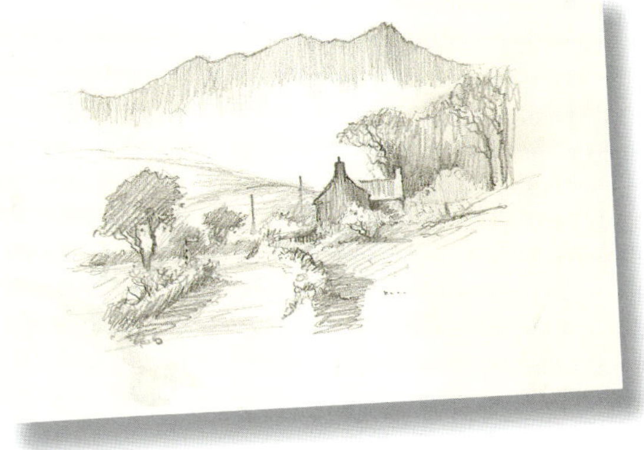

A studio sketch is an excellent way to work out your composition from photographs. In the sketch I have simplified the building and omitted those at the extremities of the photographs, as well as one of the walls crossing the right-hand field. The lane has also been made simpler.

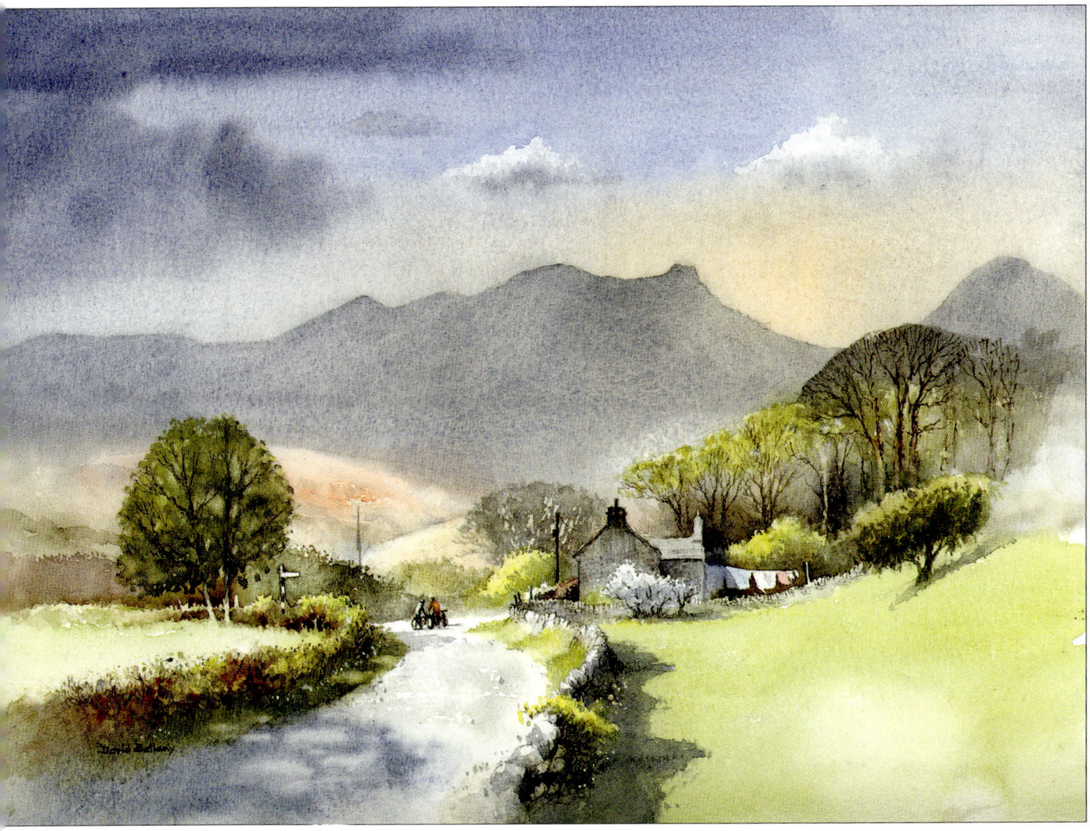

Farm near Coniston
20.3 x 25.4cm (8 x 10in)

In the painting I have tried to put across the sense of a sunny spring day, with the foreground shadows emphasising the feeling of sunlight. The main addition is the inclusion of two cyclists consulting near the farmhouse. Minor changes are always worth considering, and here you will see that I have swivelled the signpost round to point into the picture instead of the opposite direction, moved some trees and avoided the manicured look of the left-hand hedgerow. I felt the foreground mass of blossom was just too overwhelming to include.

Improving a composition

While there are a few landscape scenes that may work well without any changes, most need to be composed to a degree before they make a good image. This re-arrangement of the scene can be subtle or involve drastic alterations to the various elements and their relationships with each other. The best way to work out the composition is to do one or more thumbnail sketches in soft pencil, charcoal, watercolour or whatever suits you. Try to include the main tones as strong tonal areas have a considerable influence on how we view the composition.

I usually start with the focal point, or centre of interest, as this is the single most important feature in the scene. While you can have more than one focal point, the composition is stronger with just one, with perhaps minor ones to create a sense of balance. The focal point must stand out, and this can be done convincingly by creating your most striking tonal contrasts at that point. Bright colours and detail can also help, but by far the most powerful way is judicious use of tones.

My second concern is supporting the centre of interest with other features, such as trees around a building, a bush or prominent rock beside a waterfall, and so on. Figures and wildlife can be introduced, but they then become the focal point, so they need to be positioned near some feature of interest if possible, but not lost in detail. A further manner of support is by providing a lead-in in the form of a stream, track, dry stone wall, or whatever suits you. This should lead from the foreground directly to or close to the focal point. Gullies and ridges descending a mountainside towards the focal point also help.

Before you begin painting, check your composition for balance. If everything is placed on one side it helps to find a feature to add to the other side. Often just a simple post will suffice, but shapely bushes, trees, rocks, farm implements, or whatever seems appropriate, should fit the bill, provided it is in character with that type of landscape.

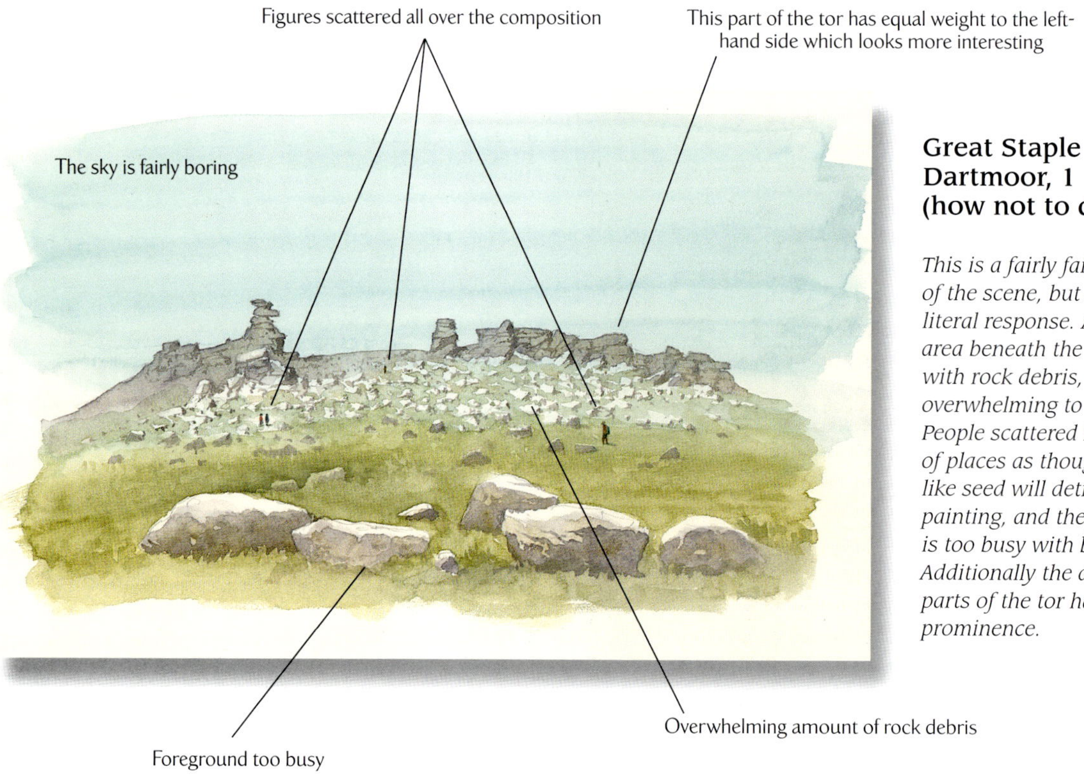

Great Staple Tor, Dartmoor, 1 (how not to do it)

This is a fairly faithful rendering of the scene, but shows a too literal response. Although the area beneath the tor is littered with rock debris, it is too overwhelming to include it all. People scattered in a variety of places as though tossed like seed will detract from any painting, and the foreground is too busy with boulders. Additionally the different parts of the tor have equal prominence.

When planning a painting, consider what sort of mood you wish to convey. If you wish to suggest a peaceful, tranquil mood then a more horizontal composition would work best, using strong horizontal emphasis in the scene and perhaps an elongated (panoramic) type format. To emphasise drama, a vertical format works well, emphasising cliffs or an abyss. A strong diagonal bias within the composition will suggest a dynamic approach and this can easily be achieved with rising mountain ridges, fallen pine trees or a series of rising crags.

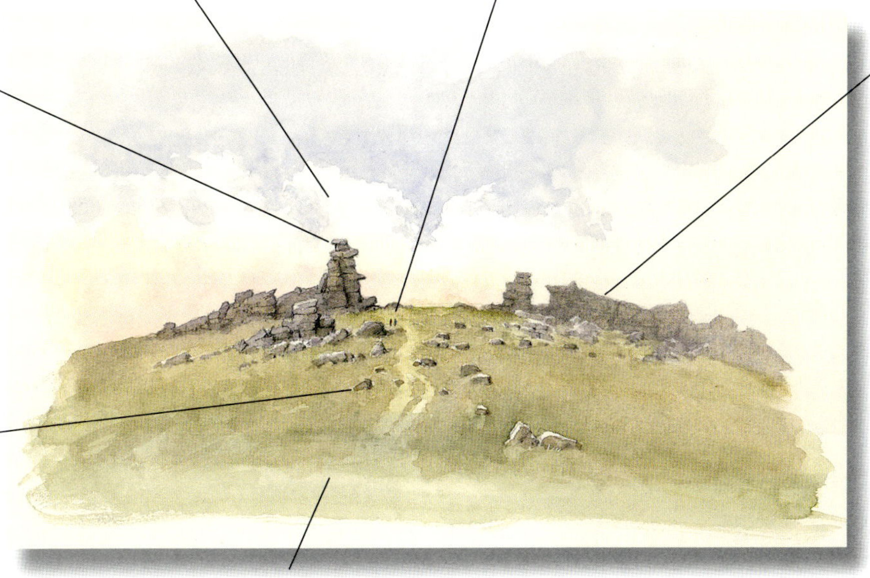

Great Staple Tor, Dartmoor, 2 (an improved response)

This is a stronger composition, with much of the rock debris eliminated. The higher part of the tor has been pushed towards the centre of the composition and the other side subdued. I now have only two tiny figures and they are positioned clearly near the left-hand tor rocks to support this as the focal point. This is further emphasised by creating a lighter track leading up to them. The foreground boulders have mainly been eliminated and the cloud structure not only improves the sky, but helps to highlight the tor.

Adding interest to foregrounds

Features that may be added:

- Puddles, preferably with a simple reflection
- Posts, perhaps festooned with vegetation
- Flowers and plants
- Rocks and boulders (in appropriate locations)
- A lead-in such as a path, road, stream, fence or wall
- Fallen tree trunk

Useful techniques to enhance foregrounds:

- Spatter with a round brush or toothbrush
- Broken colour allowing an initial wash to show through
- Dry brush effect over a lighter colour
- Shadow glaze over all or part of the foreground
- Abstraction or semi-abstraction of features
- Warm colours and strong tones to help suggest depth

Trees

Trees are often shown as a centre of interest, or as a supporting feature. They can also provide a sense of calm and shelter in an otherwise savage mountain landscape. Whether they are seen as an individual specimen or as a mass running down a mountainside, it usually pays to keep them simple and avoid trying to include every leaf and branch. Trees are also excellent when used to break up long horizontal or diagonal lines, such as the far shore of a lake, or a ridge.

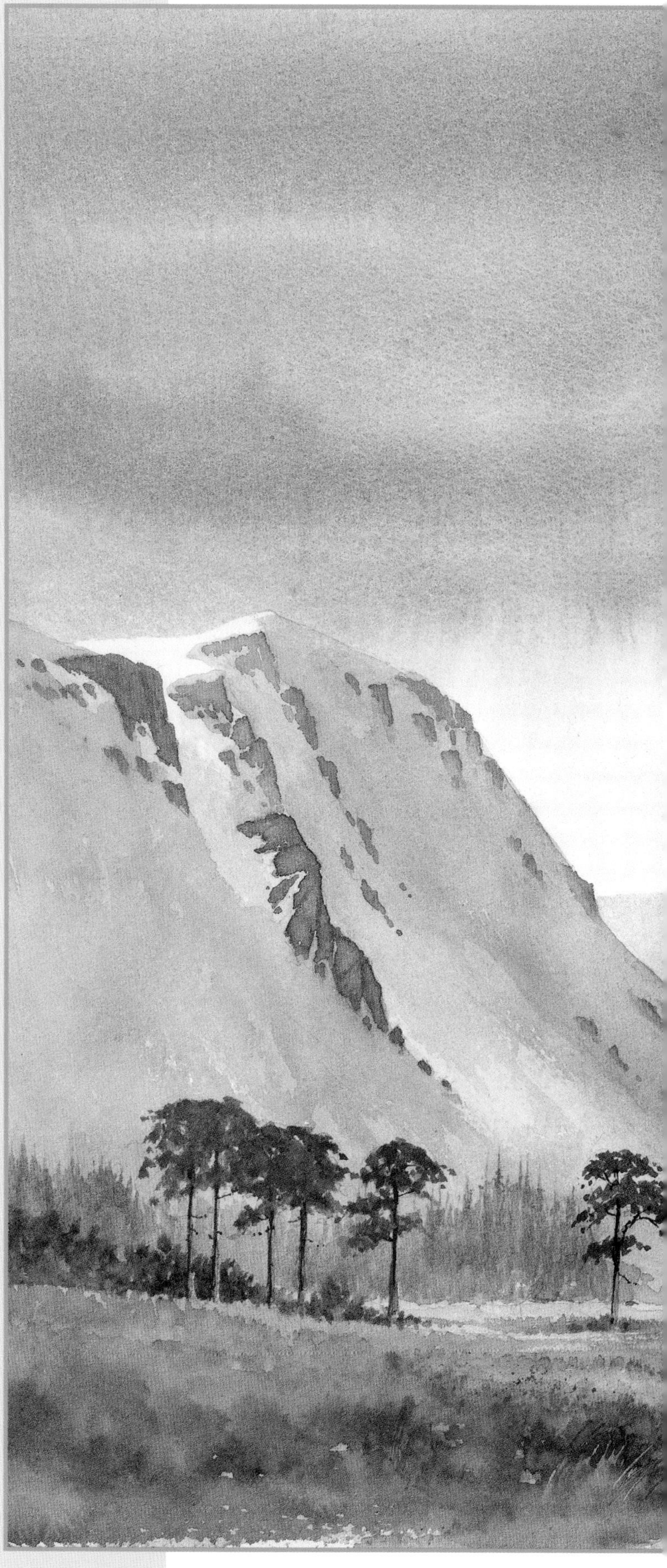

Glen Feshie
28 x 45.7cm (11 x 18in)

Although there are many larger trees in this painting, why does the small one just right of centre appear as the focal point? Look at it and try to work this out before you read any further, because it will help you ascertain what will highlight a centre of interest. Size and colour, though helpful, do not always matter as much as strong tonal contrasts. In this case the small tree is positioned almost at the end of the stream leading into the composition and is set against a light part of the painting. As well as being very dark, the tree stands on a dark section of the riverbank and is supported on the right by a line of larches. Additionally the main sweeps of the mountain slopes descend to the point where the tree stands, thus further emphasising it as the centre of interest. These are some of the devices you can use to highlight your focal point.

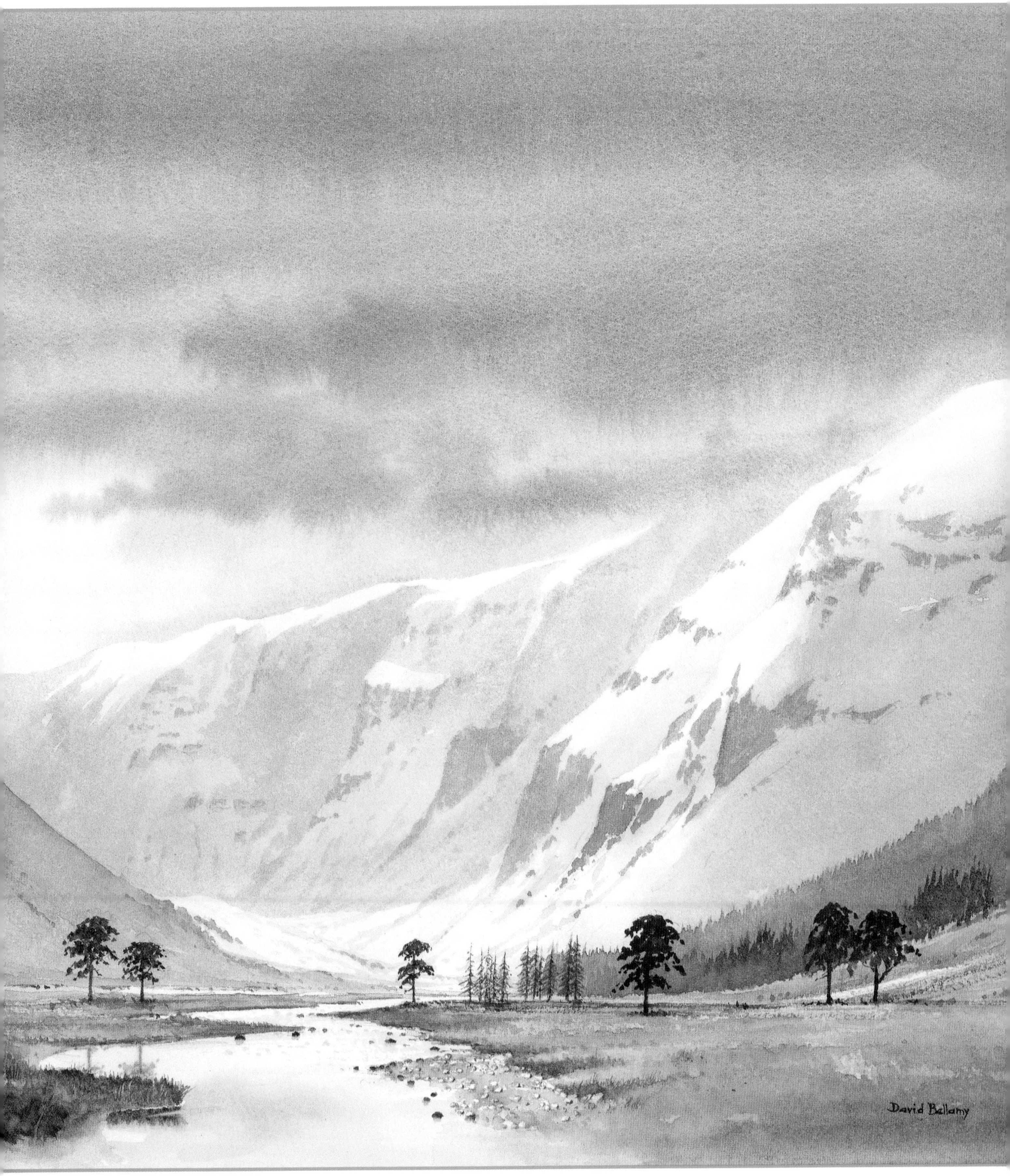
David Bellamy

Five common mountain trees

Many different species of trees adorn the mountains and moorlands, but these five are especially useful. They can be added to many wild landscapes to enhance the composition, or indeed to act as a centre of interest. Other fine trees, such as the ubiquitous birch tree, are depicted elsewhere in the book, but I have picked out these examples because they can be introduced individually or in groups into your paintings to add balance, support or as the focal point in the foreground, middle ground or far distance. It is always worth trying to work out how you can enhance a composition, and this is a superb way of doing so.

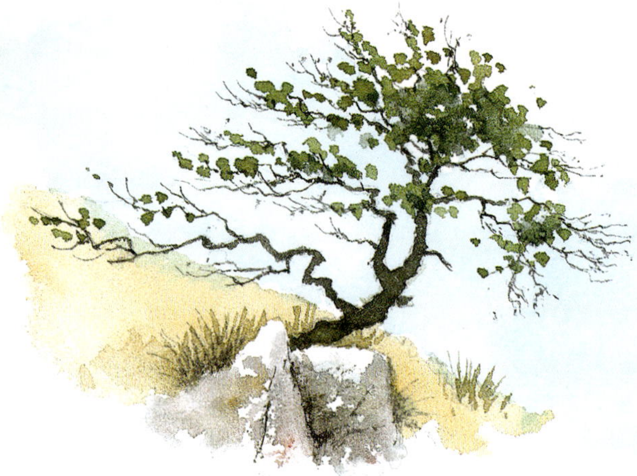

Thorn tree

These small trees, with their contorted branches, often interlocking, are so useful to include, to balance a composition, relieve the monotony of a dry stone wall, or maybe to support another feature as a centre of interest. I also like to use them to break up long ridge lines. With winter trees, and especially these thorn trees, the rigger brush is unparalleled for delineating the fine branches. As it is easy to have too much water or paint on the brush, test it on scrap paper first, twirling it across the surface to find the right strength and consistency of paint, and to achieve a fine point.

Larch in winter

The larch is a distinctive tree, with branches sweeping down to curve back upwards at the tip. In winter they provide a violent splash of orange, especially when caught in sunlight. A tall larch to one side of the foreground can provide an excellent framework to a focal point, while a stand of several of these trees makes a splendid centre of interest in itself.

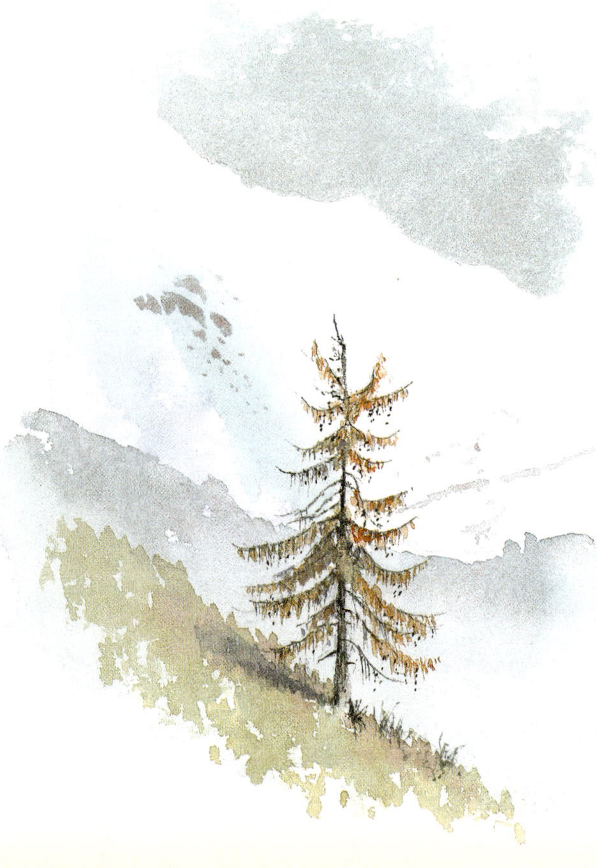

Rowan tree or mountain ash

These can often be seen growing out of cliffs or rocks, and are useful to accompany waterfalls and crags, or to punctuate bare mountain slopes where they grow at quite high altitude. In September their bright red berries flourish and can be used to add a splash of colour to a scene.

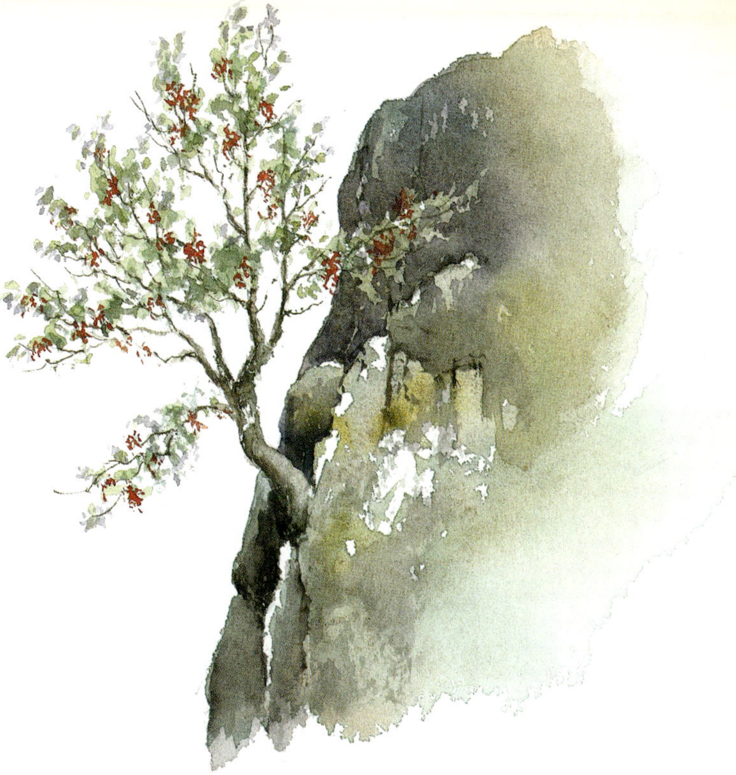

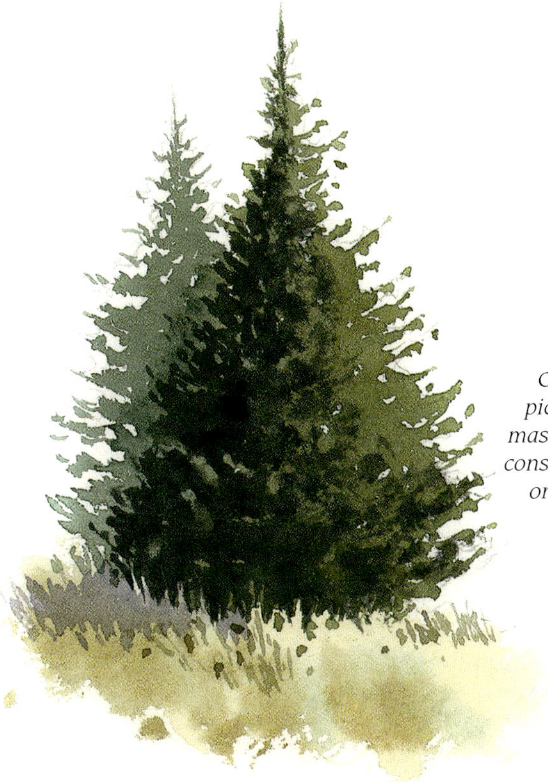

Conifers

Conifers are usually seen as a mass, but it's worth picking out one or two specimens at the edges of the mass and giving them a little more shape. They can vary considerably in size and shape, and are useful to support or highlight other features in a scene. The specimen shown here is a Norway spruce.

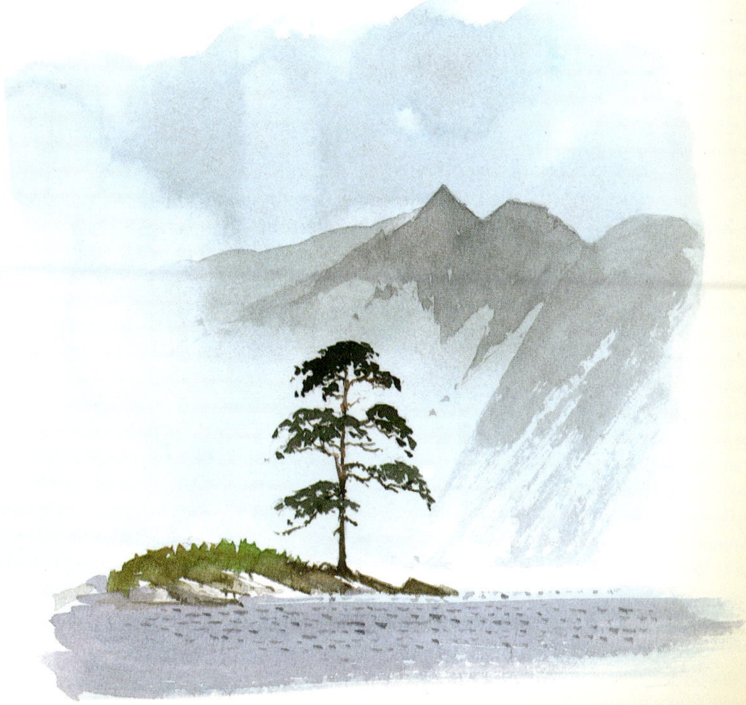

Scots Pine

Alone or in stands, these tall, graceful trees work extremely well as a focal point in many scenes, their trunks quite orange at times. Mature specimens often only show branches near the top.

Using trees as a frame

If you place a tree in the foreground, it can act as a frame to the main area of the painting, thus creating a feeling of space and distance. Sometimes it can be beneficial to step back from your subject and introduce a line of trees through which you view the focal point. A good example of this is where a lake runs for much of the way across the lower part of a composition, with a large gap between some of the trees revealing the most interesting part of the lake. One danger of having trees right in the foreground is the potential temptation to paint in every leaf. Paint large areas of foliage as a mass with a large brush and only flick a few suggested leaves at the edges of the mass.

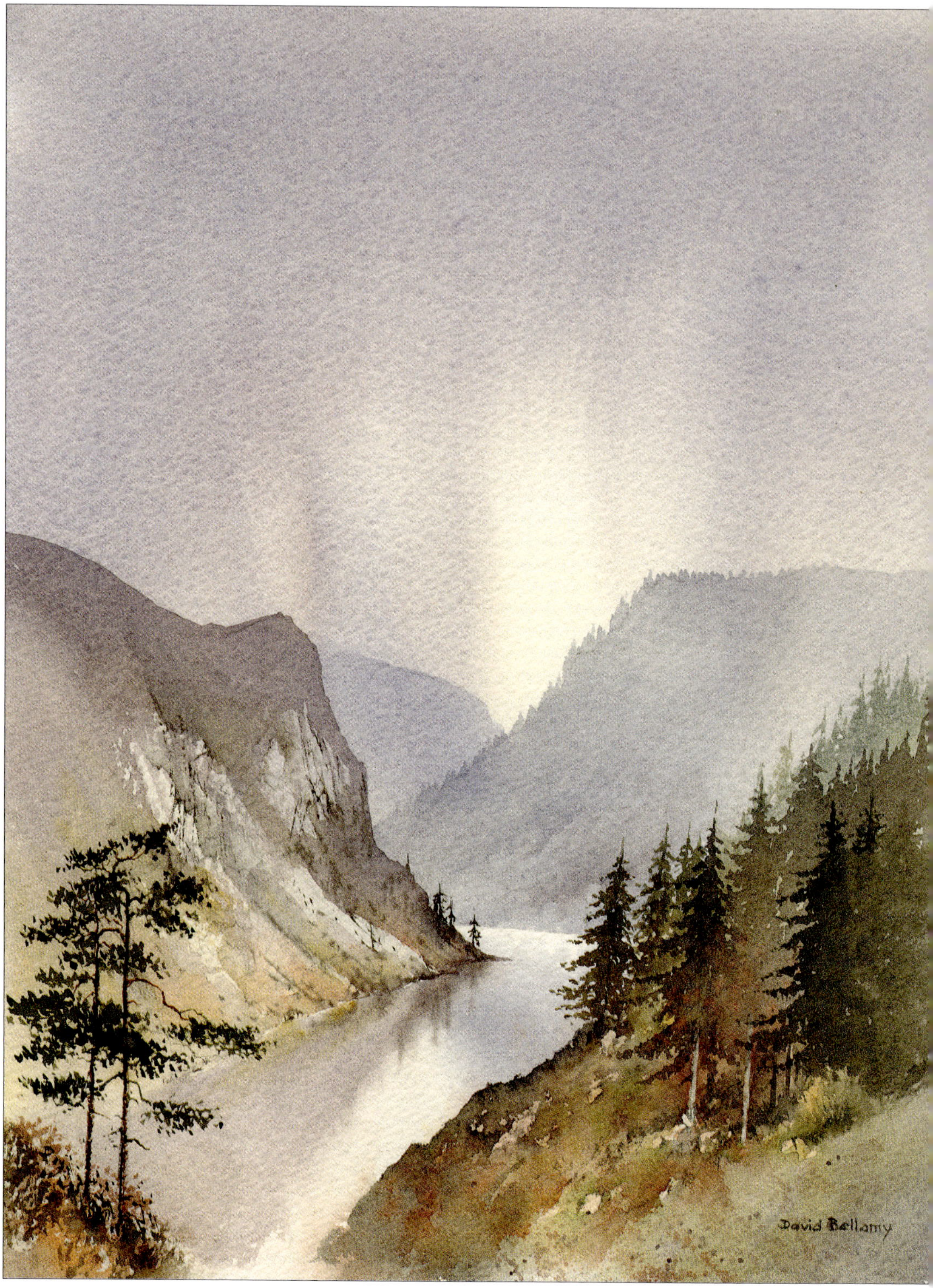

Reservoir in Cwm Elan, Mid-Wales
25.4 x 20.3cm (10 x 8in)

In this painting the tall left-hand pines have been deliberately positioned against a light background to make them stand out. Note that the sense of looking down on the lake from high up is created by the shorelines falling steeply towards the bottom of the picture.

Massed trees

Large areas of mountainsides are often cloaked in masses of conifers. These areas need not be as daunting as you may at first think. Usually the underlying ridges and gullies are betrayed by the rise and fall of the lines of conifers and we can use this to advantage. Where such a ridge runs down, the trees growing there can be given a little more prominence, such as a slightly darker row. You can soften the darker wash off gently at the bottom to join the main mass. You only need one or two of these ridges of trees, or perhaps three on a particularly large area. These can be further enhanced by mist, sunlight or shadow, which are especially effective for breaking up large passages of dull tree masses. Dropping other colours into the wash while it is still wet is another technique which works well with autumnal colours. These masses can also be broken up with one or two prominent crags rising out of the mass. Normally the rocks on such crags are lighter in tone than the surrounding conifers. A refinement on this would be to deliberately highlight a handful of pine trees at the top of the crag.

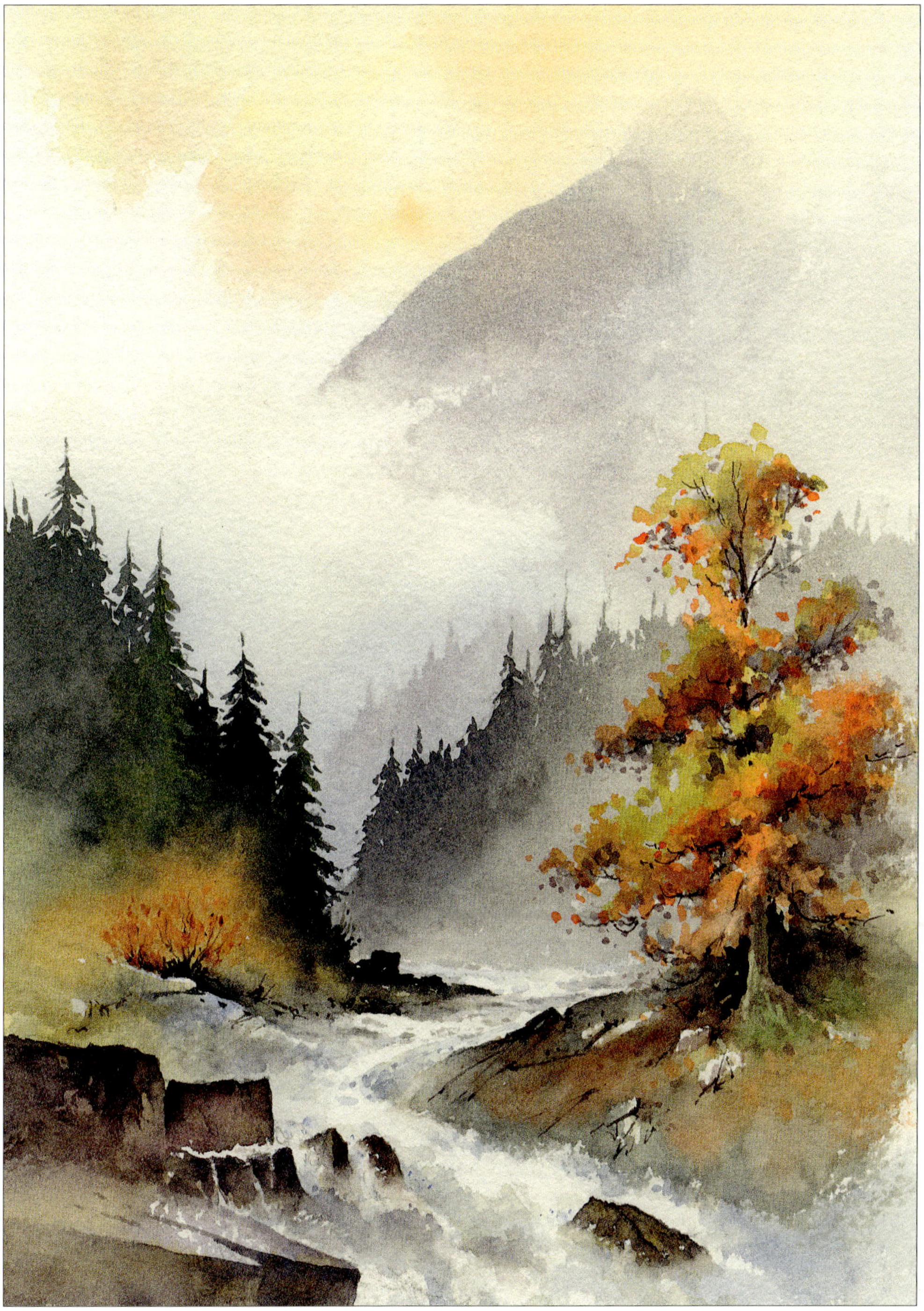

Stream in the Dolomites

22.8 x 16.5cm (9 x 6½in)

By creating a sense of atmosphere I have lost much of the tree detail beyond the tall tree on the right. The massed conifers have been rendered in a mainly flat wash with only slight graduation in the closer masses. Note how vital it is to ensure you apply the right strength of tone to suggest recession. Sometimes, if I wish to emphasise the sense of atmosphere further, I will lay a transparent glaze across the background, including the sky and both tree-lined ridges descending from the top right, before painting the dark trees coming down on the left.

Water

Water can bring life to your landscapes and in the mountains and moors we are lucky in having such a variety of tumbling water courses that include waterfalls, minor cascades, sparkling streams bubbling over a rocky water course and deep pools. Sometimes these are crystal clear and sometimes dark and sombre. There are examples of all these various types of water throughout the book, but here we will look at some of the more useful methods of rendering them.

Reflections

Reflections in water can be depicted in two ways – either by the wet-into-wet technique or by layering colours one on top of the other once the bottom one has dried. Most of the time I use the former, as in the Moorland Cascade painting, opposite. This involves laying the initial wash and waiting for it to reach a state of optimum dampness before it dries completely, before applying the reflection colour which must be barely damp, otherwise too much water will cause a runback to form when you drop it into the already-laid wash. As outlined opposite, this often needs adjustment.

The layering technique simply involves laying a wash representing the shape, tone and colour of the reflection, letting it dry then overlaying a transparent wash over the area covered by the water. Sometimes more than one wash is needed to describe a variety of reflections within the area before the final overlaid wash is applied.

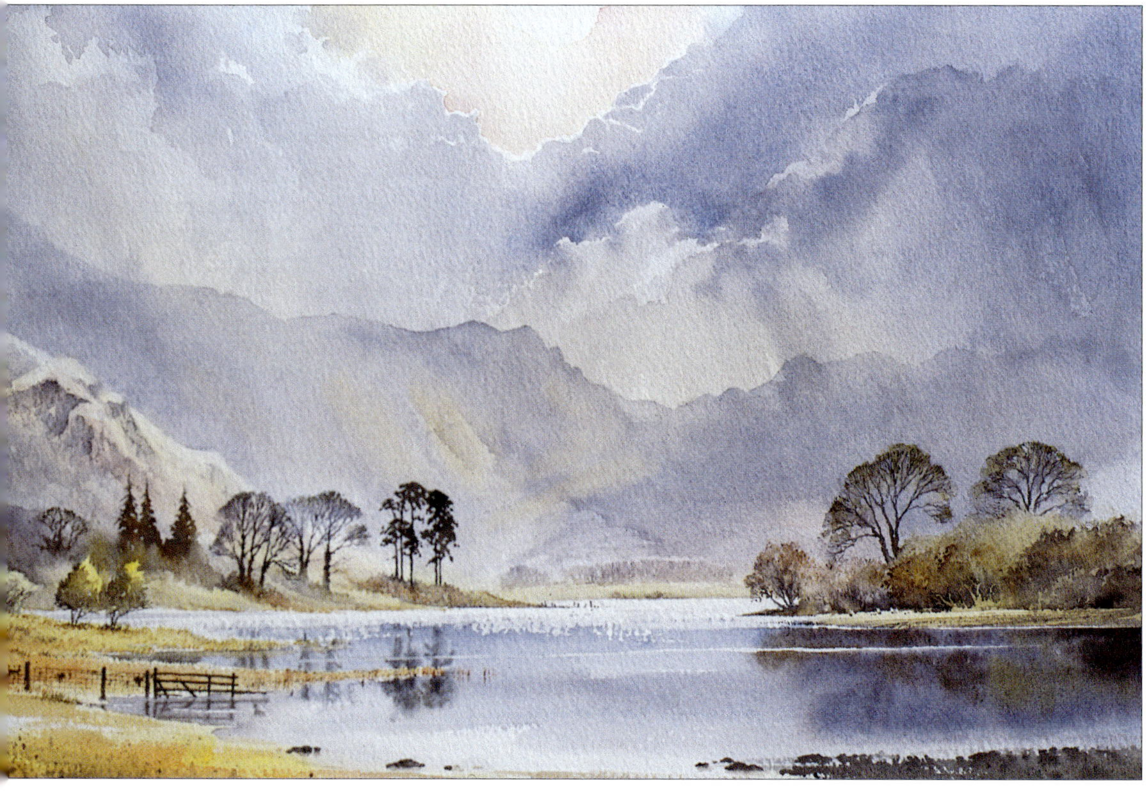

Reflections in a Lake
25.4 x 40.6 (10 x 16in)

The sparkle effect is easier to achieve if you use Rough paper, but resist the temptation to put it all over a large area of water. Here the light horizontal slivers were lifted out with a damp flat brush, and this helps to break up the reflections.

Moorland Cascade

17.8 x 28cm (7 x 11in)

Moorland cascades and pools make a delightful composition. Sometimes I add a thorn or rowan tree beside the cascade, but here it has sufficient interest with rocks and tumbling water. The contrast of hard-edged, dark rocks against the lighter water works well to highlight the water. The foreground reflections were achieved with the wet-into-wet method by dropping in the dark reflections while the pool was still damp. As so often happens, the reflections spread out too far and I had to curb them with a damp brush which I had dipped in clean water and then wiped on a paper tissue.

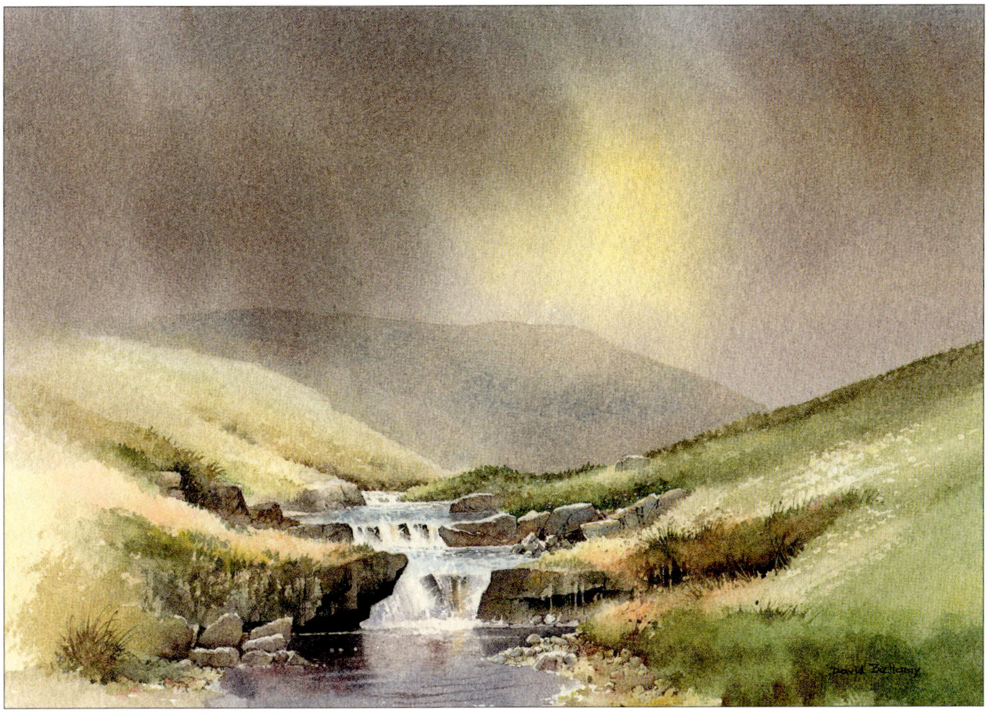

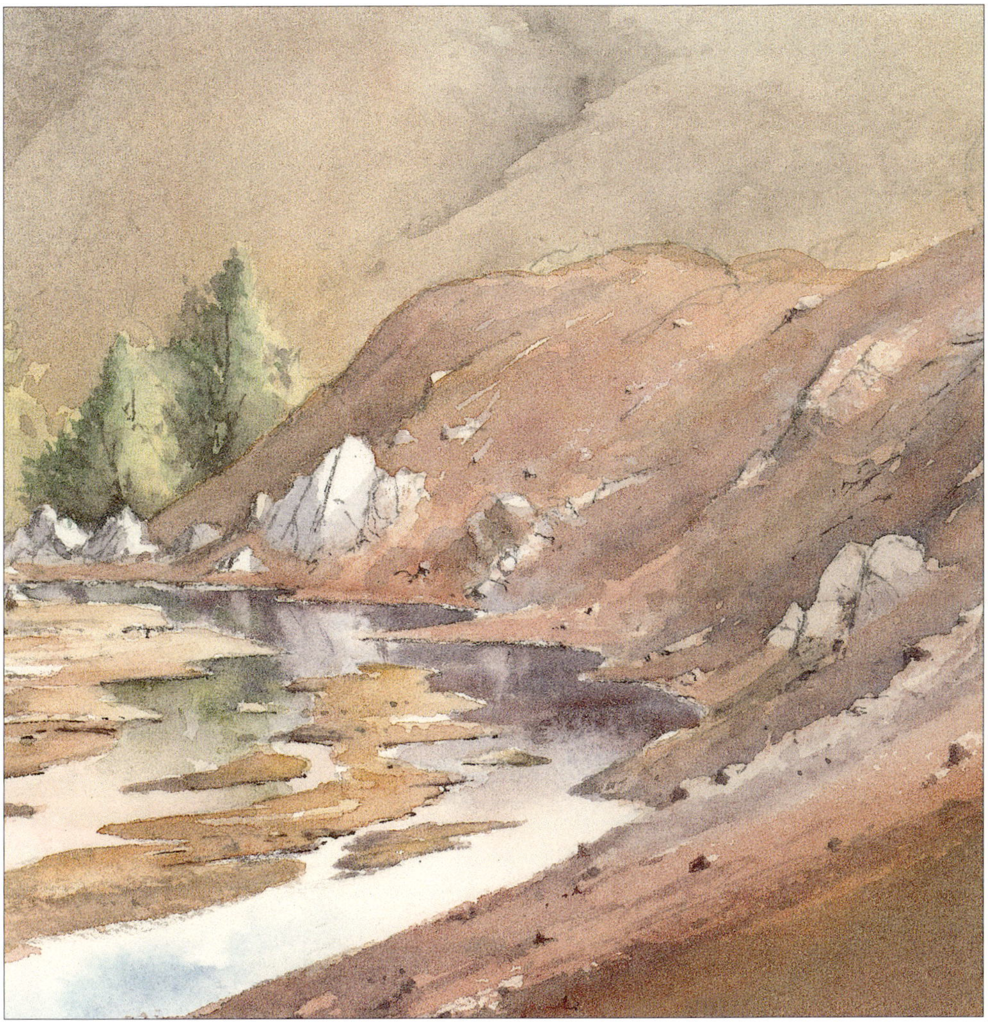

Stream in the High Atlas

I deliberately position myself with the optimum view for recording interesting features like reflections, even if afterwards I have to move to complete the composition from a slightly different angle. It is important to make the water appear to be level and not liable to run off to the side. Note how the stream edges are kept flat in the distance, but as the stream gets closer, the banks descend more sharply towards the foreground. In this scene counterchange has added to the attraction of the stream by alternating the banks to be lighter than the water in places and darker in others.

Tackling different types of water

The stretch of water you are painting might well have several different types of water: sparkling, placid, rippled, cascading, or whatever, and bringing them together can be a problem.

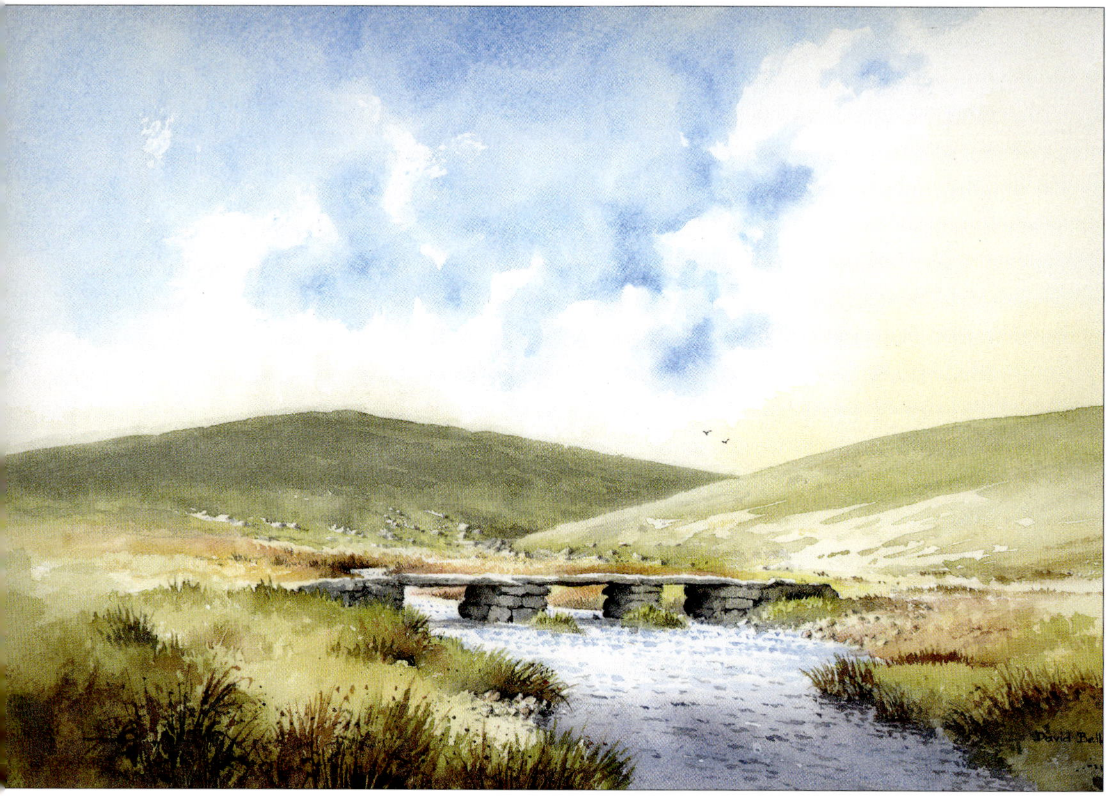

Teignhead Clapper Bridge
20.3 x 30.5cm (8 x 12in)

Here I have dabbed cobalt blue over white paper directly below the bridge, to represent the sparkling water – this could alternatively be done using the dry brush technique. When this was dry, I wet the lower part of the stream with clean water, taking it up over the bottom of the sparkling area, and then washed in a mix of cobalt blue and cadmium red, letting it drift up softly towards the sparkling water. Finally, with a stronger mixture of the same colours, I dabbed in the ripples when the wash was dry.

Glen Nevis
22.8 x 30.5in (9 x 12in)

The actual water has been kept simple with dry brush applications of colour to suggest strong backlighting falling on the water. The colour becomes stronger in tone as it gets closer, becoming darker in the foreground as it swings to the left and away from the light. I achieved this by using horizontal flicks of the brush with more liquid paint.

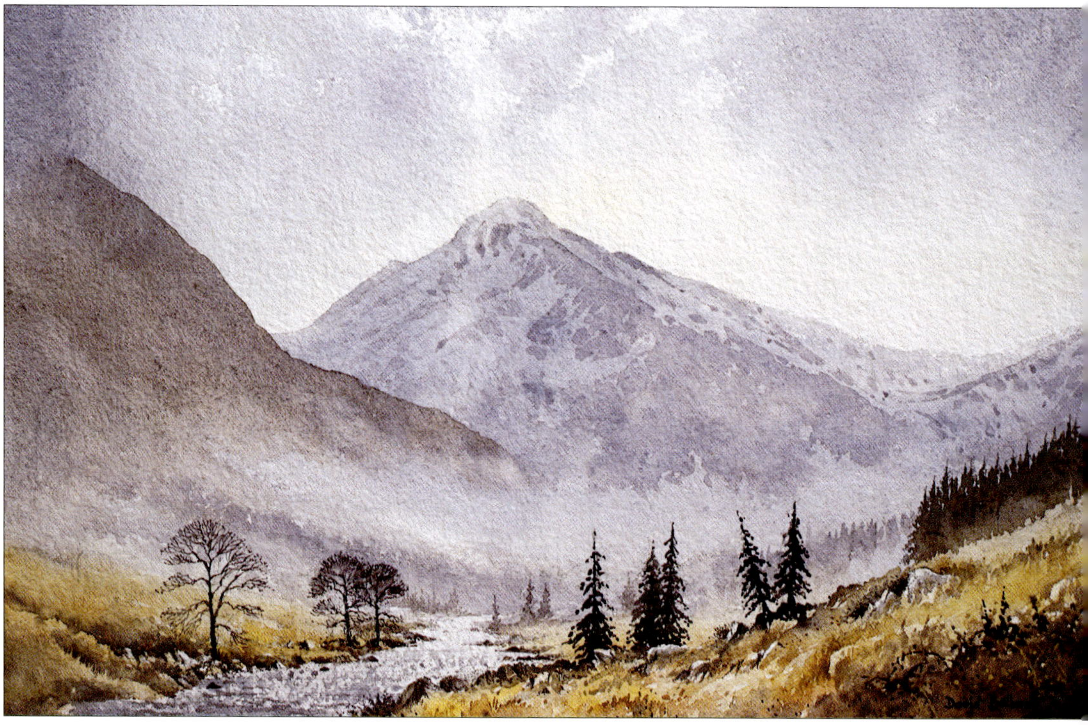

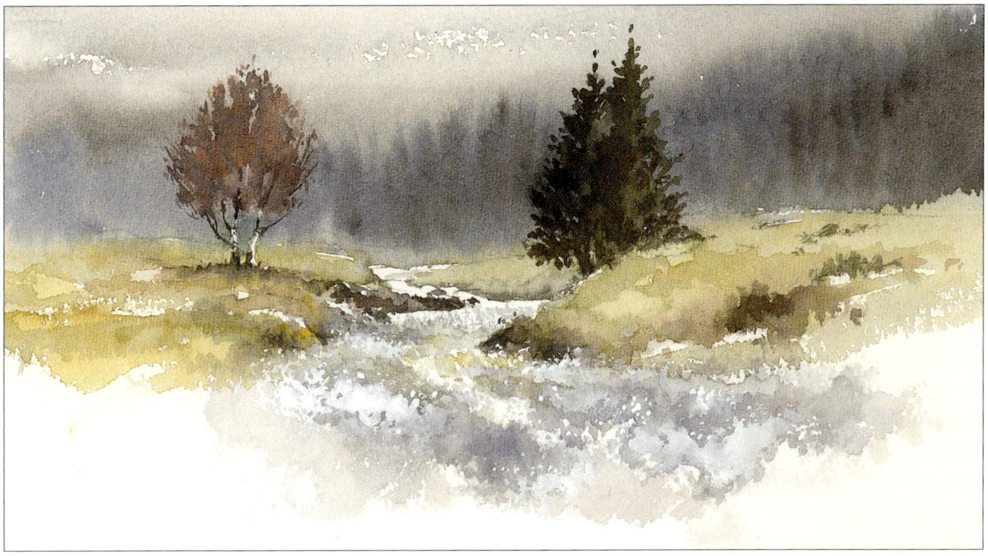

Stream in Spate

Painting water that is crashing, roaring and cascading in spate is quite a challenge, needing circular, dabbing motions with a round brush. One way to improve your chances of success is to paint in the darker tones in this vigorous, dabbing manner, leaving untouched spaces here and there, and when this is dry, apply white gouache with the side of the brush to create the lighter swirls. Just above the crests of these swirls, dab in a few white blobs to suggest drops of water as I have done in this small painting.

Tumbling Cascade

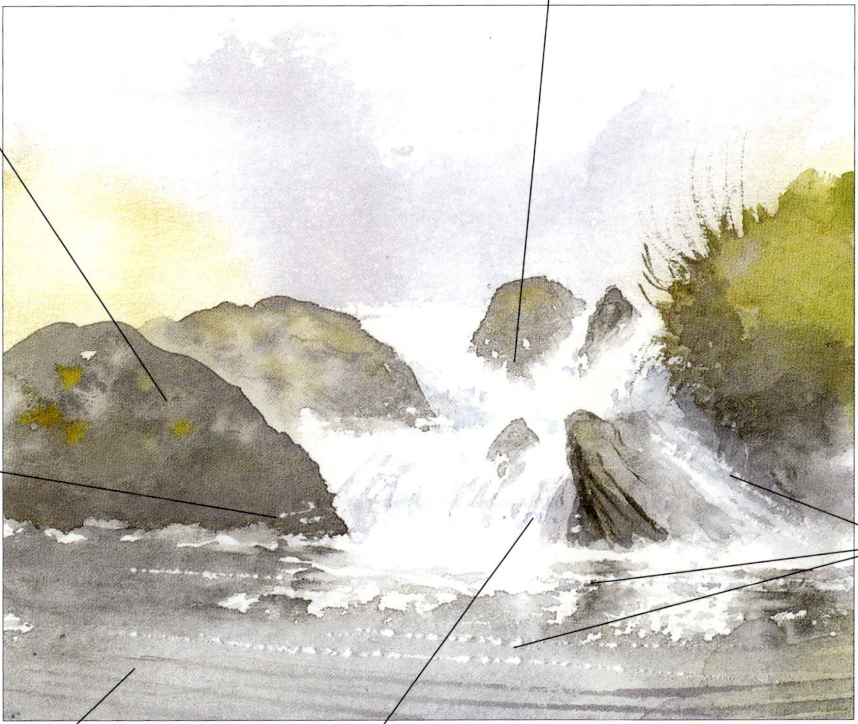

Waterfall

The contrast of light and dark tones is an important ingredient when rendering waterfalls. Here the upper section of falling water is caught in sunlight, while lower down on the left it is in shadow, thus losing its impact. Although here this is a deliberate device to illustrate how much more the waterfall stands out when the white paper has been untouched, it is also an effective means of throwing emphasis on to the upper falls. If you find it difficult to create the little white blobs with the negative painting technique as I have done here, then simply apply them using white gouache.

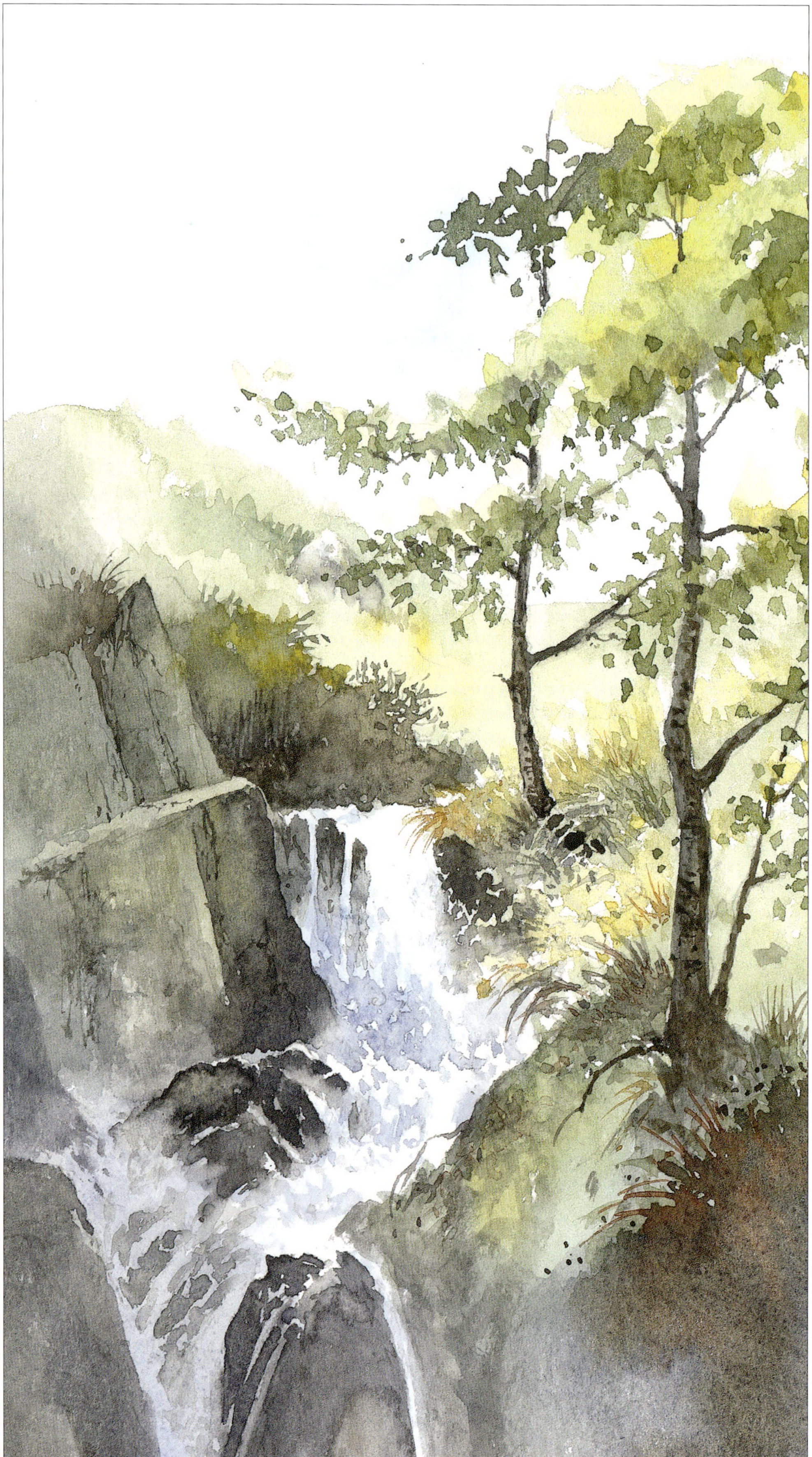

Water and rocks

We have seen how to treat falling water and rocks in the waterfall scenes, but when the water is low, we often cannot see much of it as it trickles round the rocks, and so our water course seems to be solely made up of rocks and stones. This is even more common in limestone country when the water can disappear completely until the next heavy rain. In these instances, you need to exaggerate the amount of water, seek out the deeper pools or even resort to using other references for the actual water.

L'Arveyron River

This rapid watercolour sketch was first carried out with a 4B pencil, including strong hatching for the darker tones. A few loose washes were applied afterwards. Although this has been roughly executed, the simple method of depicting water running through a mass of boulders works well. I have painted in a little more water than I could actually see, and did not bother with reflections in this case. In a finished painting I would take more care with this. Note how most of the boulders have been left as white paper – this helps the sense of sunlight as well as creating a strong contrast between water and rock.

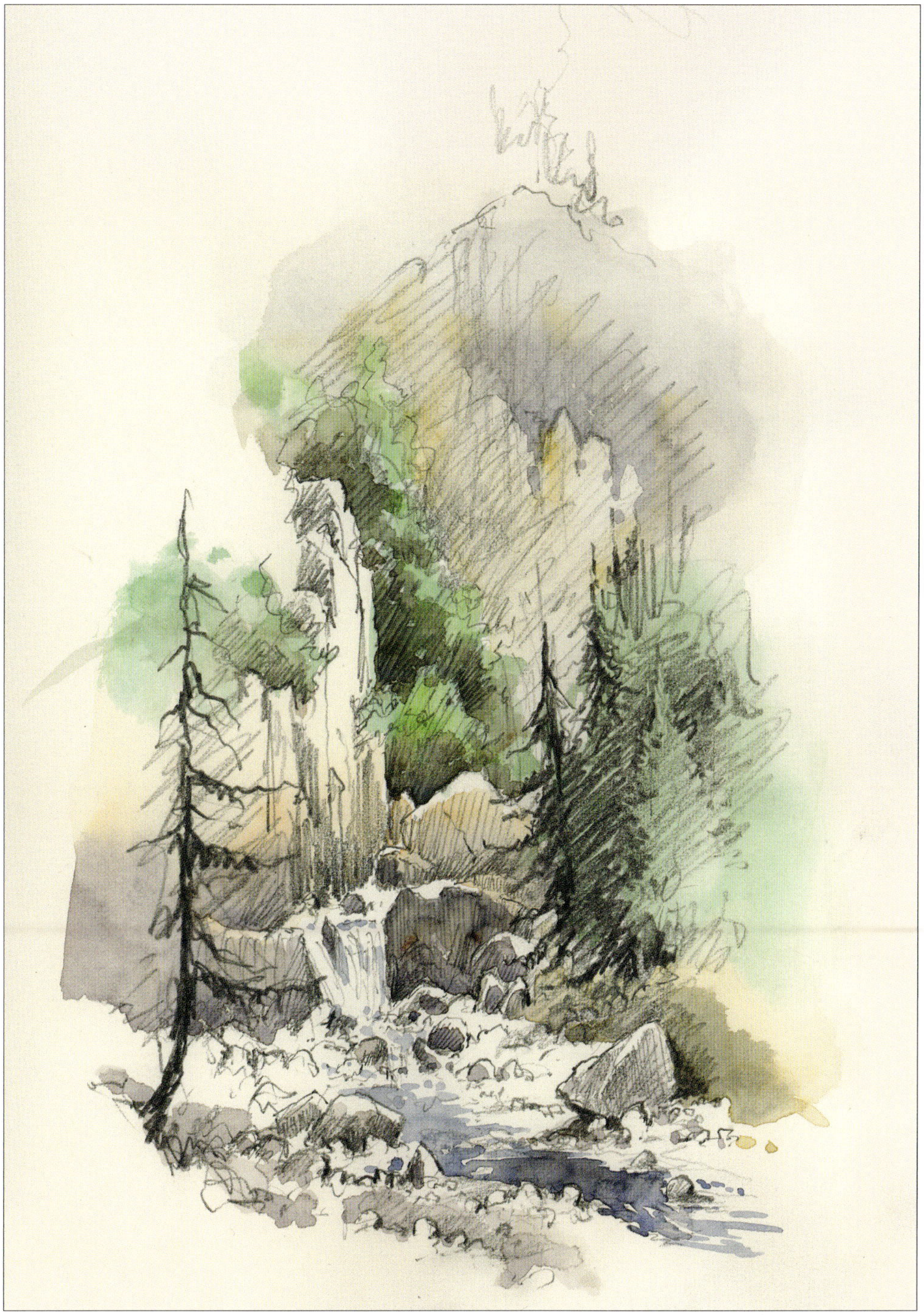

Rocks and crags

As a painter you cannot take mountains seriously without tackling rocks. These can take many forms, some shapely, others simply a crumbling mess. It pays to concentrate on the more handsome specimens that appeal to you, and although sometimes you have to include ones that are less appealing, you can subdue these and highlight an adjacent passage. Before you start painting rocks, consider the colour – is the area you are about to work on just one colour or is it variegated? Look for the main shadows, then the fracture lines, and with crags and cliffs, the fault structure. Is the main line of fault vertical, horizontal or diagonal in varying degrees? Usually you will see a tendency for the fracture lines to run in one of these directions, and translating this on to your painting can give your work a sense of authenticity.

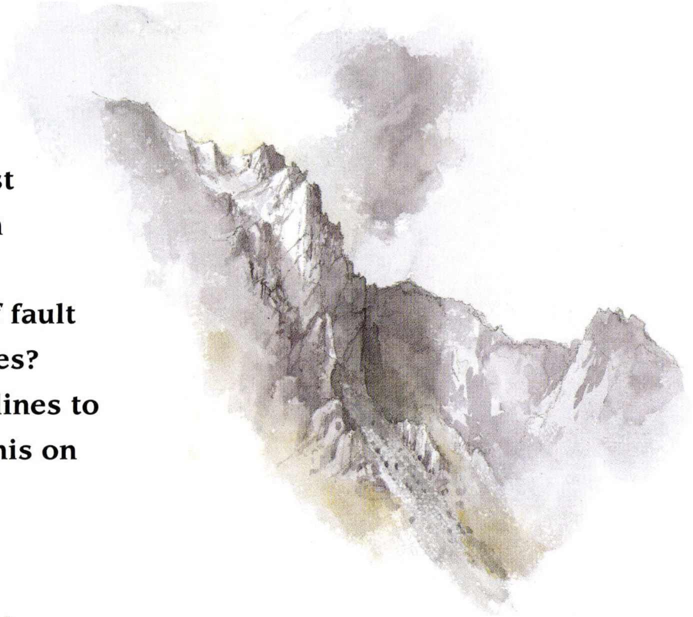

Sunlit crags

When painting rock scenery, take note of the main fault lines as well as the overall structure. Often there is a strong bias in these fractures: horizontal, diagonal or vertical. In these crags we see a definite diagonal emphasis from bottom left to top right. Try to avoid putting in every fracture line, however strong they may appear. Pick out the main ones and leave some of the face devoid of too much detail. In this watercolour sketch I have resisted the urge to depict detail on the more distant cliffs in order to suggest that they are further away.

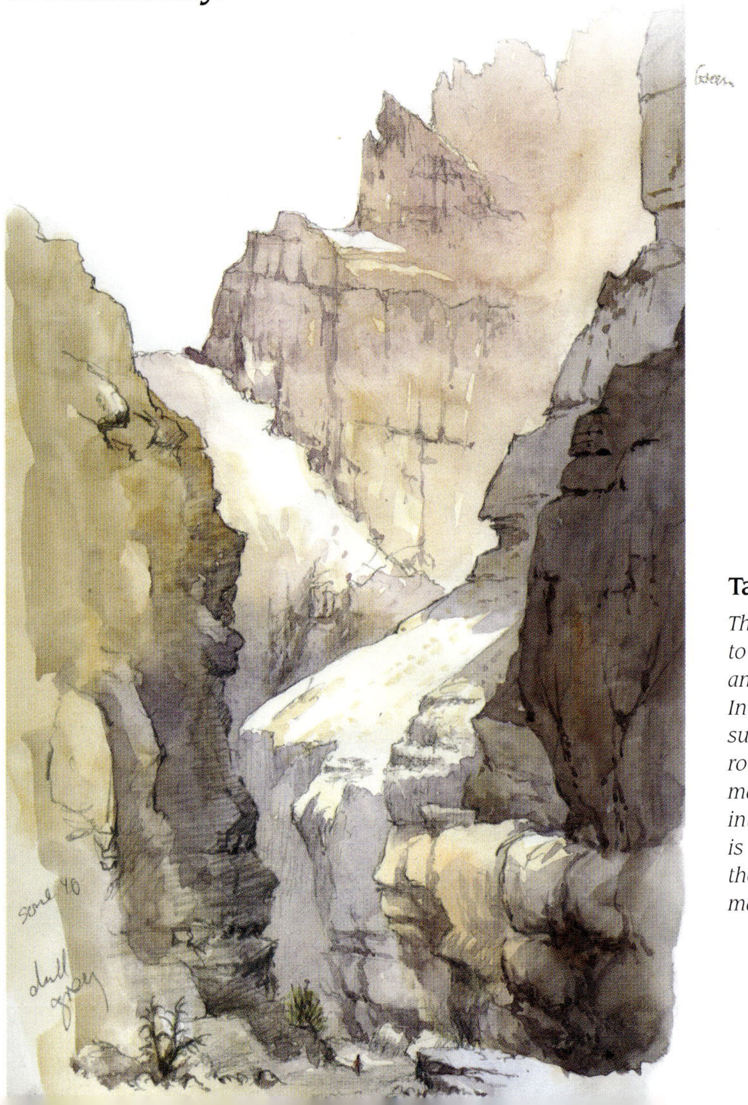

Tackling a rocky gorge

The intense sunlight catching the high cliffs fails to penetrate to the bottom of this sublime scene in Wadi Nakhar in Oman, and often the temptation is to make the lower parts too dark. In places like this, watch for strong reflected light creating subtle highlights on rock faces. Where the gorge disappears round a bend, I have kept the cliffs devoid of detail, while making the closer face much stronger in tone. Initially I intended the word 'face' to mean 'rock face', but I see there is also a profile of a human face at that point, one of three in the sketch. I included Jenny at the bottom as she provides a marvellous idea of the immense scale of this place.

Making rocks grow out of the ground

There is a danger that rocks will look as though they are plonked on top of the ground, rather than being embedded in it. This can be avoided using the method described below.

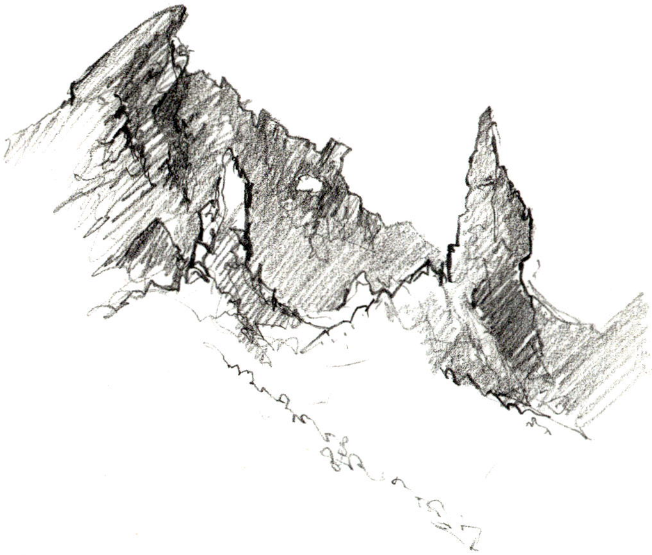

Volcanic rock pinnacles, Iceland

All the edges are hard in this sketch, except the bottom ones where the rock is secured to the cliff, thus giving a sense of solidity. In the centre is a rock window.

Dartmoor Tors

20.3 x 30.5cm (8 x 12in)

These granite tors and their satellite boulders look as though they are growing out of the ground. This is achieved by avoiding a strong bottom line to the rock and either drifting some of the ground colour up into the tor, or bringing it down into the ground below.

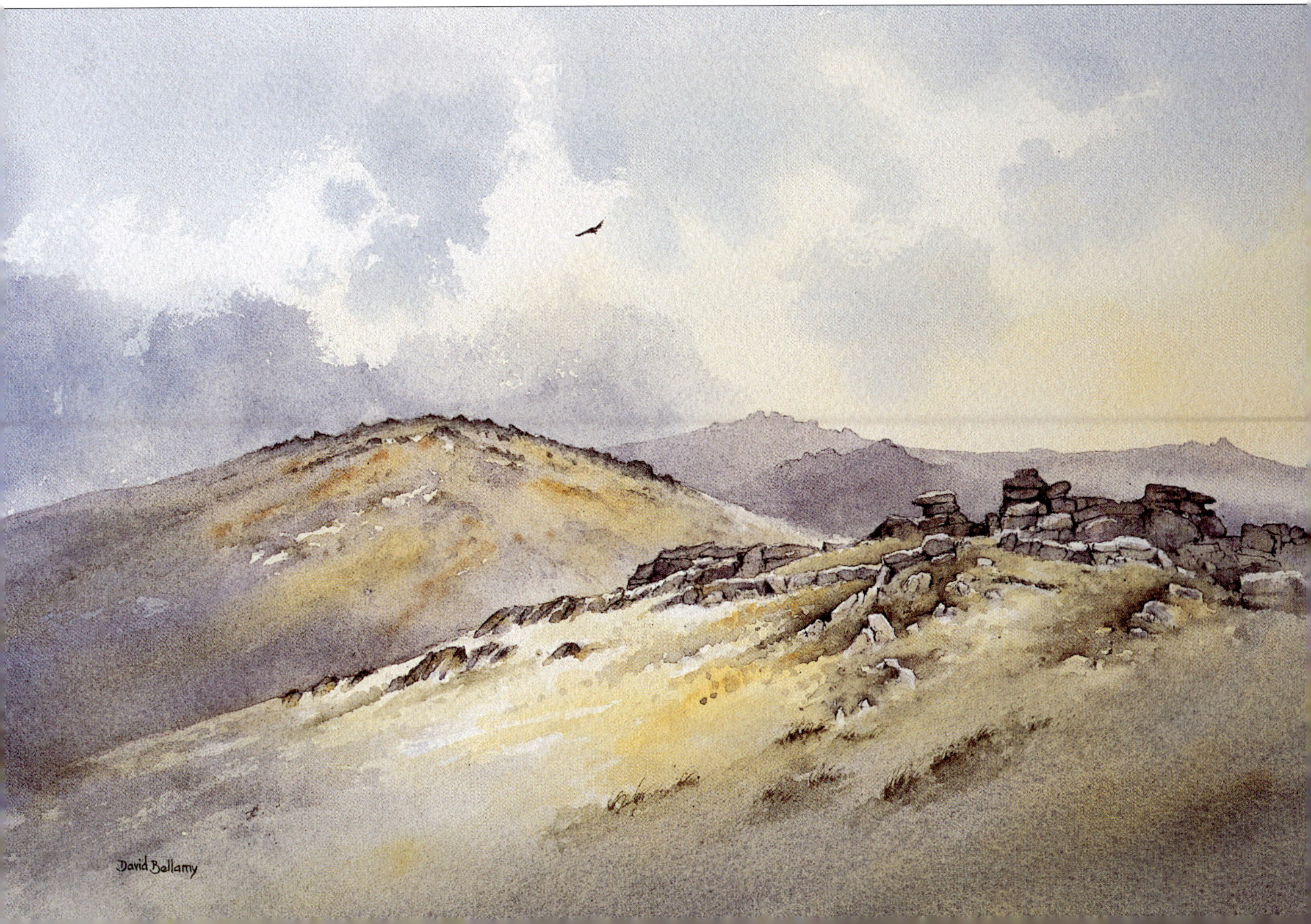

Rock textures and colours

Rocks vary considerably in shape, colour and surface texture, and here we look at the main characteristics of rocks and boulders.

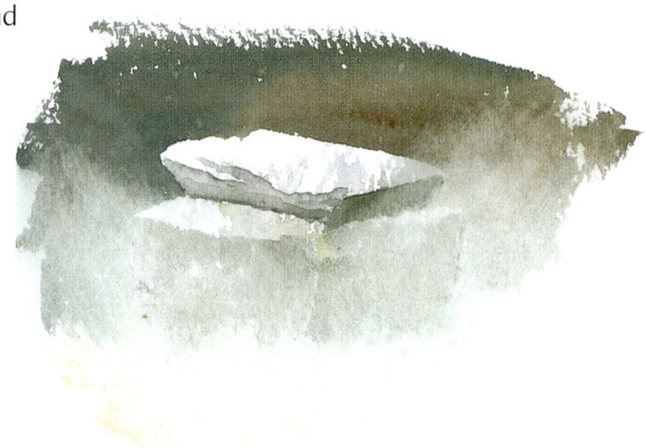

Simple texture using the dry brush method

This simple example illustrates how with the side of a no. 10 round brush and hardly any water, you can sweep colour across the paper, let it dry, then add the darker forms to suggest a rock shape. The Rough paper used in this case enhances the chances of success.

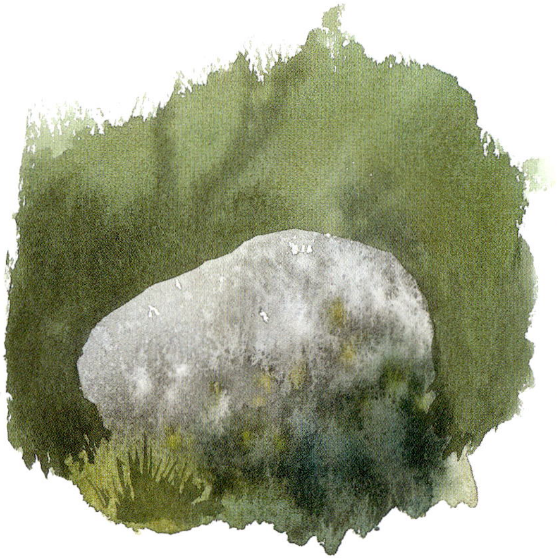

Lichen

The lichen on this rounded boulder was created by first laying a light grey wash, with some darker colour lower down to suggest the shadow area. While this was still wet, I drifted in various greens at the bottom to give the impression that the boulder had been lying in the grass for years, then I waited a few minutes. Once the drying process was well underway, I sprayed it with a couple of bursts from a small spray diffuser that can be bought at chemists, to create the fine, light spots that give a sense of rough texture. Then I immediately spattered water over the boulder to create the lichen-like blobs. A few dabs of yellow ochre added to the effect, after which I let it dry completely before painting the darker green around the top of the boulder. Try experiments on scrap paper with this method of working, slightly varying your timings and the distance from which you spray.

Fissure lines

A certain amount of care is needed when defining fissures – I have seen some horrors occur on courses where these appear more like emaciated worms than fractures. In this illustration you can see the variation in the width of the lines, the thin ones achieved with a rigger, the widest with a no. 3 or 4 round brush. In most cases I applied varying pressure to the brush to create more interesting fractures. Try not to make them too regular – vary the distance between the lines and leave some parts untouched. Have the lines emerging from a larger crack or strong shadow area as much as possible, rather than stopping and starting in the middle of a blank rock face.

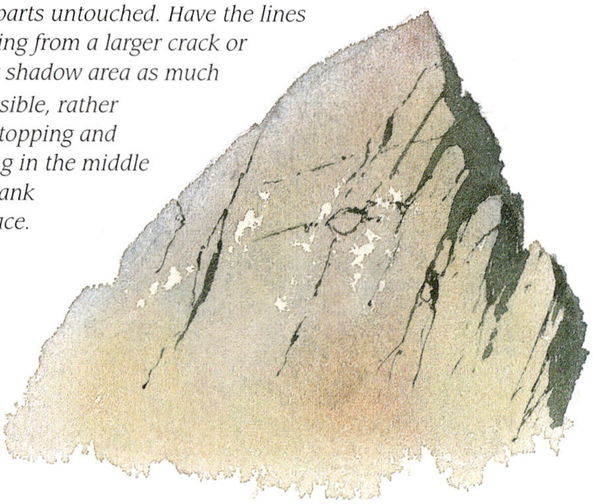

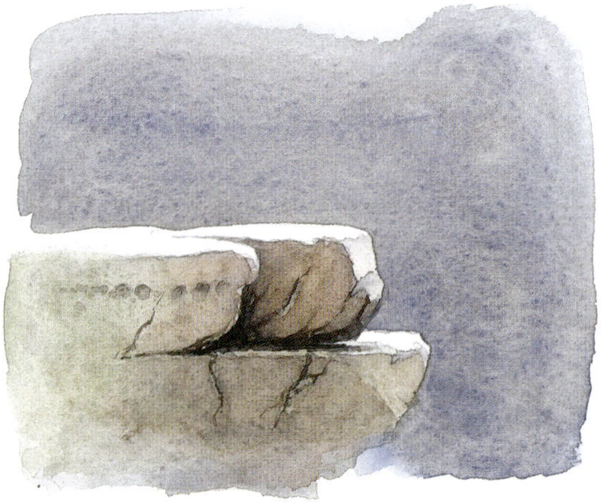

Colour in rock

Allow colours to run loosely into each other, then let the paper dry before describing the fracture lines and shadows. Here I began with a weak wash of French ultramarine and cadmium red over the rock apart from the light tops, then dropped green into the left side of the wet wash plus some raw sienna for the light right-hand ends. Once this had dried, I applied some light red with a touch of the French ultramarine mix to define the stronger reddish area to the right. I left the raw sienna prows untouched, and faded the reddish mix into the left-hand side. Finally the dark shadows and fracture lines were rendered with French ultramarine and burnt umber, and the blue-grey background added.

Boulders and loose rocks

Boulder fields and scree can be daunting to render as there are so many individual shapes. Much simplification can be achieved by reducing the number of those shapes, losing edges, just suggesting some definition and leaving quiet areas. It also helps to break up the monotony of massed boulders with bushes, an occasional tree, a fallen trunk, or even an animal. One device I often employ is to lay a transparent shadow across part of the boulder field – French ultramarine and cadmium red works well. It is also a good idea to highlight one or two boulders, thus varying the emphasis.

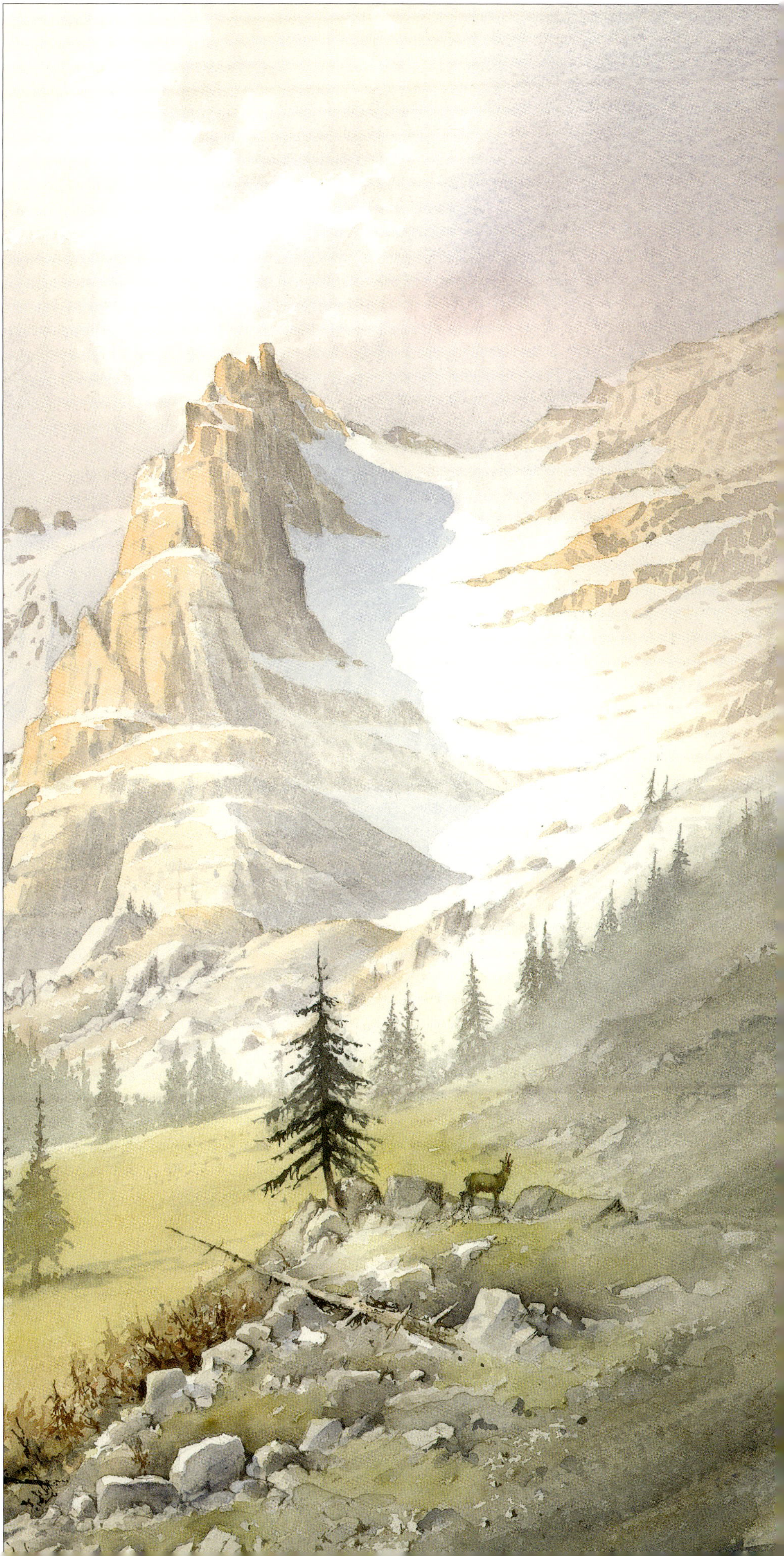

Foreground rocks and boulders

Note how in this Alpine scene dark vegetation and ground has been used to highlight the tops of the boulders, while the bottoms are faded into the ground unless there are other rocks in front. Some are rounded, some angular, and a fallen tree provides a little relief from the mass of rock shapes. If you wish to vary the boulders further, then dropping colour such as yellow ochre or cadmium red into them while they are still wet gives a convincing appearance.

Buildings

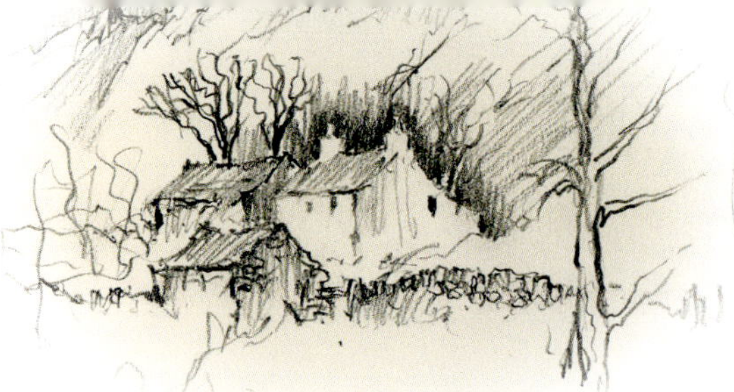

If you enjoy painting rustic old buildings then you are probably more likely to find good examples of these in the mountain regions than anywhere else. The added complication here, though, is that many of them are built on uneven ground, sometimes with almost every side appearing to be at a slightly different level. This is not necessarily a great problem, and rather than correct it so that the building looks as though it has been built on flat ground, use these sloping angles to advantage, even exaggerating them if you like.

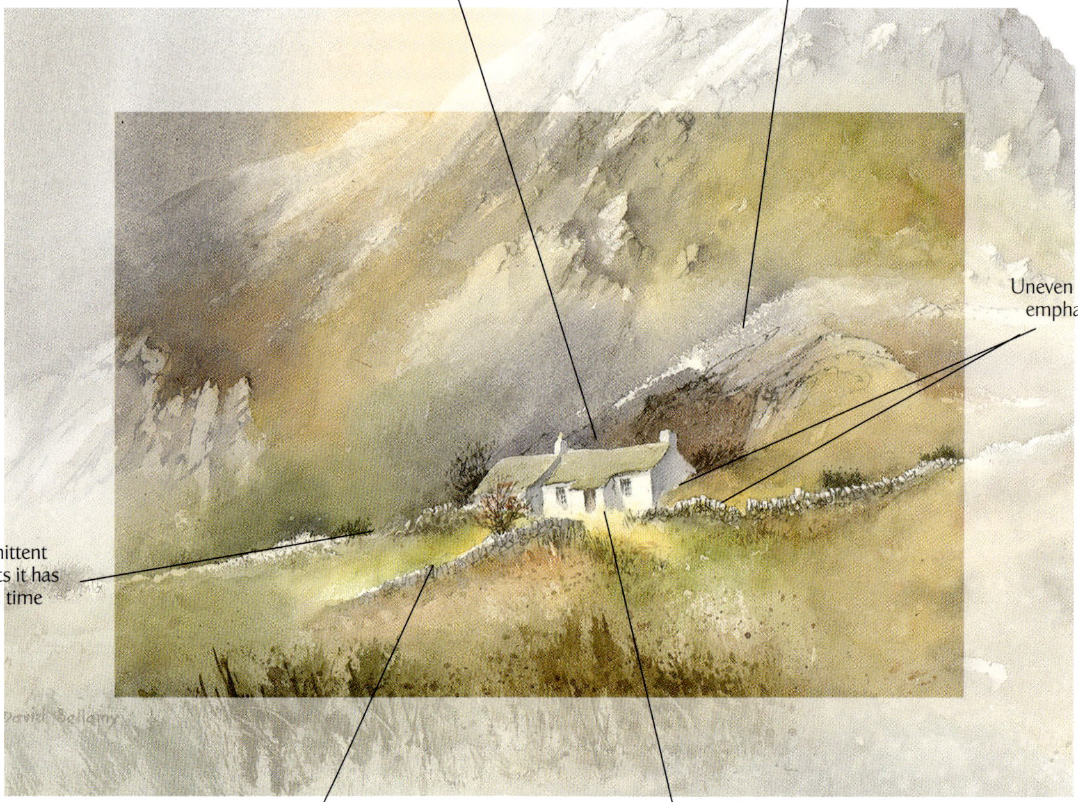

Cottage in the Hills

How often I see students painting a stone cottage scene on a mountain slope, but totally ruining the effect by placing the building itself on what looks like a billiard table! As with rocks and boulders, we need to make hillside buildings look as though they are growing out of rough, uneven ground.

Perspective on hillside buildings

In many situations where the ground is rough and sloping, keen observation of the structure lines is more important than following rigid perspective rules. I normally prefer to enhance the sense of character instead of correcting any wonkiness, but a simple studio sketch or two will usually guide you to the right answer.

The further away you are from a building, the more the perspective problems will diminish, but in the scene below, the viewer is well below the subject, so the closer barn needs particular care.

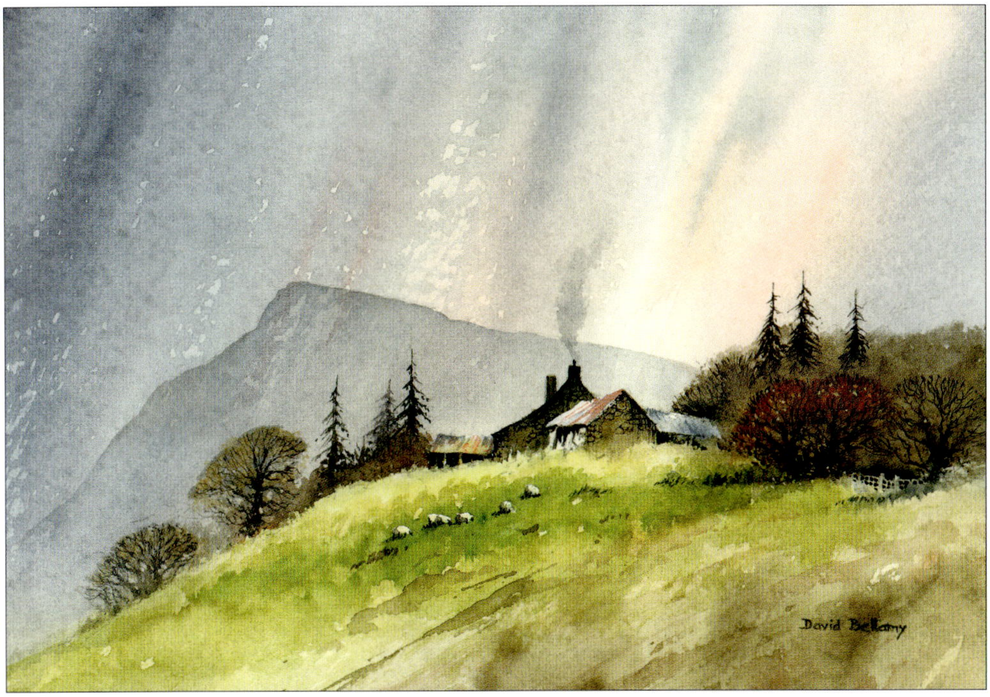

Hill Farm
17.8 x 22.8cm (7 x 9in)

The barn in this painting is set at a different angle to the house, with two sides showing, so we need to portray the roof lines as sloping slightly downwards as they recede to the left. The accompanying diagrams illustrate how to tackle this, but many of these ancient rustic buildings do not conform exactly to the laws of perspective, which often adds to their charm. Make full use of the sloping ground to show up the uneven floor levels.

Perspective diagrams

These diagrams give an idea of how the angles of the horizontal lines (mainly on the roof here) are seen by the viewer both below and above the subject.

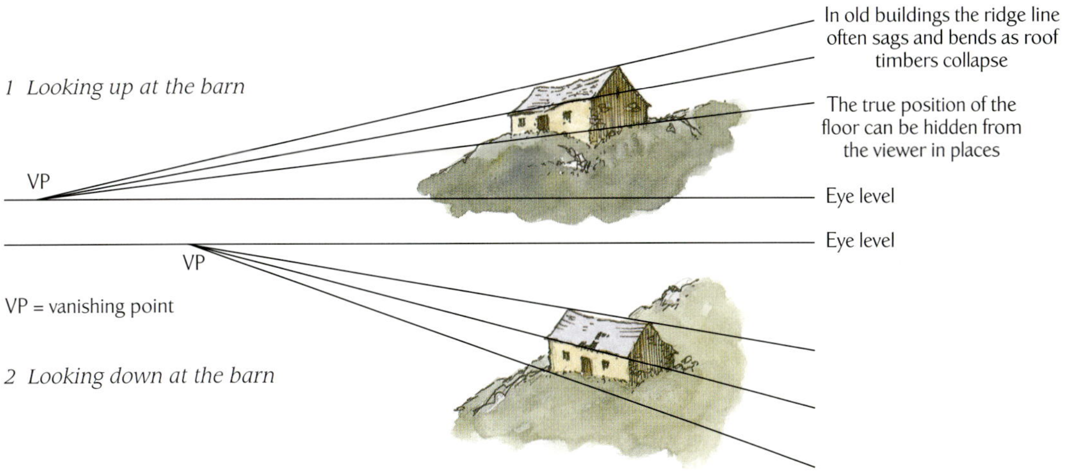

Pen and wash buildings

A technical drawing pen or fibre-tip one can be extremely effective both for sketching and for producing pen and wash paintings. A dip pen is excellent, but can be impractical outdoors. If you feel that drawing is your strong point, and laying colours perhaps less so, then working in pen and ink may well suit your temperament better. Here I use it on buildings, but it can be equally good for rocks, trees, bridges and many subjects. If you are a little nervous about diving in straight away with a pen, then outline the subject in light pencil first, and only when you feel confident, proceed with the pen. Doodling is an excellent way of overcoming this problem.

Himalayan mountain huts

In this sketch I have used a brush-pen with a black ink cartridge. Not only does this give an extremely varied width of line according to the pressure applied, but it can be used on all manner of surfaces, however rough, unlike an ordinary pen which will scratch on Rough paper. One technique I use with these brush-pens is to draw a line or two, and before it has time to dry, swipe a finger across it in the desired direction to create a textural graduated tone. This technique works well on Rough paper. You can see the effect here on the gable end of the right-hand hut where I have used a downward stroke of the finger, though it is not so prominent because this has been done on smooth cartridge paper.

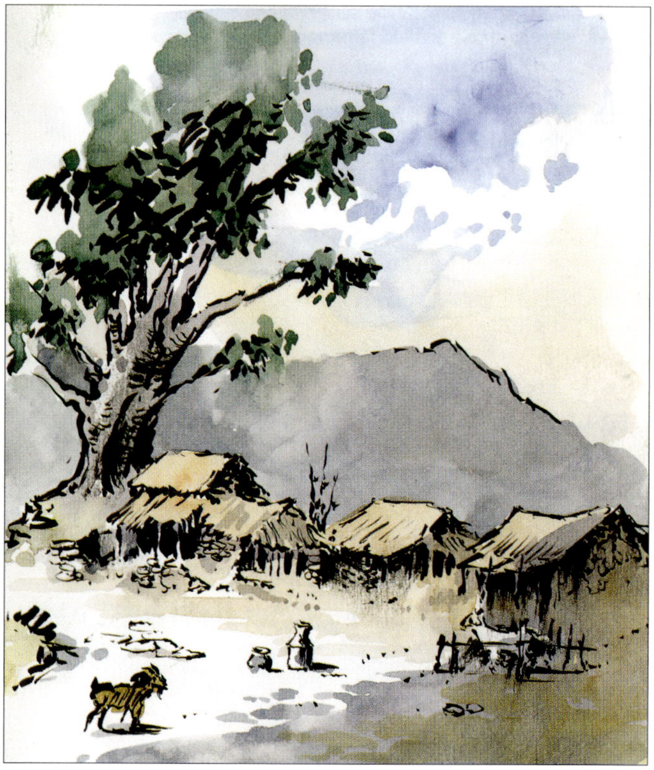

Fivizzano, Tuscany

Here an ordinary fibre-tip pen has been used to draw in the scene before applying washes. On the distant mountain outlines, I have used a broken line as this helps to suggest distance, but often, when drawing with a pen, I omit an outline for distant mountains and clouds and simply paint them in directly. The right-hand tower was more of a sandy colour, and almost invisible when not in direct sunlight, so I have left it white to give it more prominence.

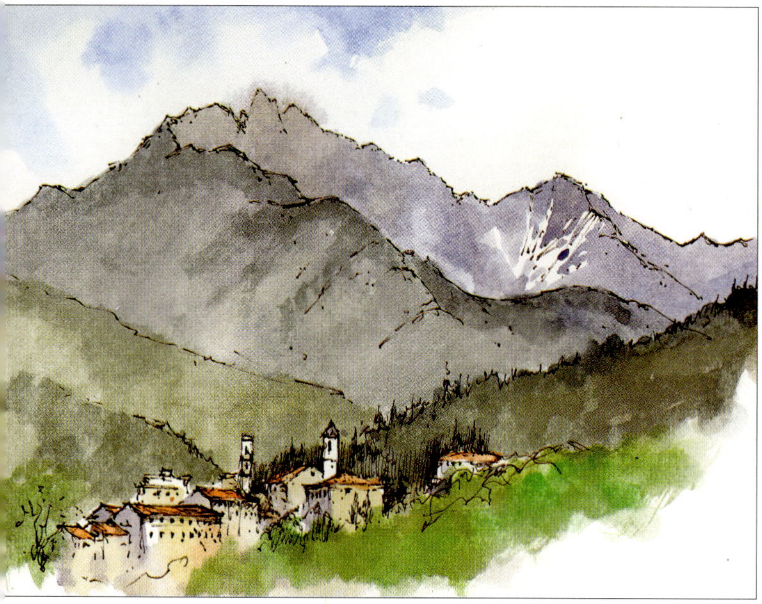

Opposite

Alpine village

22.8 x 17.8cm (9 x 7in)

The combination of Alpine buildings with their flowers and plants and a backdrop of a shapely mountain provides an irresistible composition. The original pencil sketch was devoid of figures, but the scene called out for some life. If you enjoy painting villages and towns, make sure you work on figures, however small, to enliven your compositions.

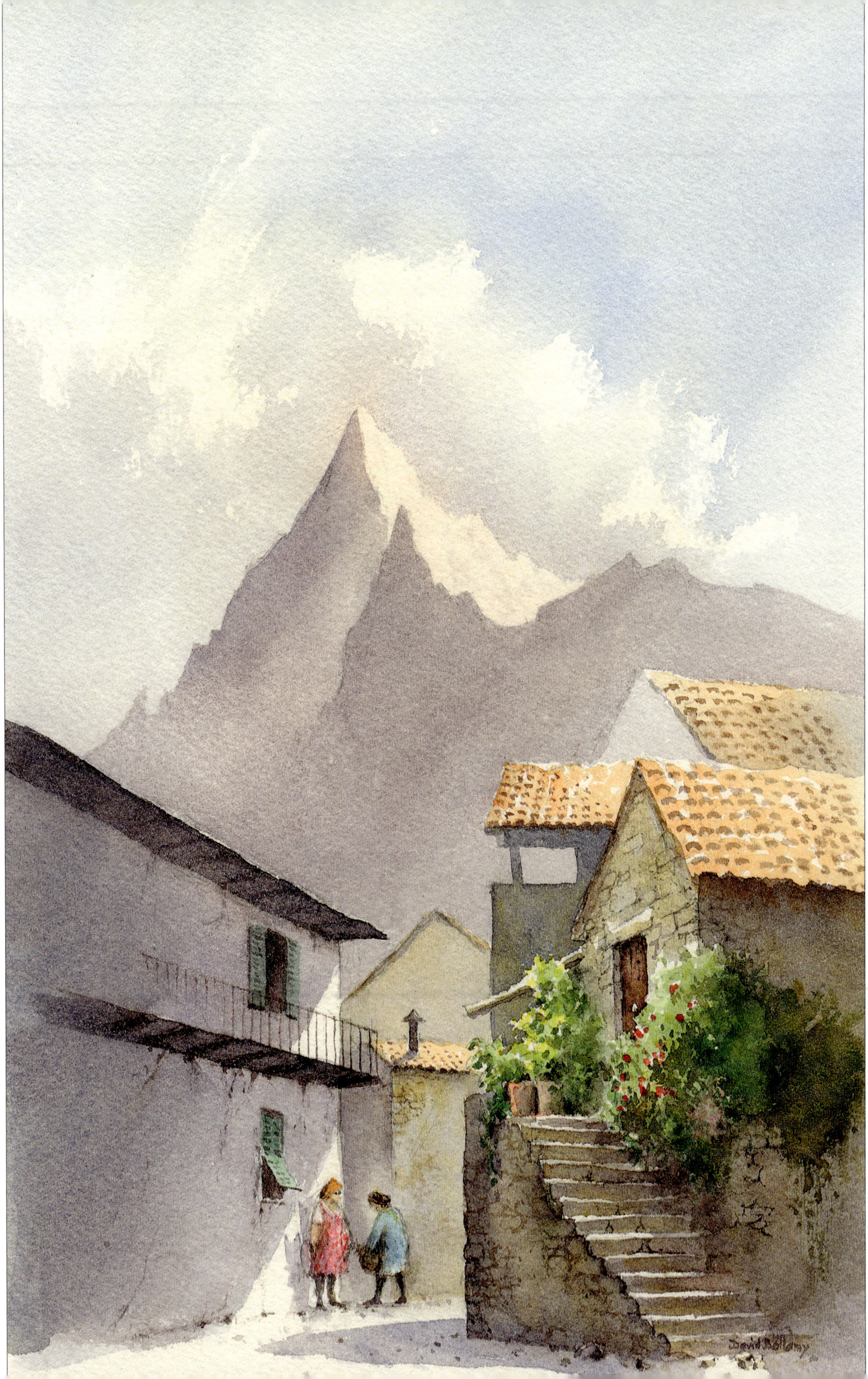

Moorland scenes

Moors can range from pleasant valleys to dreary, high, mist-clad acres of peat-hags, with some hills rising to almost mountainous proportions, capped by rocky tors and outcrops. Out on the high moors you occasionally come across little gems, perhaps a stone packhorse bridge over a tumbling stream, or some shapely crags rising above the surface of a heathery slope. Here we will look at how even the more mundane parts of the moor can be livened up, starting with a simple rendition of a moorland scene using broad washes in three easy stages.

King's Tor

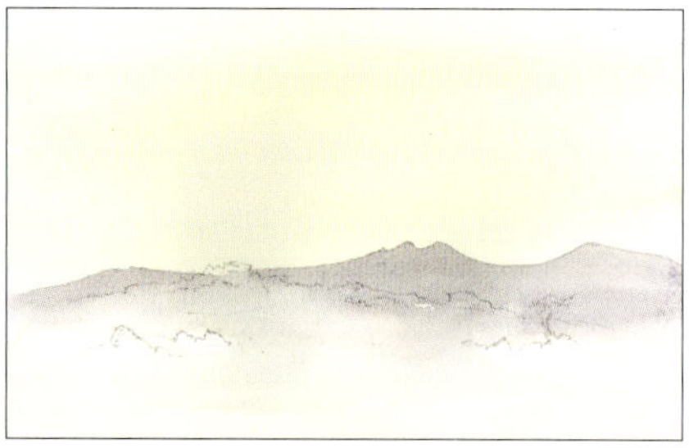

1 Firstly I laid a weak wash of cadmium yellow pale over the sky, bringing it down over most of the paper. When the paper was dry, I applied the distant ridge using a fairly weak mixture of French ultramarine and Indian red, and softened the wash off at the bottom.

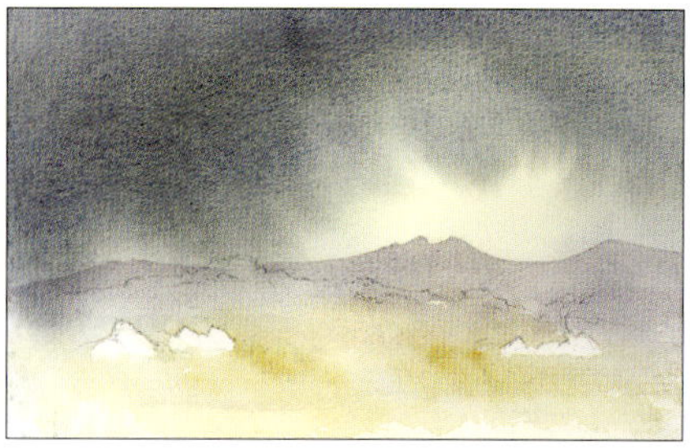

2 Once the paper had dried completely, I re-wet the whole surface and dropped in a strong mix of burnt umber and French ultramarine over the sky, allowing it to run down over part of the distant ridge to suggest a rain squall. I added yellow ochre to the lower part of the wash in the foreground.

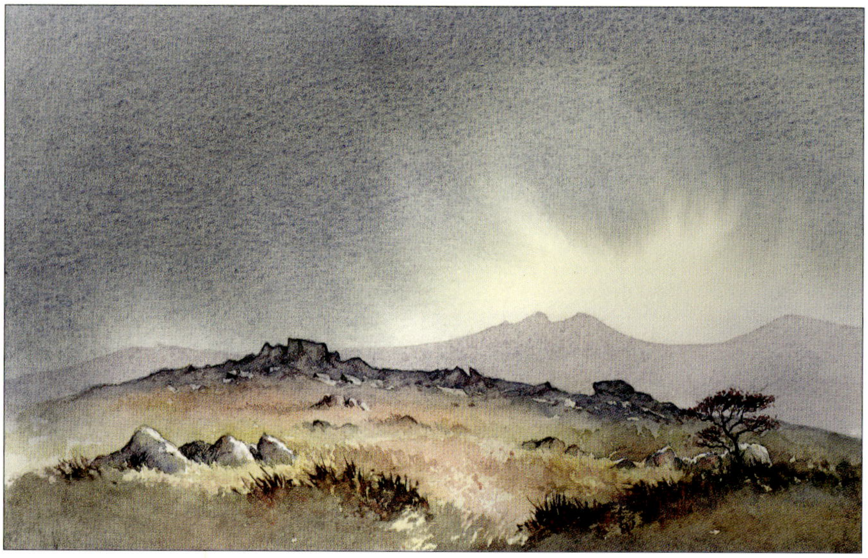

3 For the main tor I painted a wash of stronger French ultramarine and Indian red, dropping in a little yellow ochre, then some light red below the rocks, blending it all in. Then I painted the foreground rocks, while the thorn tree was rendered with a rigger. The dark grasses were applied using a mixture of French ultramarine and burnt umber. Some Indian red was dropped in.

Creating moorland textures with wax resist

One superb method of suggesting rough moorland and mountainside textures, or intermittent snow lying on the ground, is by using a candle or wax crayon to create a resist effect. Wax repels watercolour washes and on Rough paper the textural effect will be even more pronounced. Lay the wax on first, then apply the wash over the top. While you will not get highly accurate detail with this technique, it does give a marvellous spontaneity and uninhibited appearance. Naturally if you want to suggest snow, a white or off-white colour is recommended, but otherwise any colour of wax crayon can be used to create the effect you desire, including an abstract passage. As with all new techniques, try this out on scrap paper first before you commit to it in your full watercolour painting.

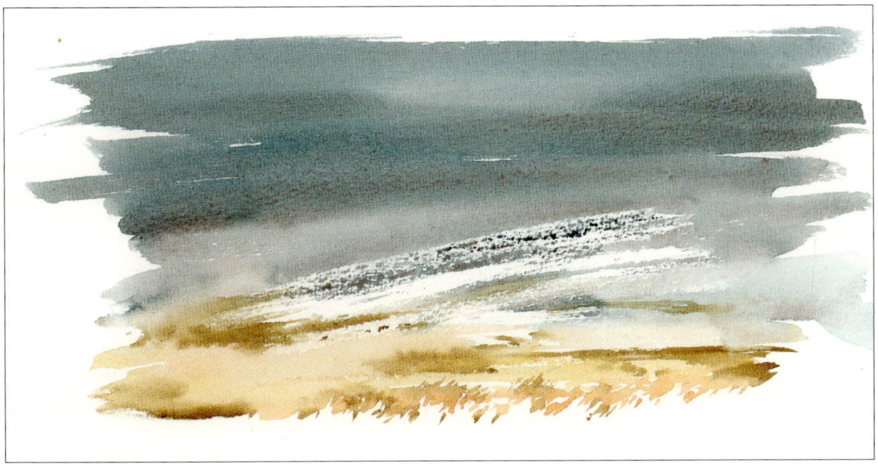

1 To achieve the suggestion of a moor partly covered in snow, I began by dragging a candle across the paper in a shallow diagonal to suggest the slope, then applied a wash of blue-grey across it. Part way into the candle wax area, I introduced some yellow ochre and brought this down to the foreground area. The wax resists the watercolour to create the required effect.

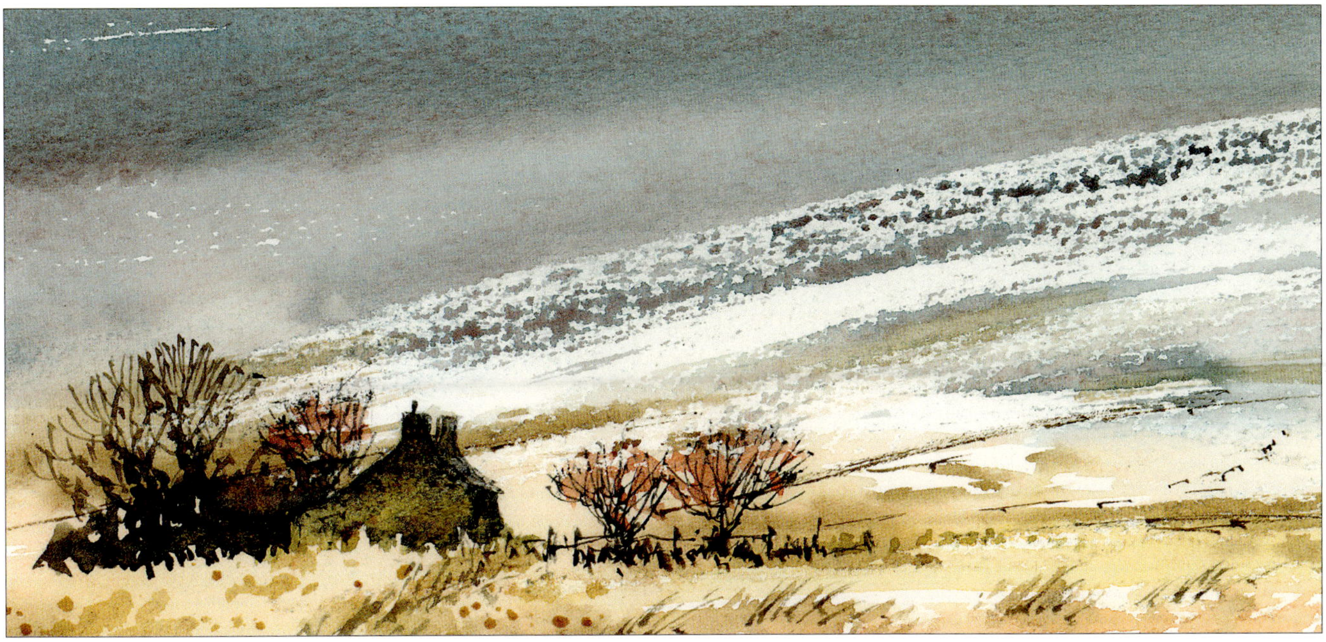

2 The cottage and trees have been added to complete the scene. Naturally, when laying on the candle wax, I avoided the area where these features were to appear. Try experimenting with wax resists using a candle or wax crayons.

Adding interest to simple moorland scenes

There are a number of techniques that can be used to liven up a simple scene. Below I have shown how counterchange can be used to beef up a scene, without actually changing the subject itself, and how you can choose a centre of interest from several options and then emphasise it to give it prominence. Try introducing these ways of working to some of your own scenes.

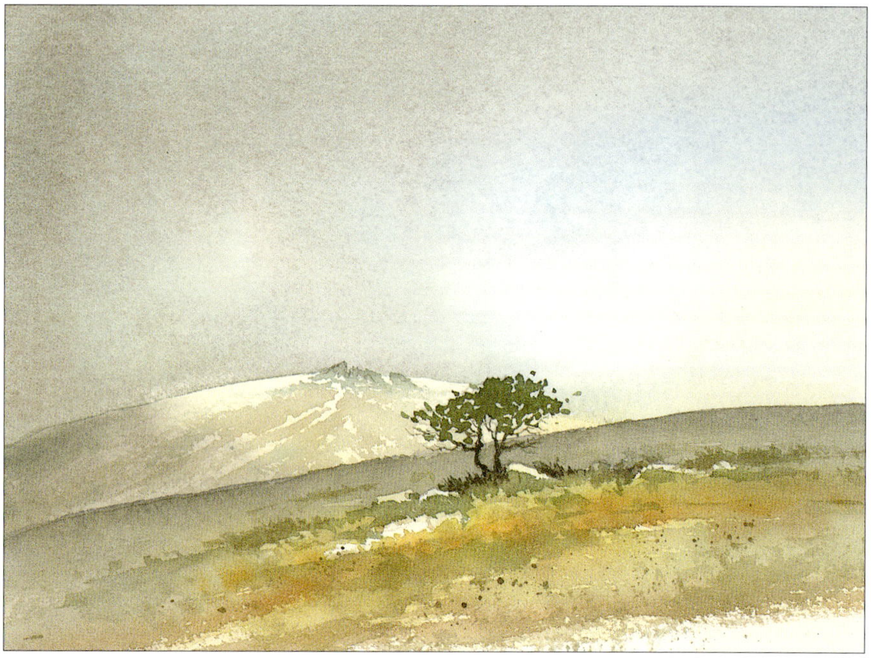

Using counterchange

Here I have used counterchange to add interest to a scene with fairly mundane moorland slopes, a useful technique where you wish to give the scene a bit of zip. Note how the background whaleback ridge goes from light to dark. Counterchange also throws the emphasis to a point of your choosing.

Emphasising a focal point

This sketch of rocks and aloe plants at Spioenkop in South Africa illustrates how I have taken a few rocks, plants and bushes and made them into a centre of interest within a wide landscape. You can always add to the number of these features, or simply make them larger to suit your needs. In the actual landscape there were many of these clumps of rocks and vegetation: I chose the clump that appealed most to me.

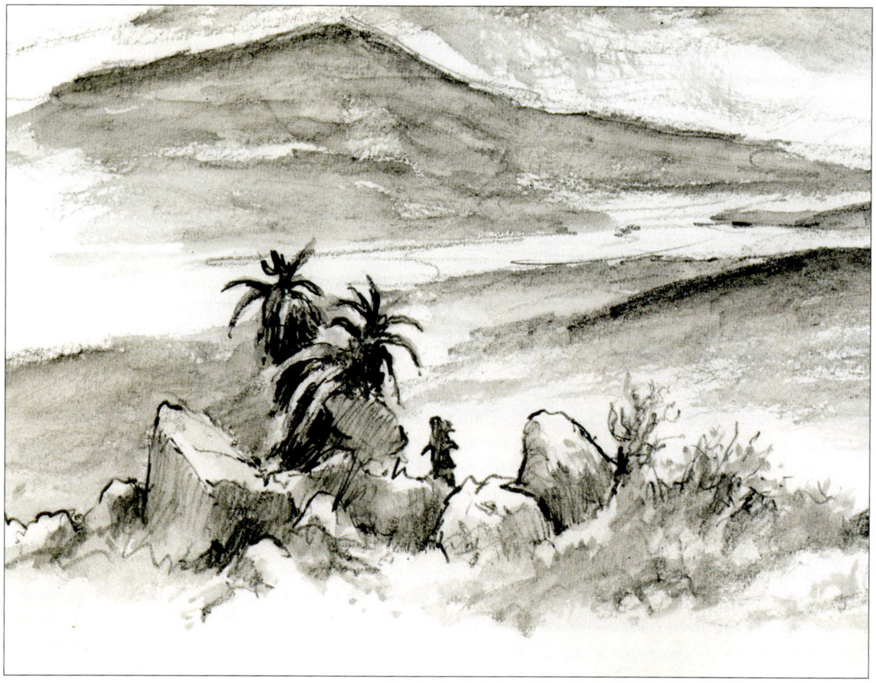

Using birds as a focal point

Either in flight or on the ground, birds can create an excellent focal point for a moorland scene, as shown in the two examples below.

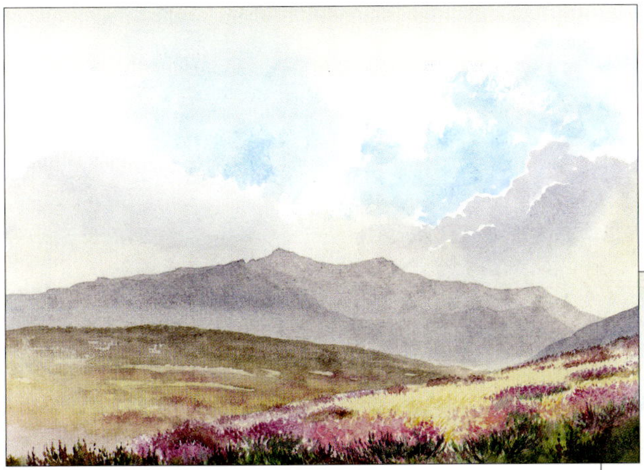

Here the subject, moors south of Cadair Idris in North Wales, is lacking a focal point, sometimes a problem with open moorland, even if, as in this case, Cadair Idris mountain can be seen looming in the background.

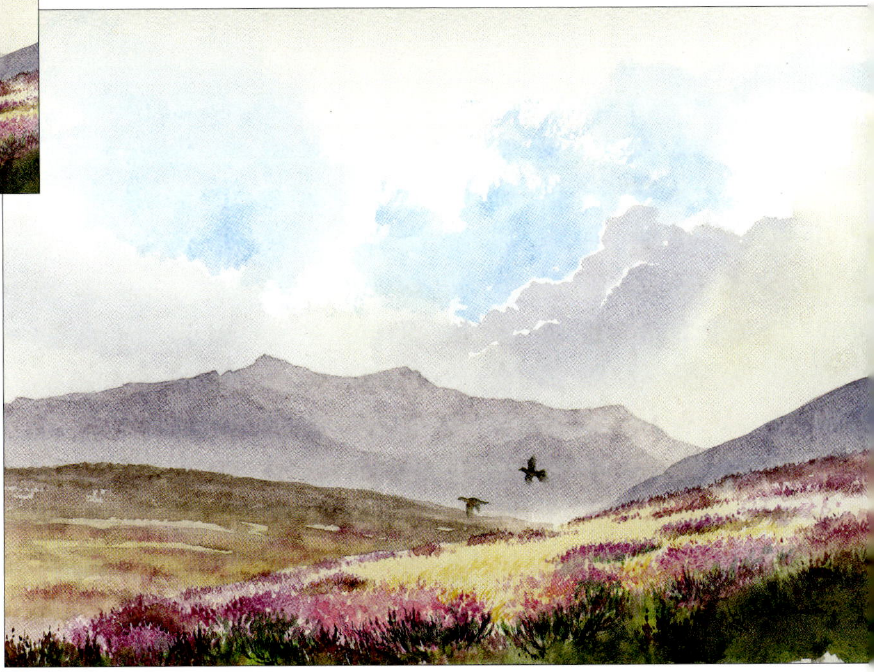

Moors in Snowdonia, Wales
22.8 x 30.5cm (9 x 12in)

The addition of a brace of grouse flying low over the moor has effectively introduced a focal point to the scene. Birds or animals can often be of help in this way. Note how their wings are blurred to suggest the frenetic wing movement of grouse taking off.

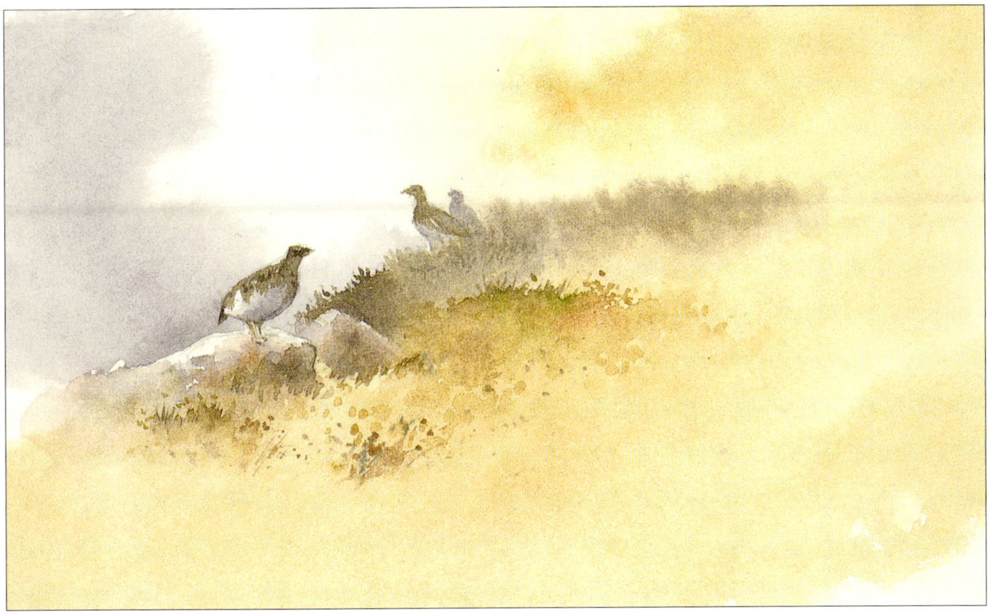

Ptarmigan

Ptarmigan are high-level birds and change their plumage in winter. On the ground they can form an excellent focal point, or they can simply be used within a composition to add life. As they are rather curious birds and come quite close, they are fairly easy to sketch.

Painting large skies

The flatter moorland terrain tends to demand more expansive and interesting skies that complement the subject. I like to arrange the sky so that the most detailed part is close to the focal point. A light area within swirling cloud formations can be used to highlight a tor or crag sticking up from the moor. Sometimes it is worth adding birds in flight near the centre of interest, and where you may have a more distant hill or moorland swelling, think about bringing down a rain squall over it. A well-executed sky can more than make up for a poor centre of interest amidst a barren landscape.

Moorland Farm
28 x 43.2cm (11 x 17in)

Make use of the wide expanse of sky so typical with moorland subjects. Here the blue-grey washes were painted on dry paper to achieve the hard, ragged edges to the white clouds, then, when dry, they were reinforced in places with a slightly stronger wash of the same colour, which I ran out at the top to blend in with the rest of the sky. This has the effect of sharpening up the more important clouds, leaving the remainder subdued. Sheep add life and interest into a foreground, especially one as large as this.

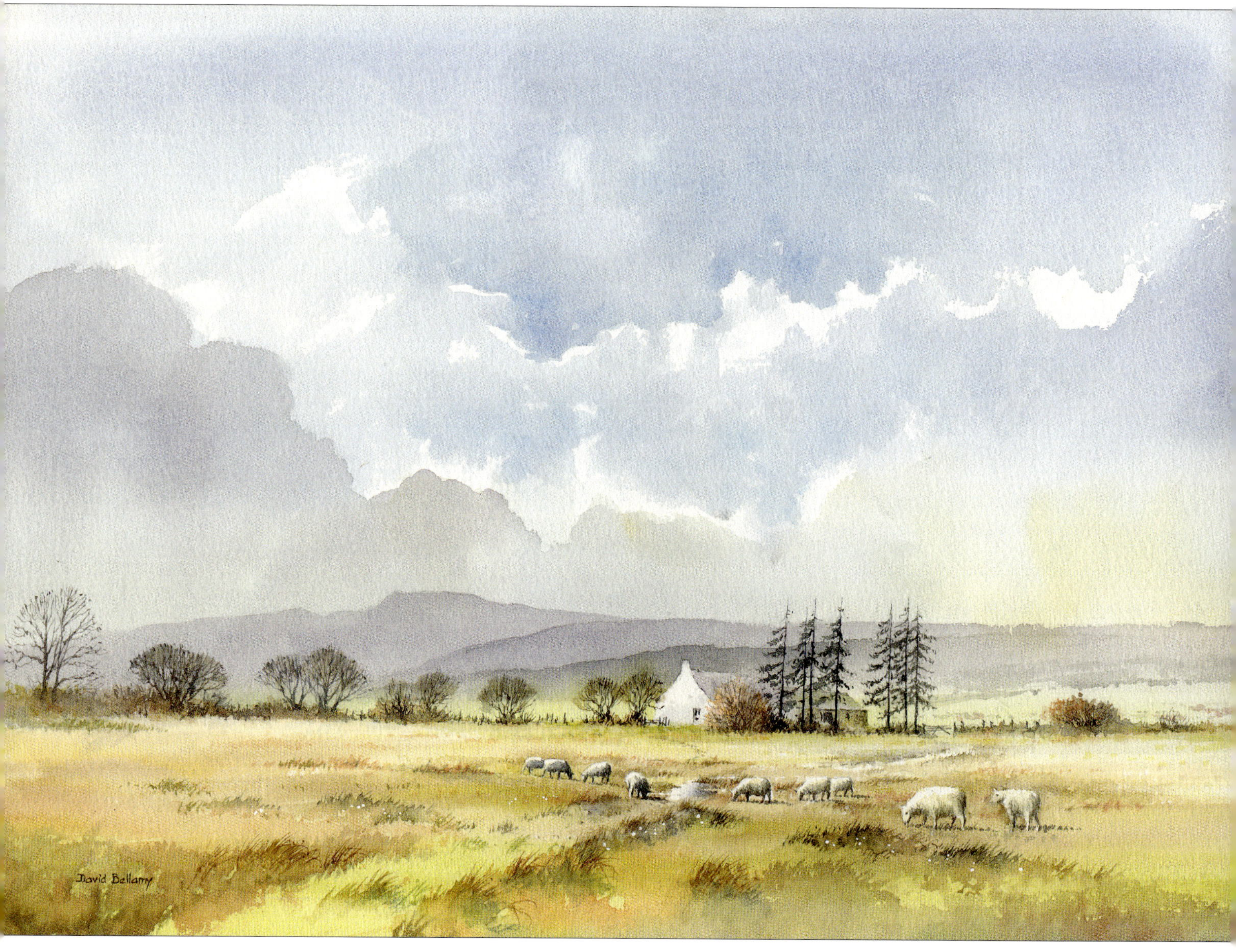

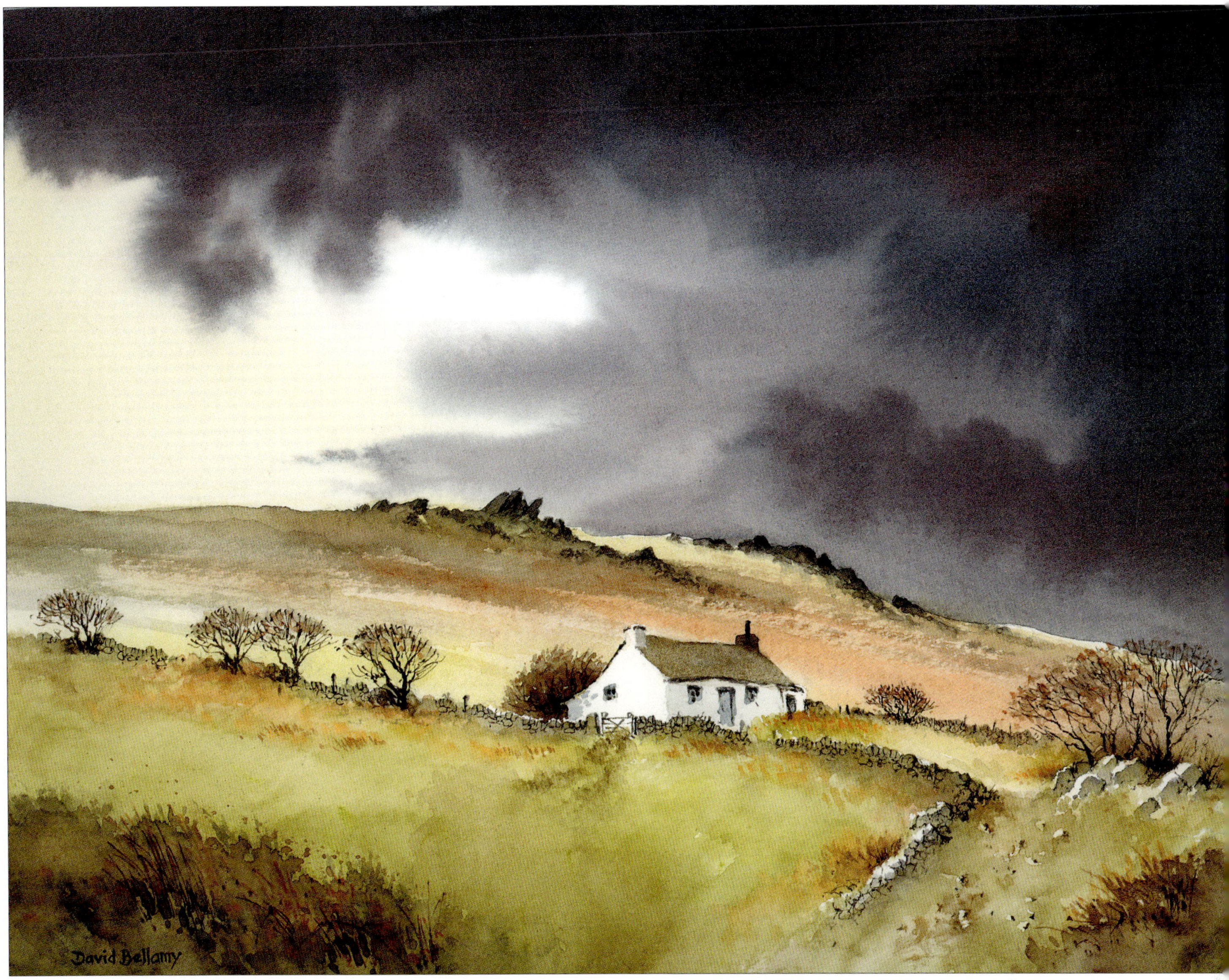

Mood and colour
20.3 x 30.5cm (8 x 12in)

Emphasising strong colours can bring a painting to life. In this painting, the various diagonal washes of light red, yellow ochre and cadmium yellow pale across the background slope overlap each other. After applying a mix of light red and French ultramarine to the crags, I then brought a slightly weaker version of this mix down diagonally over part of the yellow ochre and light red in a rapid, dry brush fashion. This is an excellent manner of suggesting rough ground, and the result can best be seen just above and to the right of the right-hand chimney.

The moody sky was begun with a fluid wash of Naples yellow across the left-hand half, followed immediately by a medium-tone wash of Indian red and French ultramarine over the right-hand sky, taking it across the top to the left. Without pause, I then applied a stronger version of the same colours to form the darkest clouds that dropped into the Naples yellow on the left. In contrast to my normal way of working, the sky was done after I had painted the yellow ochre on the moorland and allowed it to dry. The crags were painted after the sky had dried.

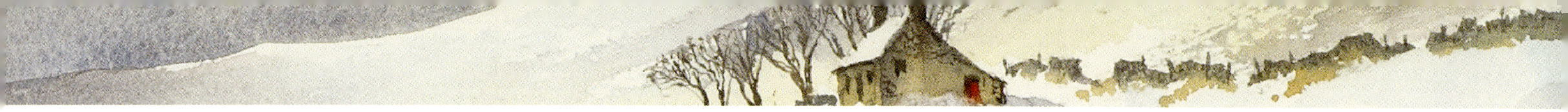

Chapel le Dale

When painting a snow scene like this one in Chapel le Dale, Yorkshire, try to introduce some warm colours to avoid an overall cold result. This can be done in the sky, reflections, vegetation or in a building. In this demonstration I show how to add warm reds and yellows to a winter moorland landscape.

Materials used

Saunders Waterford High White, 300gsm (140lb) Not watercolour paper

Brushes: squirrel mop, no. 7 and no. 4 round, no. 1 rigger, no. 1 round and 6mm (¼in) flat

Colours: Naples yellow, cadmium yellow pale, cadmium red, French ultramarine, cobalt blue, yellow ochre, burnt umber

Paper tissue

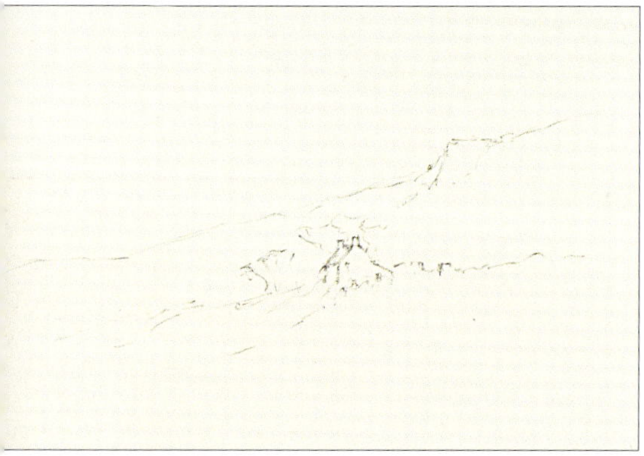

1 Draw the scene.

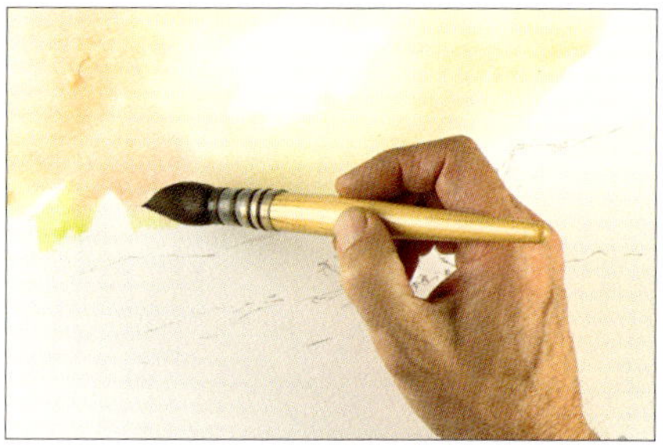

2 Use the squirrel mop to paint a touch of Naples yellow around a central white space in the sky, then while this is wet, drop in cadmium yellow pale, then cadmium red.

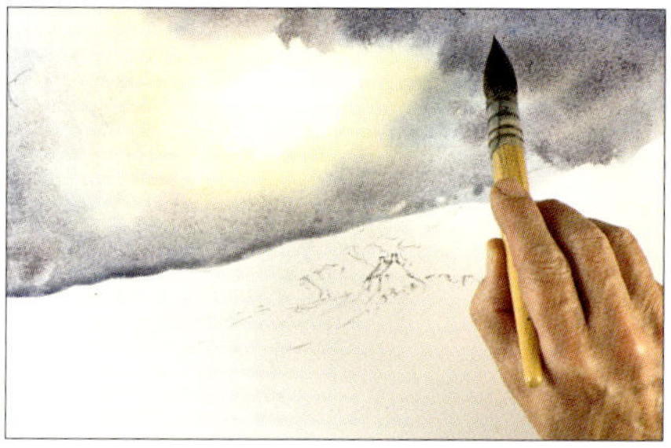

3 Drop in ultramarine around the edges of the sky, then a mix of ultramarine and cadmium red, and then a stronger mix of the same colours at the very edges of the sky.

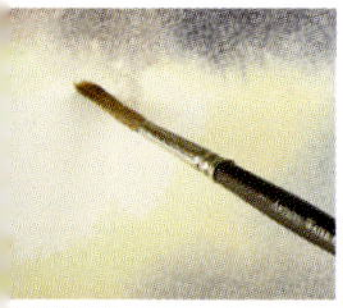

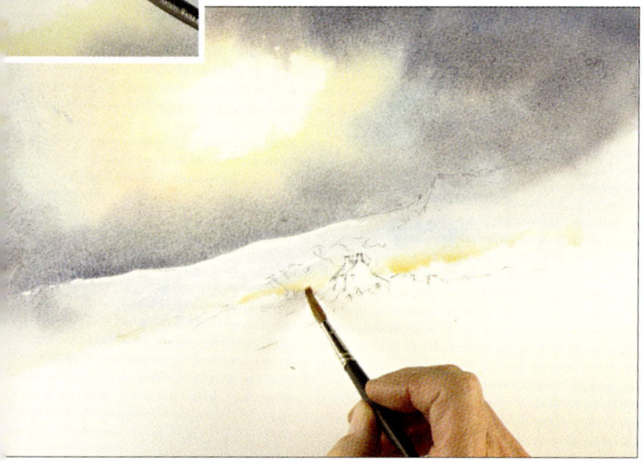

4 Change to the no. 7 round brush to soften the cloud colour into the dry white area. Then use a clean brush with water to bring the cloud colour down into the snowy area on the far left. Use a dry brush to paint a wash of cobalt blue across the distant snow, leaving highlights white, then add yellow ochre and allow to dry.

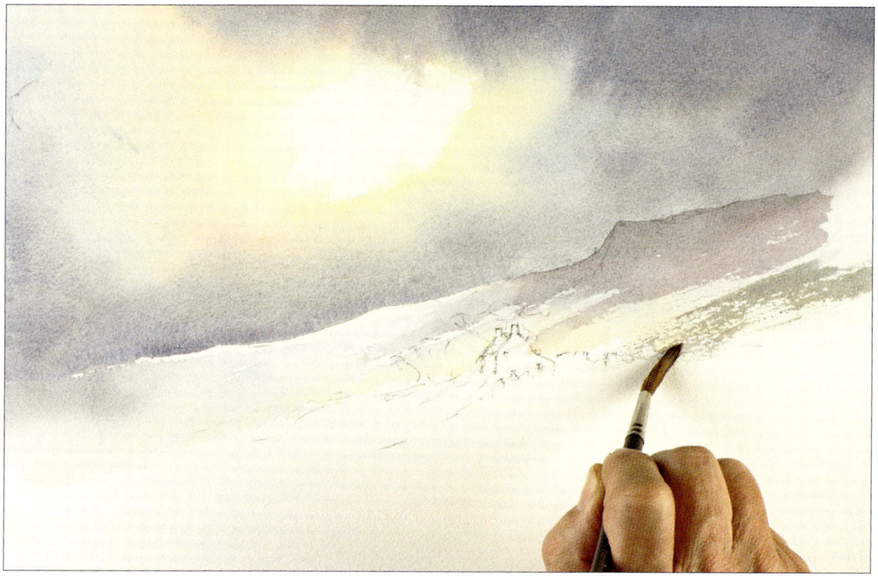

5 Paint the distant moorland with a mix of ultramarine and cadmium red, then use a mix of burnt umber and ultramarine with the dry brush technique to paint the partly snow-covered area further forwards.

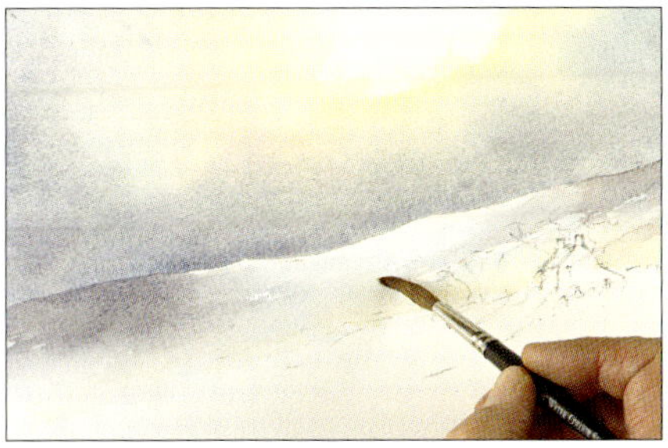

6 Wet the far left-hand side with clean water, then bring ultramarine and cadmium red across to emphasise the light in the centre. Feather the darker area off with clean water towards the centre.

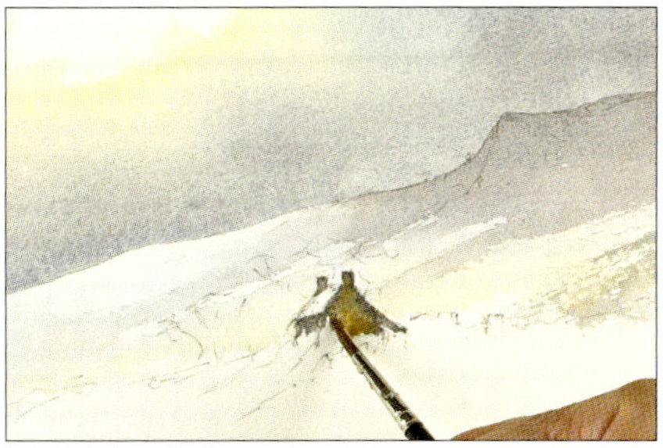

7 Use the no. 4 round with a weak mix of ultramarine and burnt umber to paint the building. Drop in yellow ochre lower down and this will spread upwards, creating texture. Allow to dry.

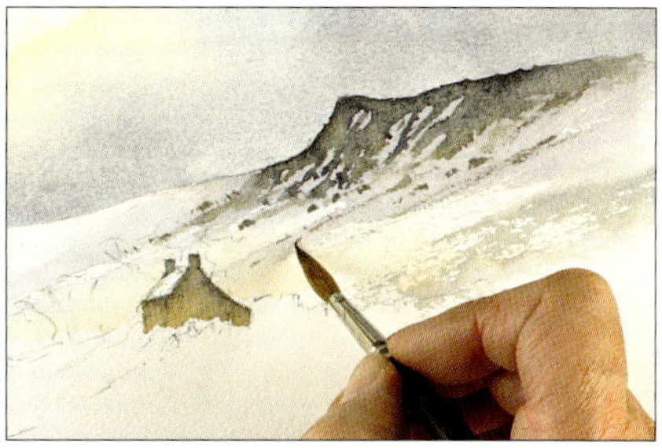

8 Use the point of the no. 7 brush and a mix of ultramarine and burnt umber to paint the strong darks on the crag, suggesting the structure. Drop in yellow ochre while still wet. Drag a mixture of ultramarine and cadmium red down from the crag to link it with the house and create texture.

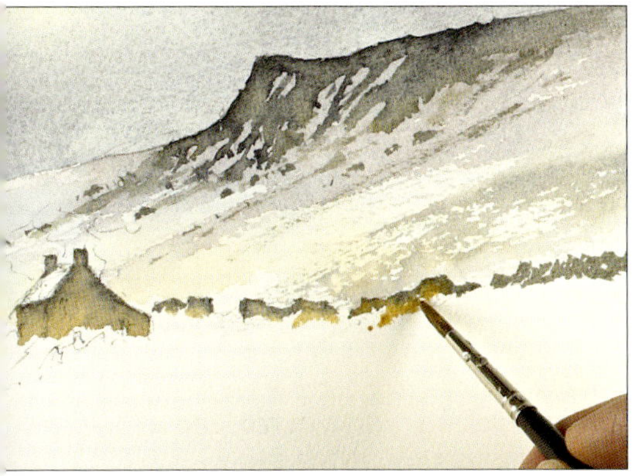

9 Use the point of the no. 7 brush and a mix of ultramarine and burnt umber to paint the intermittent dry stone wall, then change to the no. 4 round and drop in yellow ochre beneath the wall, suggesting grasses.

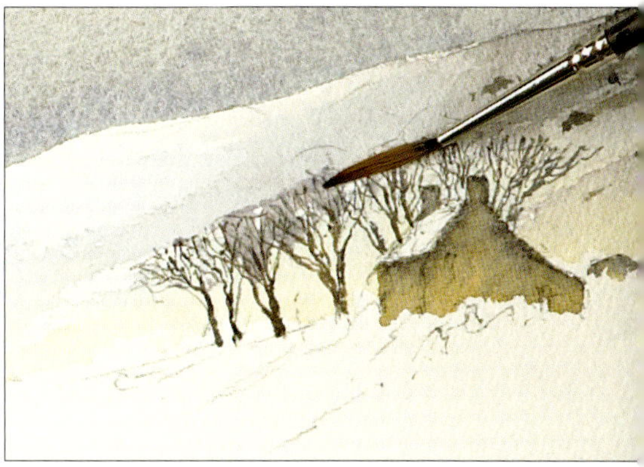

10 Paint the trees around the house with the no. 1 rigger and the ultramarine and burnt umber mix, working from the bottom upwards. Then pick up a mix of ultramarine and cadmium red and use the side of the brush to create the mass of twigwork, this time working downwards from the top of the trees.

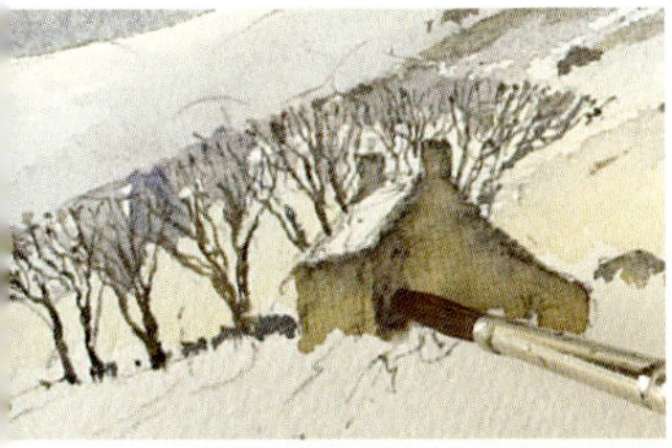

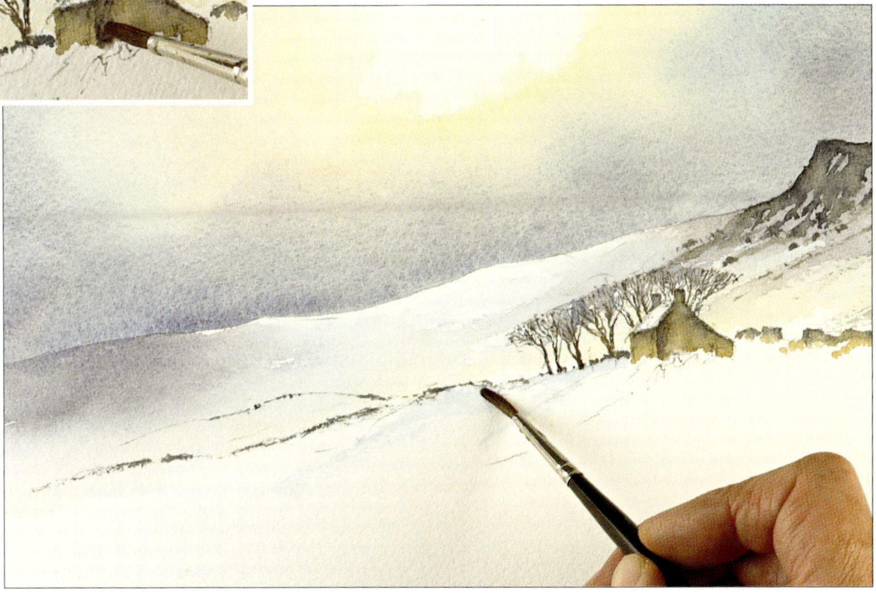

11 Use the same brush and mix to paint the continuation of the dry stone wall, and another wall coming to meet it. Then use the no. 4 brush to paint the shadow on the house with ultramarine and cadmium red, to define the corner. Fade off the colour to the right with clean water. Paint snow shadows with a thin wash of cobalt blue, suggesting the undulating land.

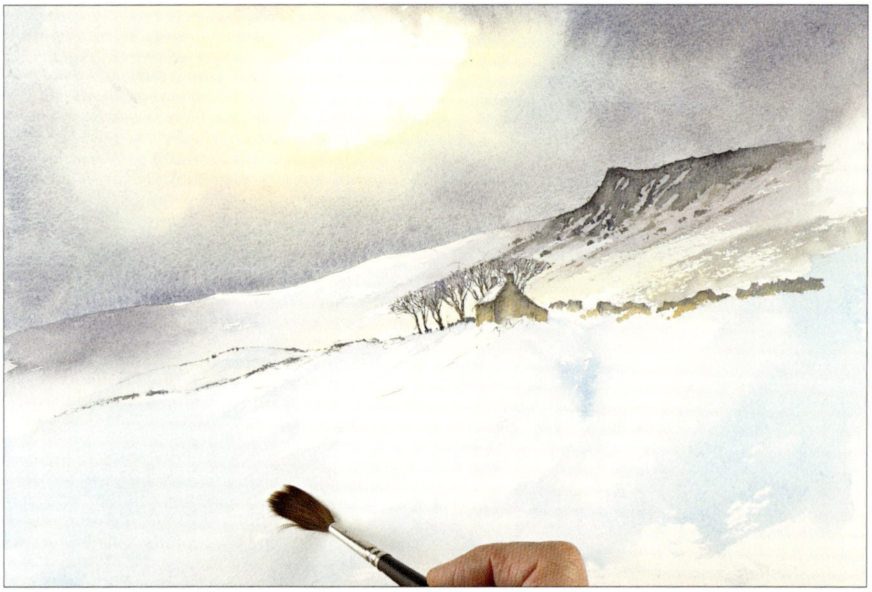

12 Create a lead-in to the scene by suggesting a snow-covered track leading to the house, using the same brush and wash. Add ultramarine to the wash and soften the track with clean water. Continue describing the snowy land, changing to the no. 7 brush and painting darker shadows at the edges of the scene, reflecting the dark-edged sky. Allow to dry.

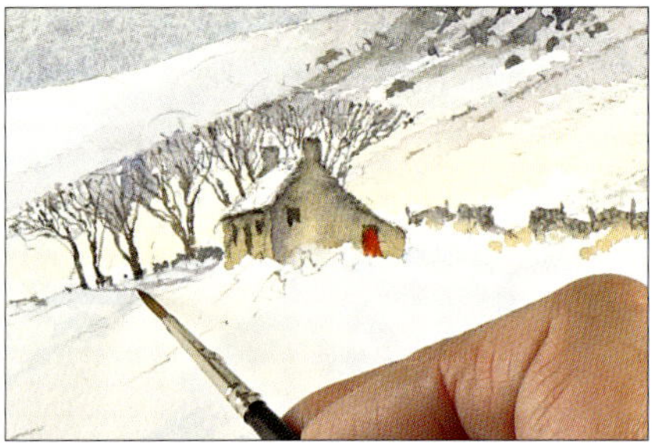

13 Use the no. 1 round brush and a dark mix of ultramarine and burnt umber to paint the posts by the wall and to hint at stonework. Paint the details of the house in the same way, then drop in cadmium red for the door while the dark colour is wet. Paint cast shadows from the house with ultramarine and cadmium red.

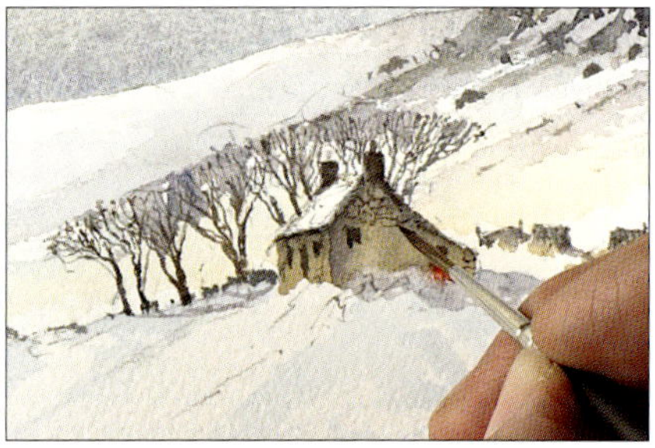

14 Strengthen the chimneys with ultramarine and burnt umber, then use the no. 1 rigger to suggest the stonework of the house.

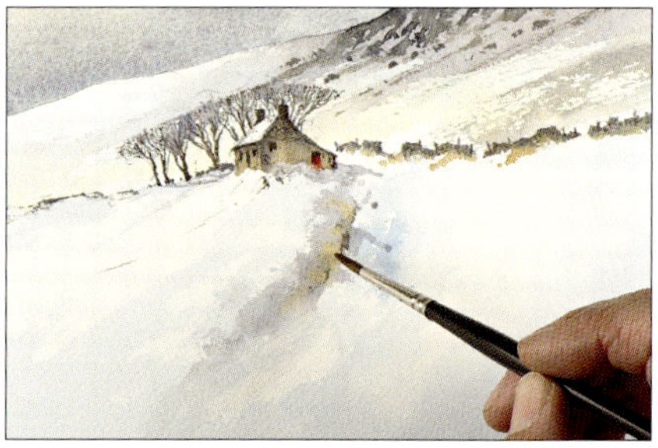

15 Darken the shadow on the bank beside the track with the no. 4 brush and ultramarine and cadmium red. Use the side of the brush to create a ragged effect, then drop in a touch of yellow ochre.

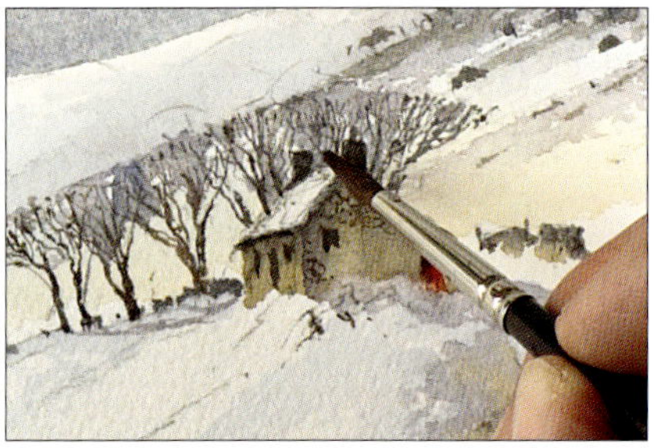

16 Define the snowy ridge of the roof by darkening the background behind it with ultramarine and cadmium red.

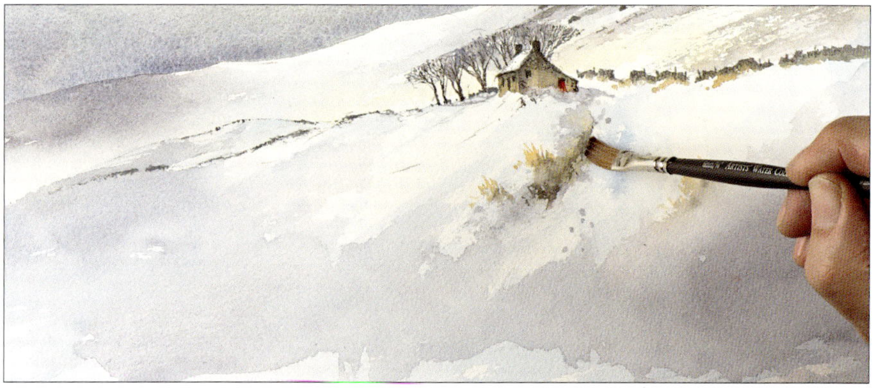

17 Darken the left-hand and right-hand sides of the snow with ultramarine and cadmium red on the no. 7 brush to emphasise the lighter area of the focal point, then use the no. 1 rigger and yellow ochre to suggest grasses. Darken them in places with burnt umber and ultramarine. Use the edge of the 6mm (¼in) flat brush and clean water to soften the track.

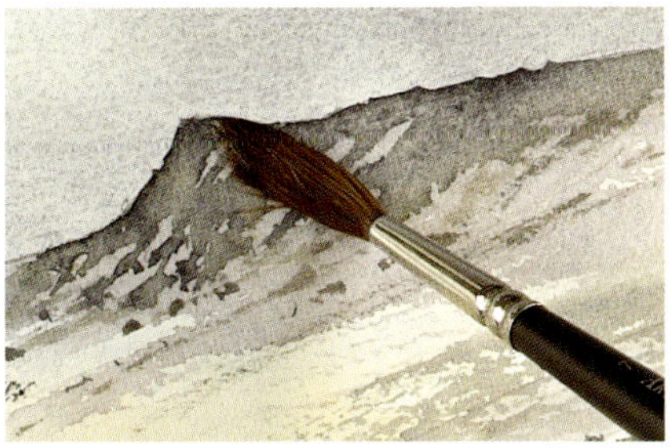

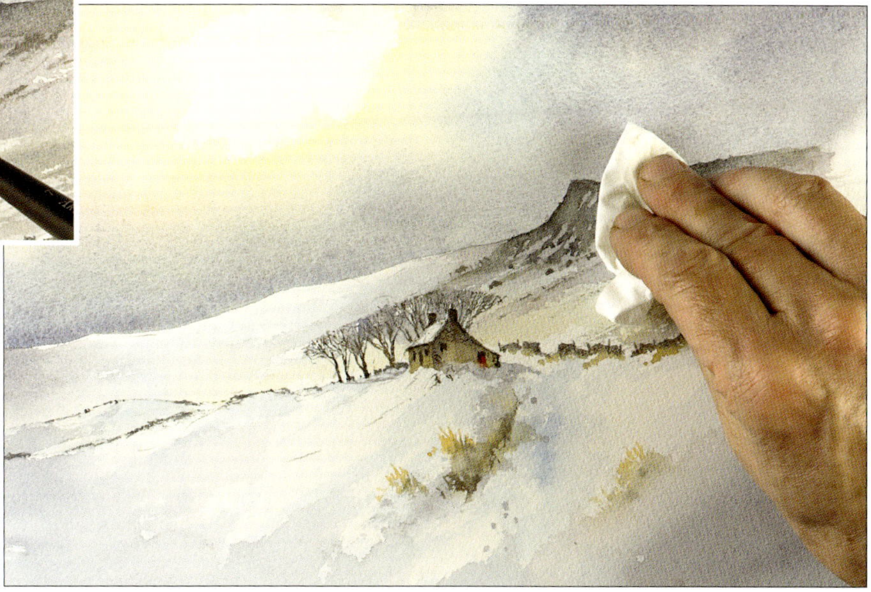

18 Use the no. 7 brush to float clean water over the distant crag, then dab it with a paper tissue to soften it a little.

The finished painting. At the final stage, I erased the pencil lines to keep the white clean.

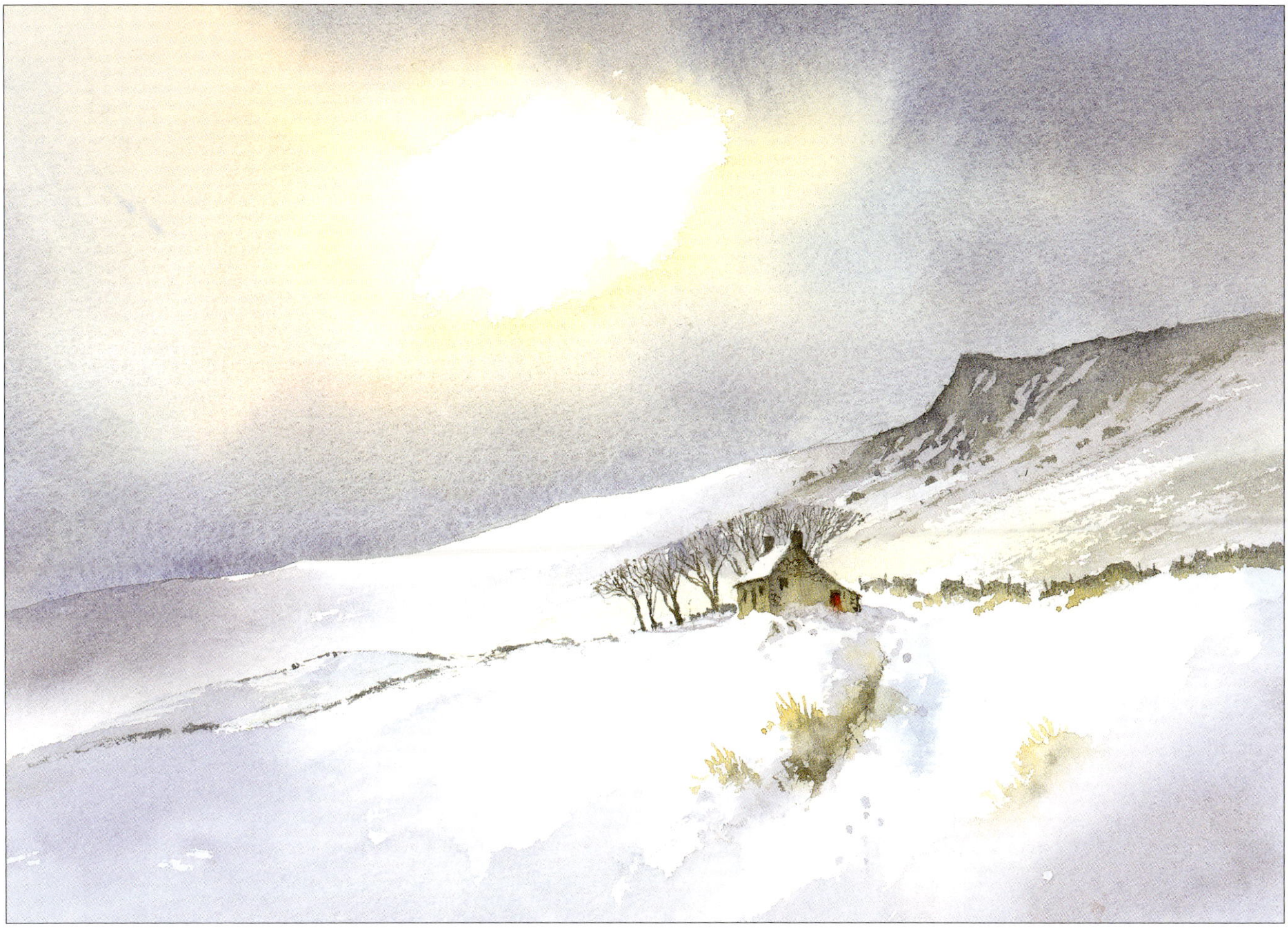

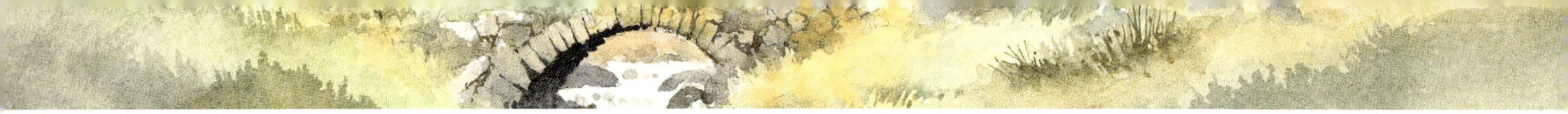

Moorland Bridge

It can be a challenge to maintain interest in large areas of open moorland. In this demonstration I show how to enliven these various parts of the scene, and throw the main emphasis on to the focal point.

Materials used

Saunders Waterford 300gsm (140lb) Rough watercolour paper

Brushes: squirrel mop, fan brush, no. 7 and no. 4 round, 6mm (¼in) flat, no. 1 rigger and no. 1 round

Colours: Naples yellow, French ultramarine, burnt umber, cadmium red, yellow ochre, raw umber, cobalt blue, viridian, new gamboge, cadmium orange, perylene maroon

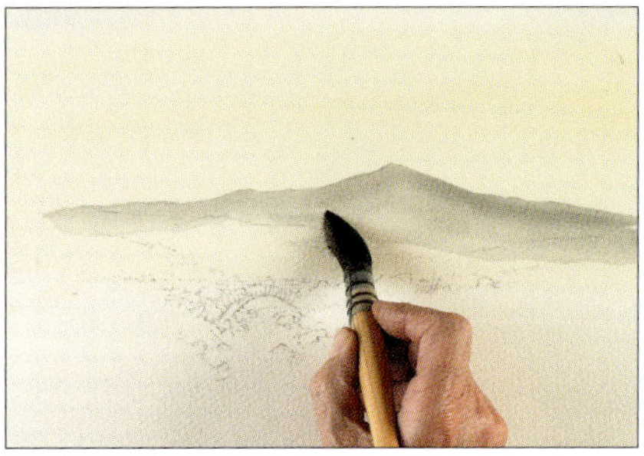

1 Draw the scene. Wet the sky area and distant ridge with a squirrel mop and clean water, then sweep a wash of Naples yellow across the same area. Allow to dry. Paint the distant ridge with a pale mix of ultramarine and burnt umber. Allow to dry.

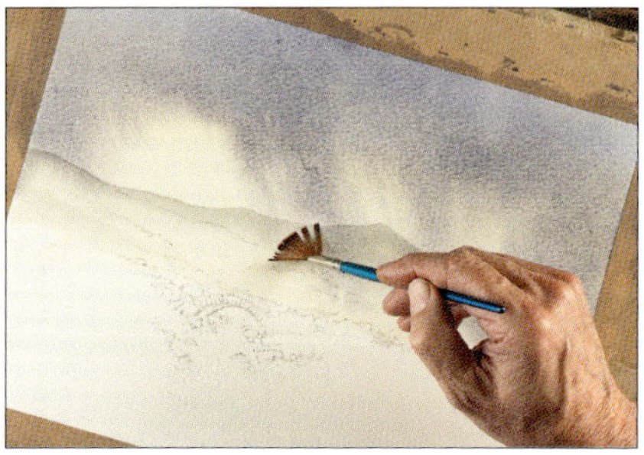

2 Prop your painting board up at a steep angle. Cover the sky and distant ridge with clean water, then paint a mix of ultramarine and cadmium red into the upper sky. This should run down to create a rain squall. A damp fan brush is effective if you need to encourage its downward progress. Allow it to dry naturally. Lift out colour with a clean no. 7 brush if it creeps too low.

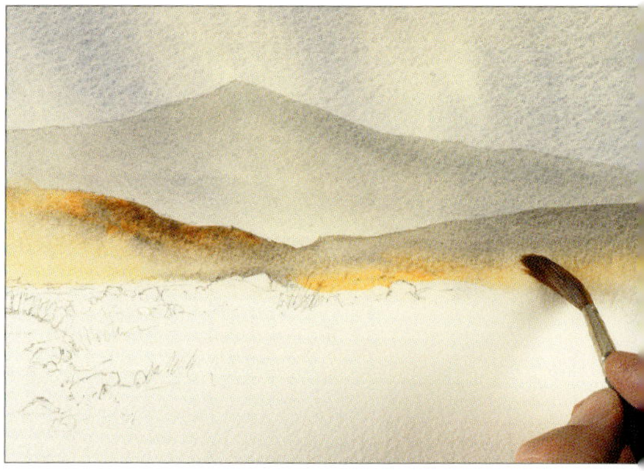

3 Paint the next line of hills in front of the ridge with the no. 7 brush and yellow ochre. Drop in raw umber in places. Paint a mix of ultramarine and cadmium red into the left-hand side, against the light of the sky, then a stronger mix in the middle, in front of the lighter distant ridge, then more of the paler mix to the right. Drop in yellow ochre lower down.

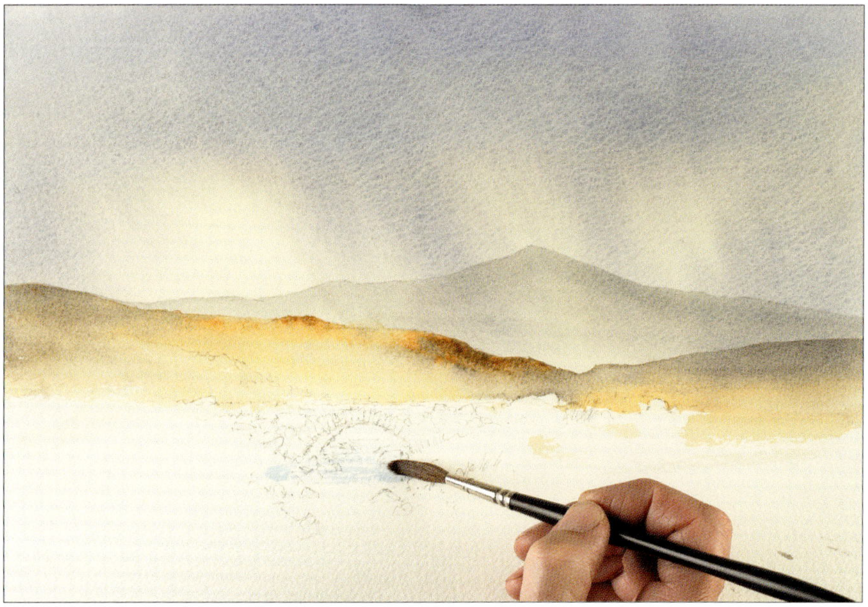

4 Pick up a cobalt blue wash on a dry brush and sweep this across the water area beneath the bridge. The dry brush technique should create a sparkling effect with the Rough paper.

5 Use the no. 7 brush to paint the green of the grass with viridian and new gamboge, then bring in yellow ochre, down to the bottom, and allow the colours to merge. Use the no. 4 brush to drop in cadmium orange to create brightness here and there. It will lose its intensity in the wet background. Allow to dry.

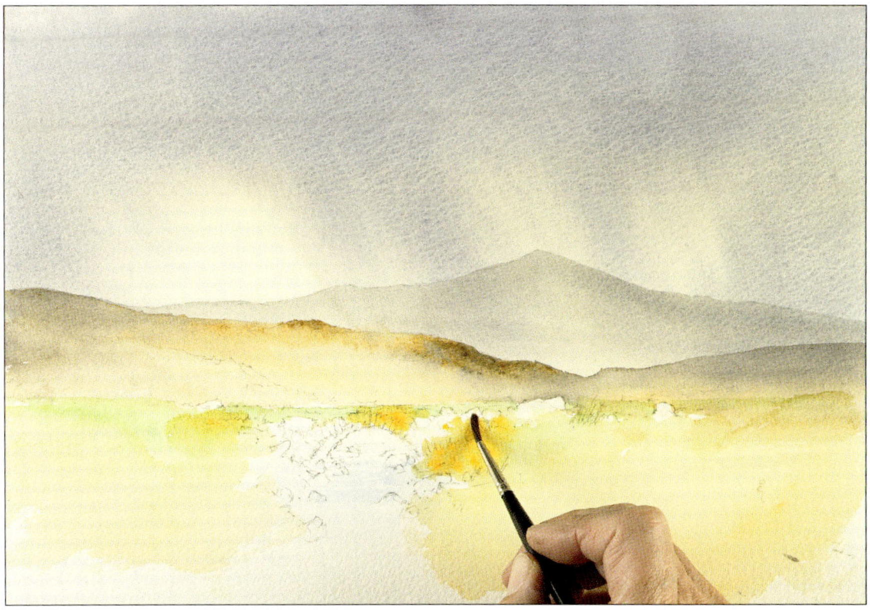

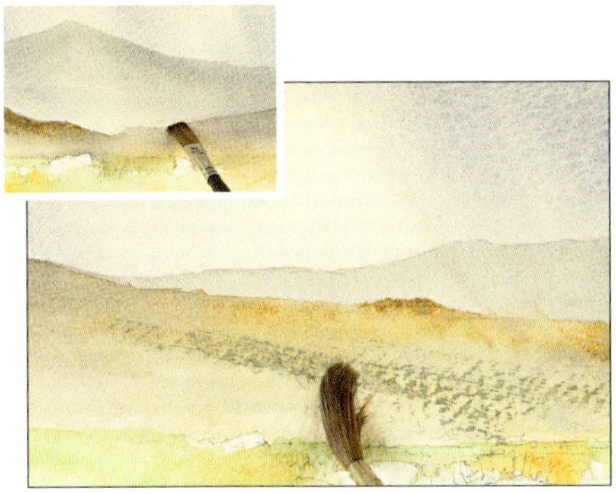

6 To increase the sense of distance, soften part of the middle distant ridge with the 6mm (¼in) flat brush and clean water. Use the no. 7 brush with ultramarine and raw umber to create moorland texture with the dry brush technique, then soften the edges of this with clean water.

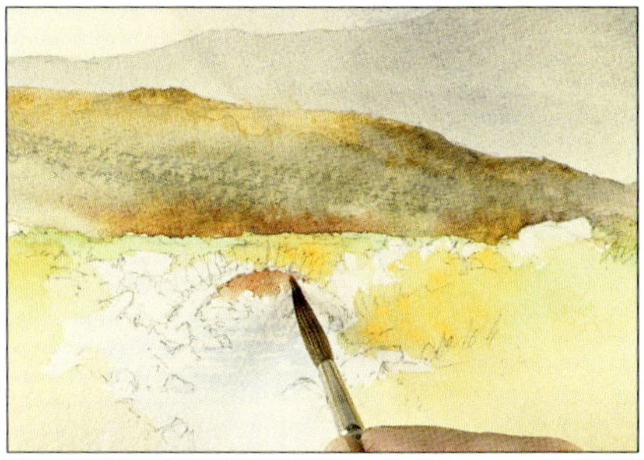

7 Paint more raw umber behind the bridge to highlight the top, then drop in perylene maroon. Vary this with yellow ochre in places and drop in perylene maroon under the bridge.

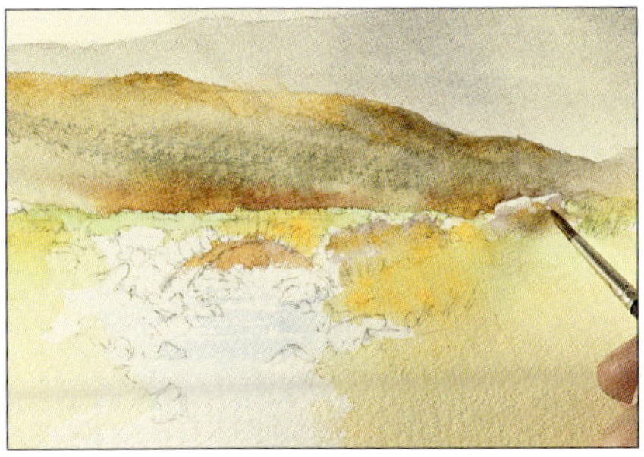

8 Use the no. 4 brush to paint rocks with ultramarine and cadmium red. Soften them at the bottom with clean water, then drop in yellow ochre. Leave white highlights on the tops.

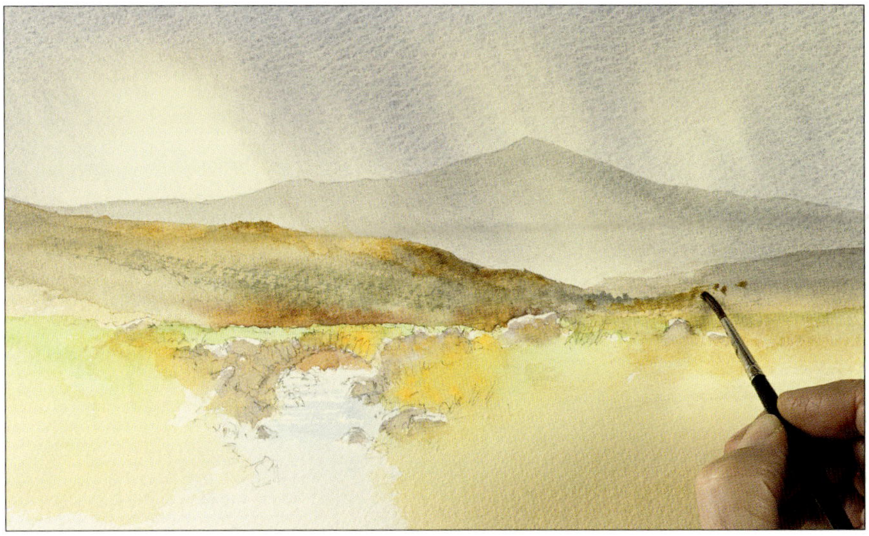

9 Suggest more distant rocks with the same method, blending them into the moorland at the bottom.

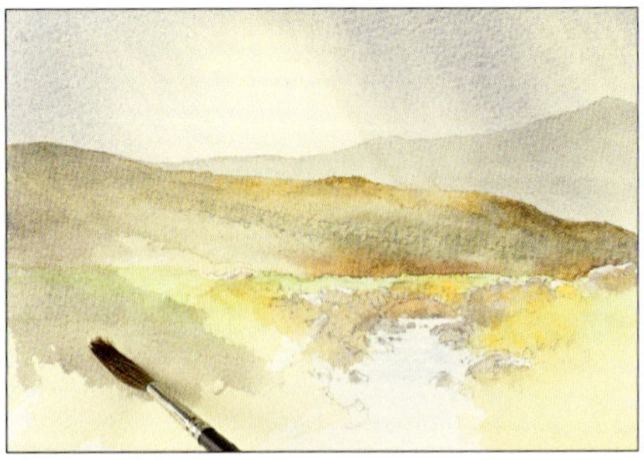

10 Use the no. 7 brush to paint a shadow over the left-hand moorland with ultramarine and cadmium red. Allow to dry.

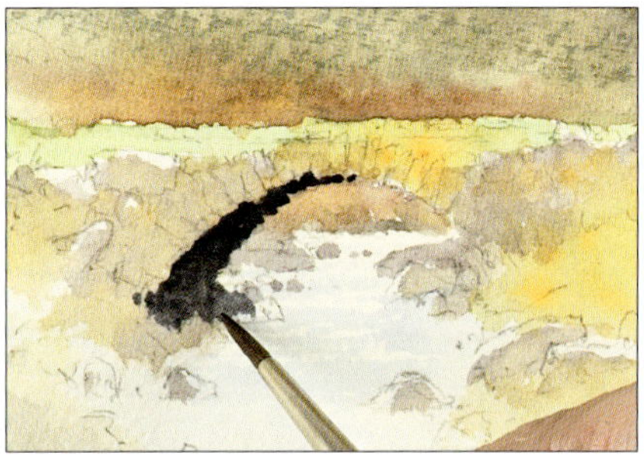

11 Use the no. 4 brush and a dark mix of ultramarine and burnt umber to paint the strongest tone in the painting: the shadow under the bridge. Add water lower down to suggest reflected light.

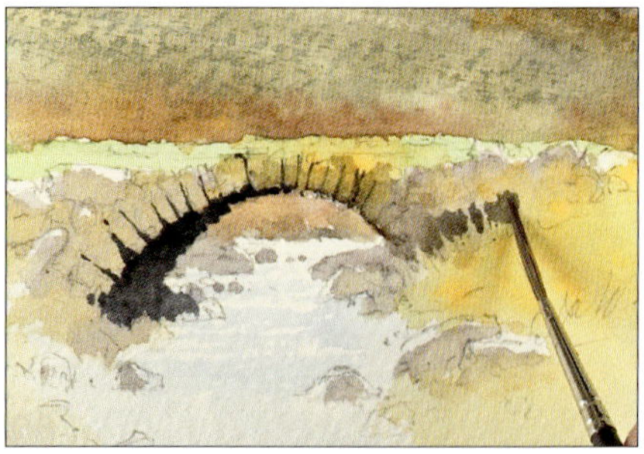

12 Change to the no. 1 rigger. Twirl it across a piece of scrap paper to get a good point and use the same mix to paint the stonework of the arch. Vary the pressure to get a natural look. Darken the right-hand side of the bridge a little with a wash of ultramarine and cadmium red, making it darker still to the right, behind the bright grasses.

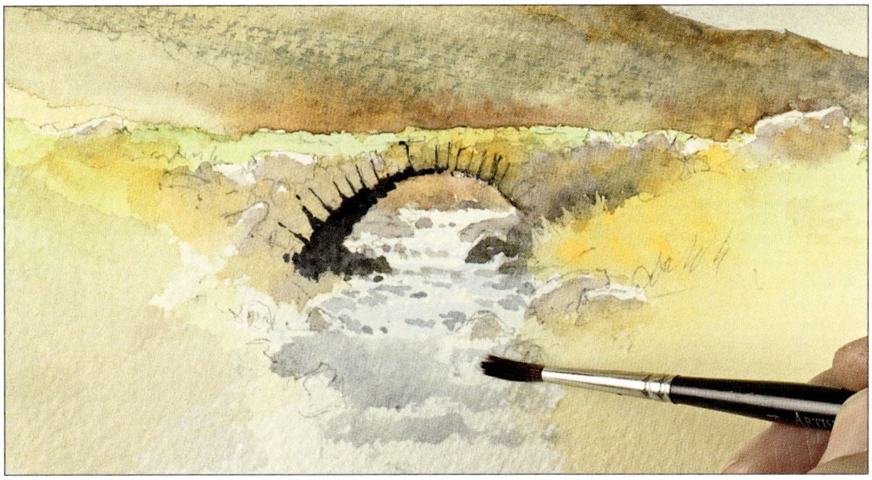

13 Paint rocks under the bridge with the no. 4 brush and a mix of ultramarine and burnt umber. Use the point of the brush and a bluer, paler mix to paint ripples in the water, then use the side of the brush to paint the water.

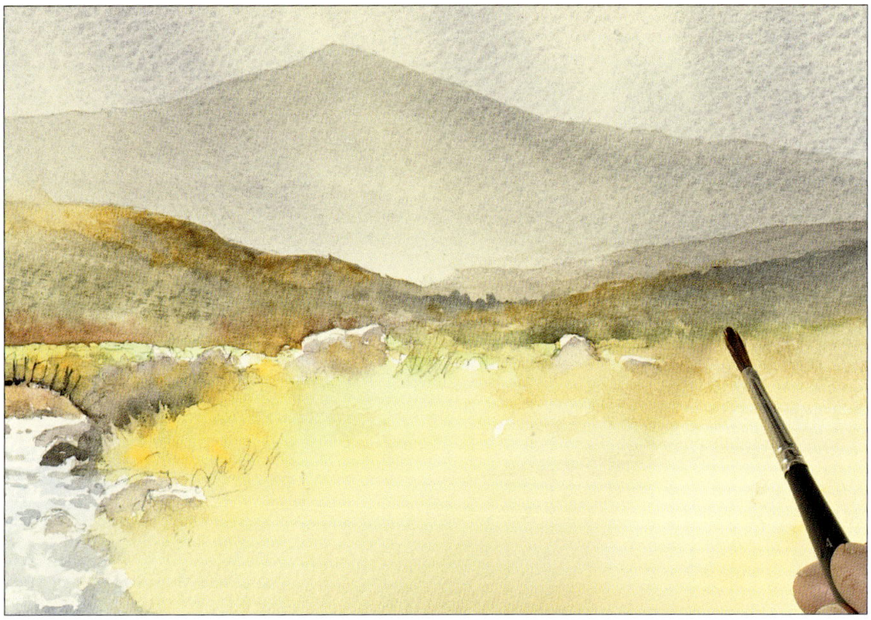

14 Define the line of the ridge sloping down towards the bridge with a mix of ultramarine and raw umber, then blend this in with clean water.

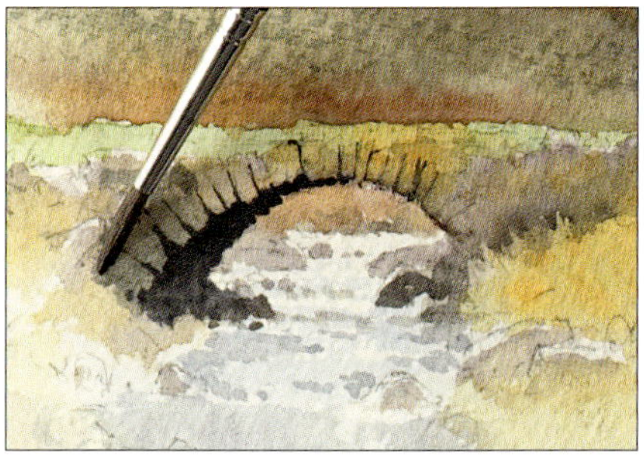

15 Drag the same colour across the lower part of the bridge.

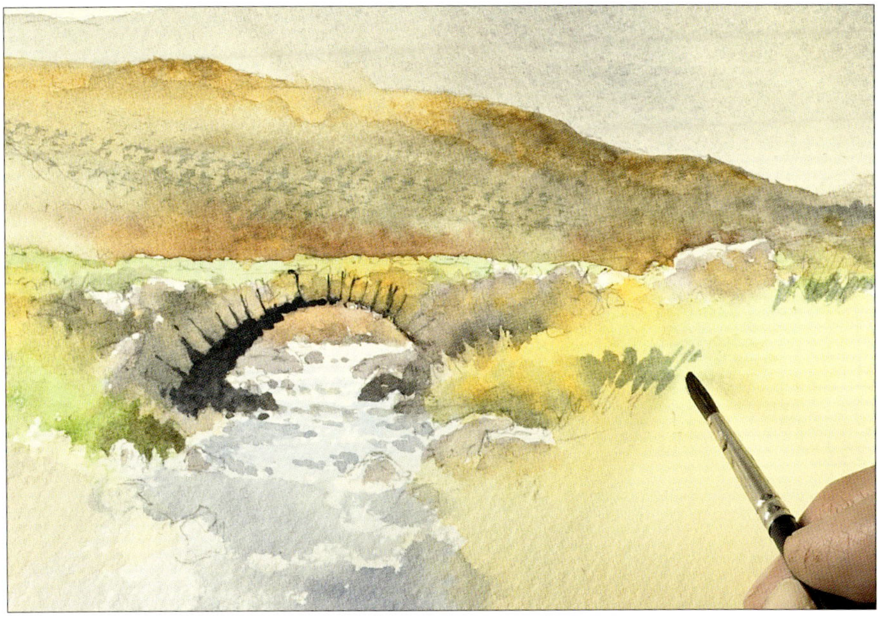

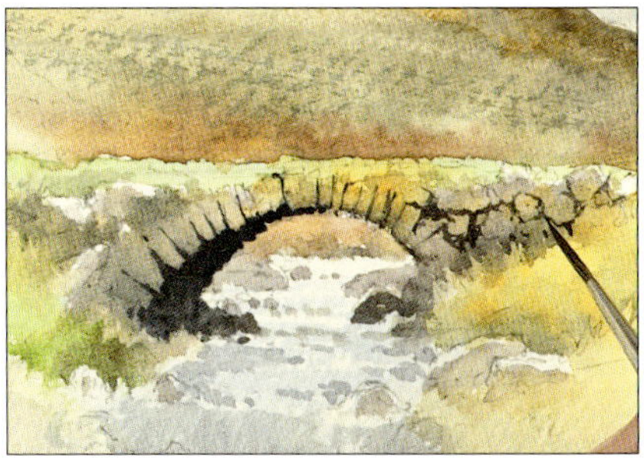

17 Use the no. 1 rigger and a dark mix of ultramarine and burnt umber to paint the remaining stonework of the bridge, varying the pressure to create a natural look.

16 Add bright green to the grass on the left-hand bank with viridian and new gamboge, then paint a little raw umber behind the rocks on the right-hand bank to emphasise them. Suggest grasses with ultramarine and raw umber.

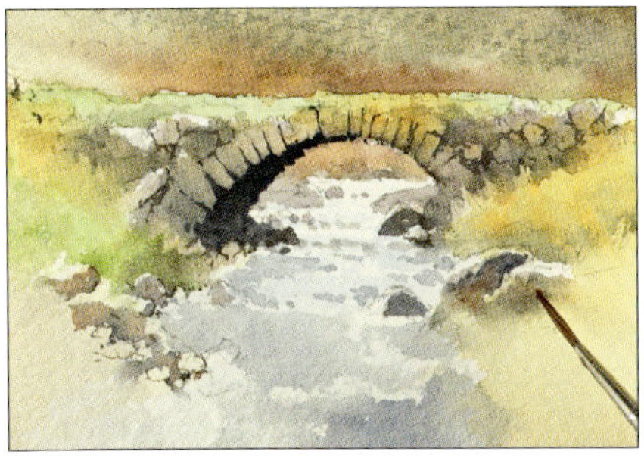

18 Suggest stones on the riverbank in the same way, then add tone with a paler wash of the same colours. Drop in perylene maroon in places.

19 Add shadow to some of the more distant rocks with the ultramarine and burnt umber mix.

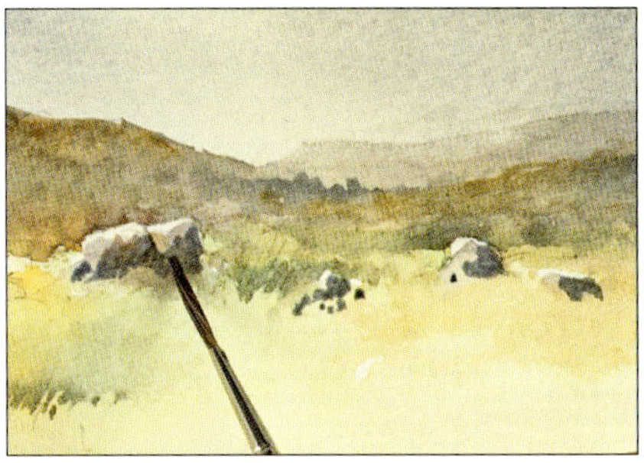

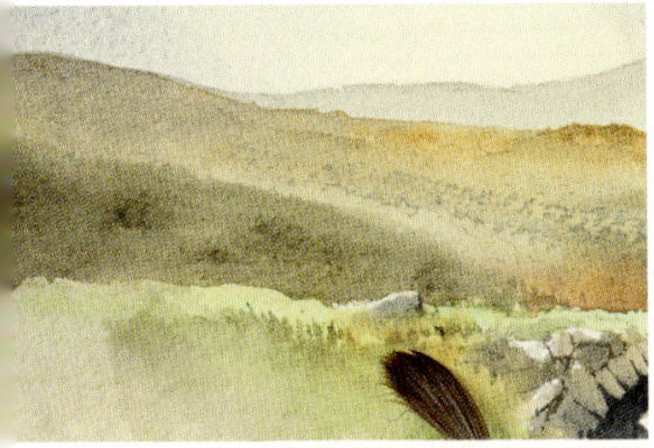

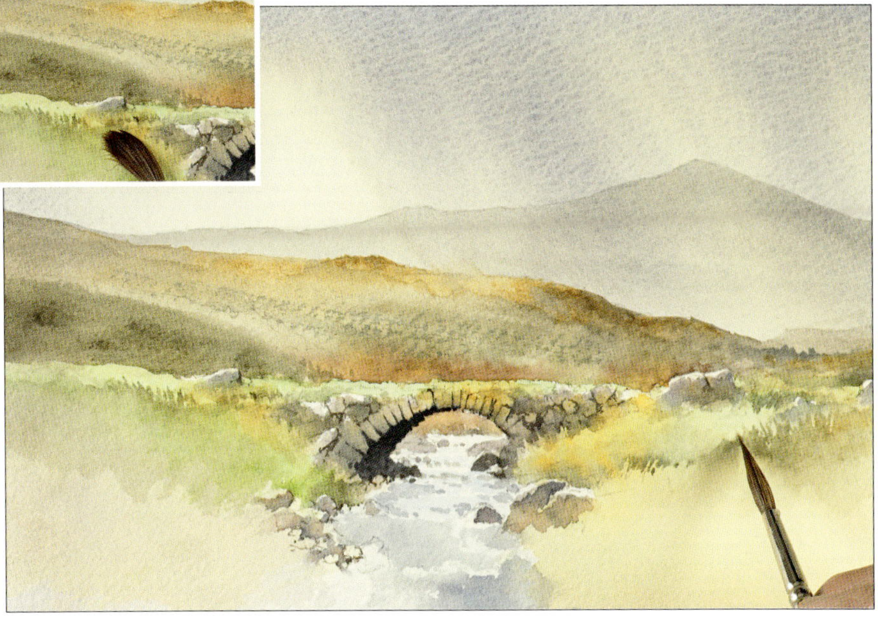

20 Paint the dark ridge on the left of the scene with the no. 7 brush and a mix of raw umber and ultramarine. Add grasses on the lighter foreground green, using the point of the brush. Sweep the brush over the base of the grasses to soften them in. Repeat to add a ridge of grasses on the right-hand side.

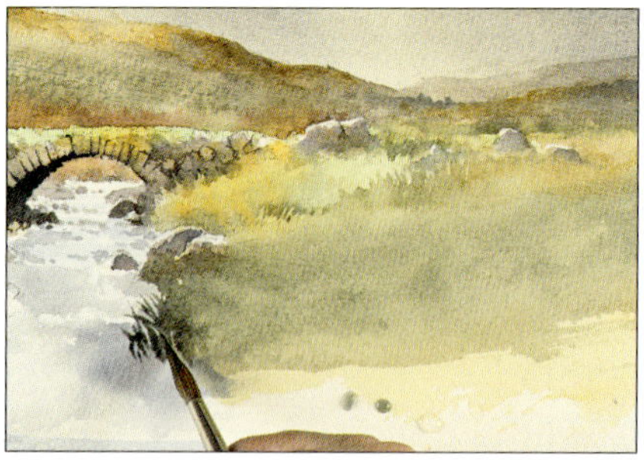

21 Darken the right-hand side of the painting with a wash of ultramarine and raw umber. Use a darker mix and the point of the brush to paint grasses at the water's edge.

22 Darken the left-hand side in the same way, and drop in yellow ochre.

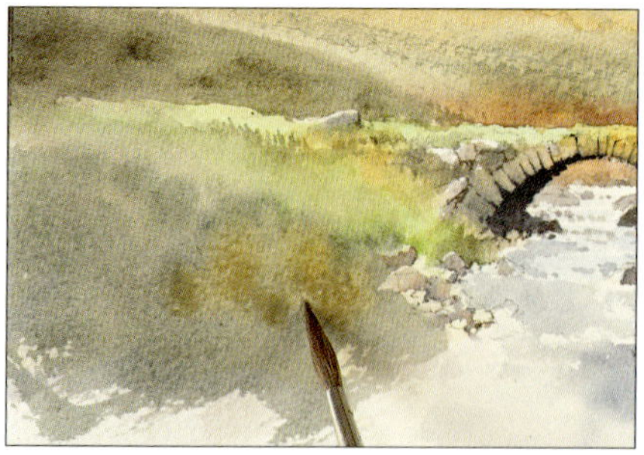

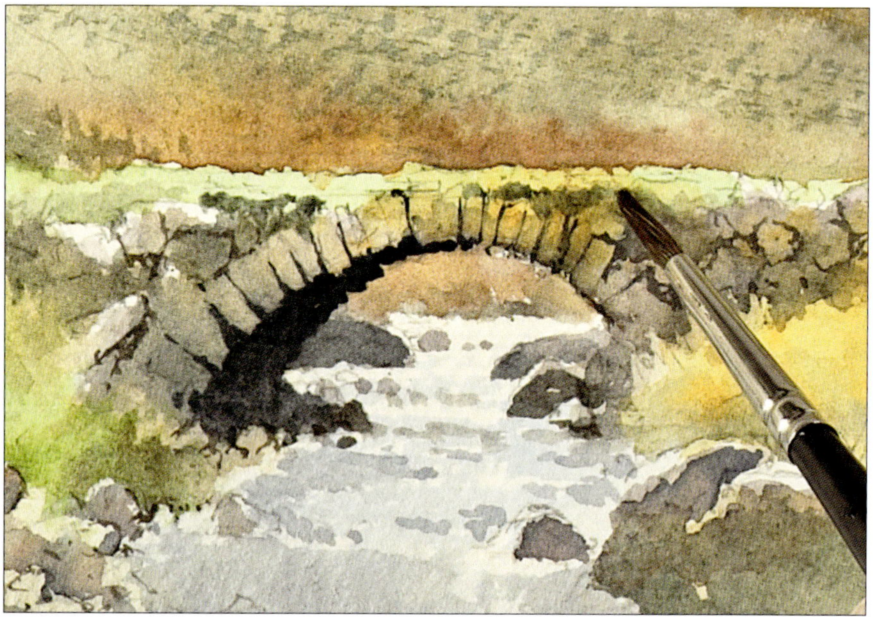

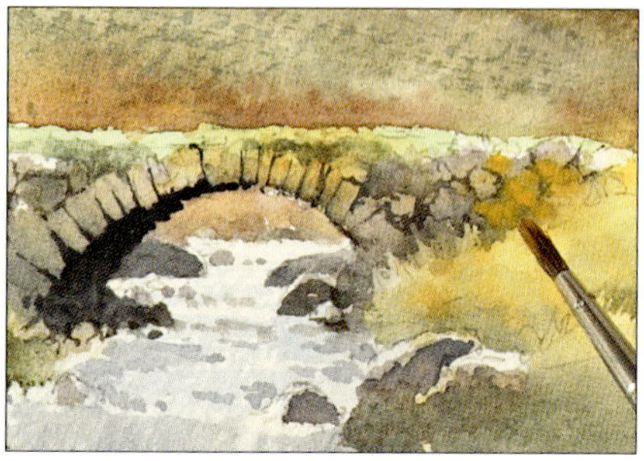

24 Wet the area to the right of the bridge and drop in cadmium orange.

23 Strengthen the rocky area visible through the bridge with the no. 4 brush and a mix of ultramarine and burnt umber. Add detail above the bridge with the same mix and soften it in with clean water.

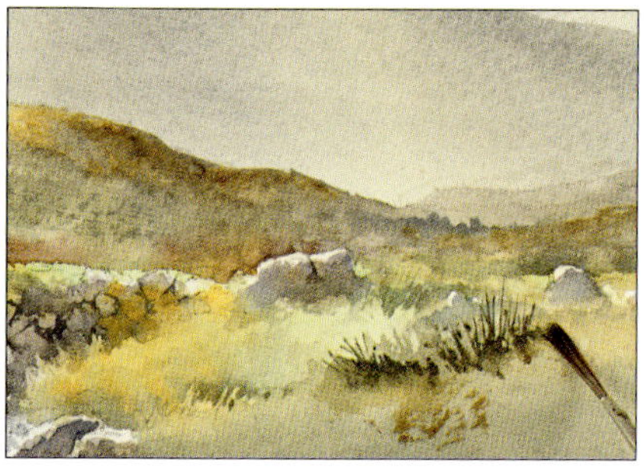

25 Use the no. 1 rigger and a mix of ultramarine and raw umber to paint reeds, and soften them in.

26 Paint a wash of ultramarine and raw umber across both sides of the foreground and drop in cadmium orange on the left.

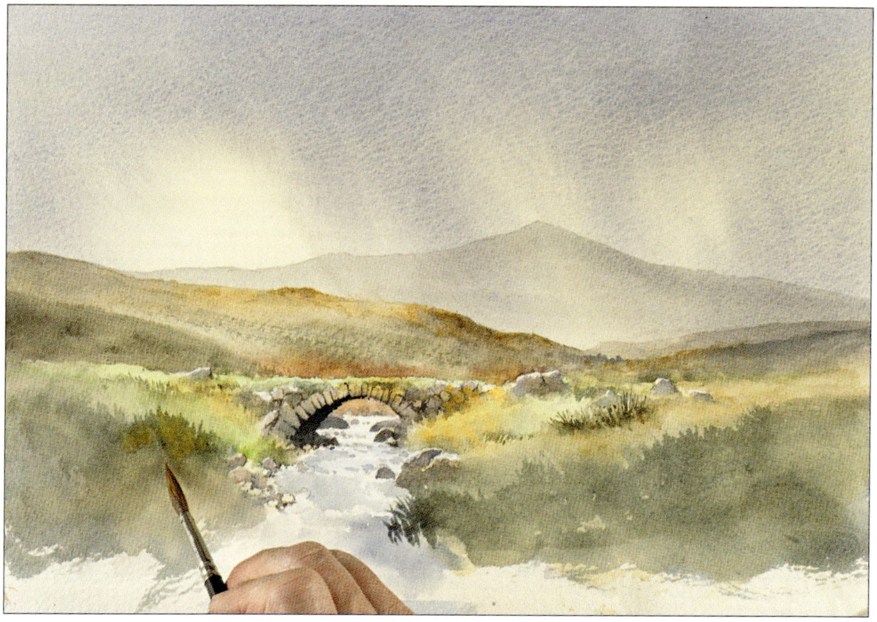

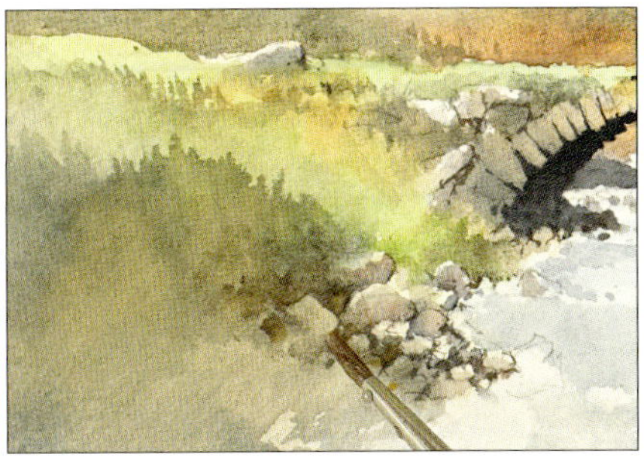

27 Add dark tone around the rocks on the left-hand bank to emphasise them, using the no. 1 round brush and burnt umber and ultramarine. Drop in yellow ochre.

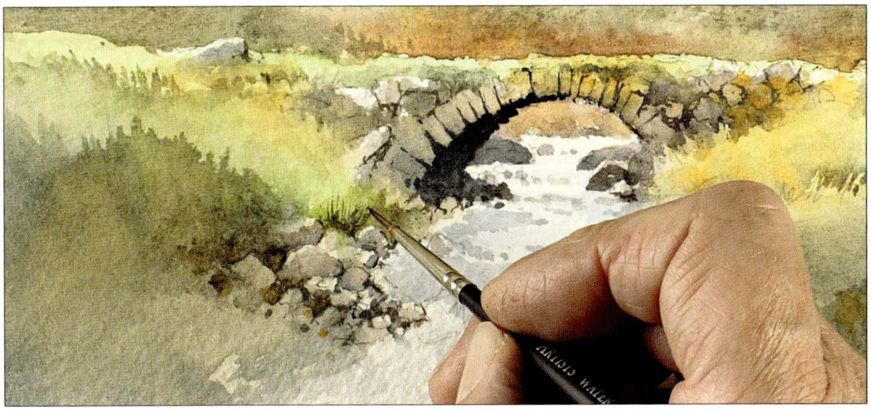

28 Finally, paint reeds with perylene maroon and burnt umber.

The finished painting.

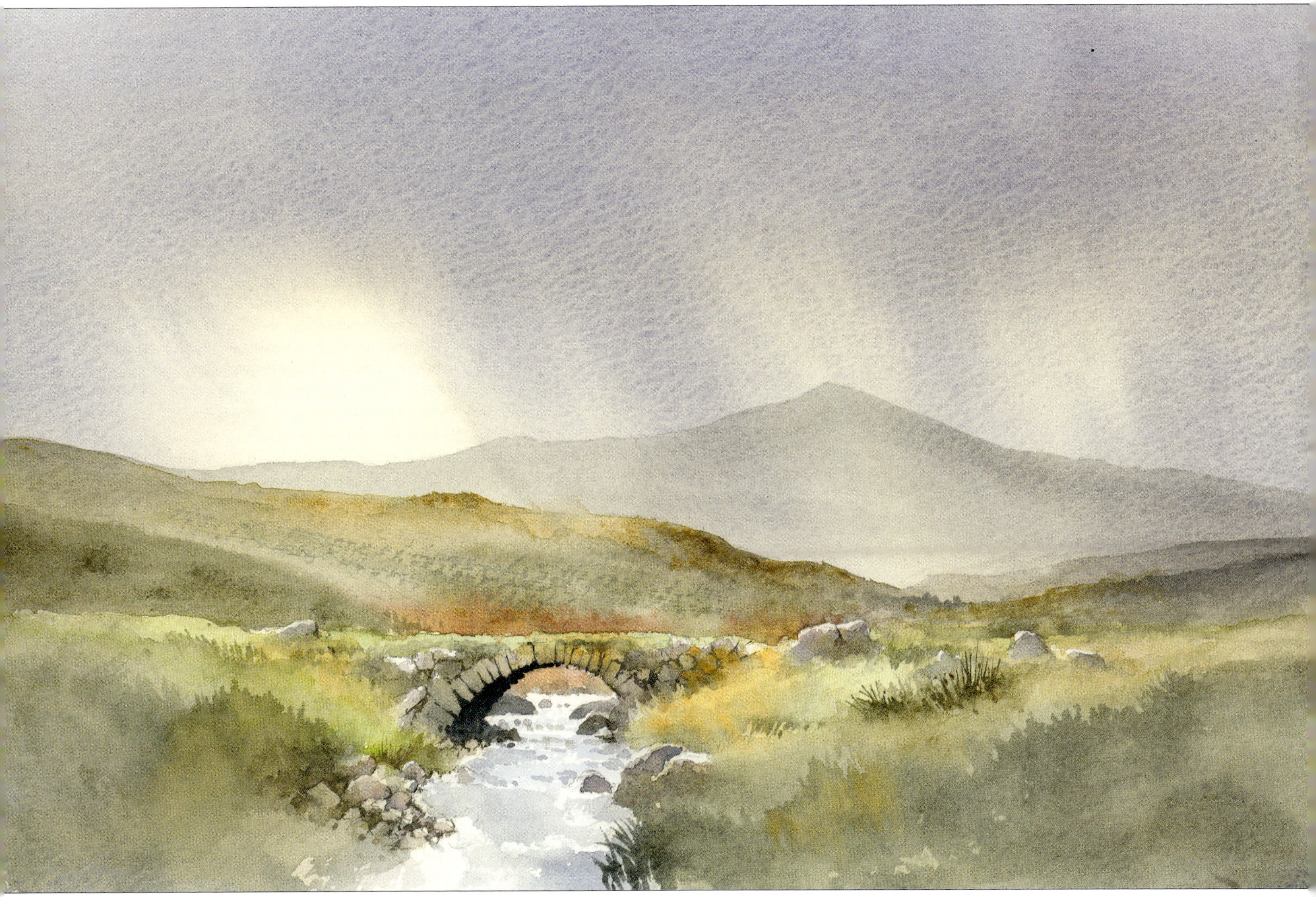

Mountain scenes

Mountains can often be painted without you needing to be anywhere near the subject. In this chapter we take a closer look at them, as well as paint them in the distance. Often, even climbing just a few hundred metres up a path will offer you a much improved perspective, and give you a more intimate relationship with rocks and crags. If you are painting a portrait of a particular mountain, often the optimum viewpoint is around halfway up the opposite mountain.

I cannot emphasise enough how important it is to move around to seek out the best angle to paint your subject. Ask yourself questions such as, 'Should I move further away from the shepherd's hut to give it a greater sense of isolation, or is it more important to show up the textures on the stone wall?'; 'Do I want to emphasise the savagery of this place by including only boulders and crags in the foreground, or would a softer approach with trees suit it better?'; 'Is this viewpoint dramatic enough or should I move closer to the abyss to highlight the sublime nature of the place?' Whatever your choice, make sure you at least photograph each of the possibilities so that you have a record of them all.

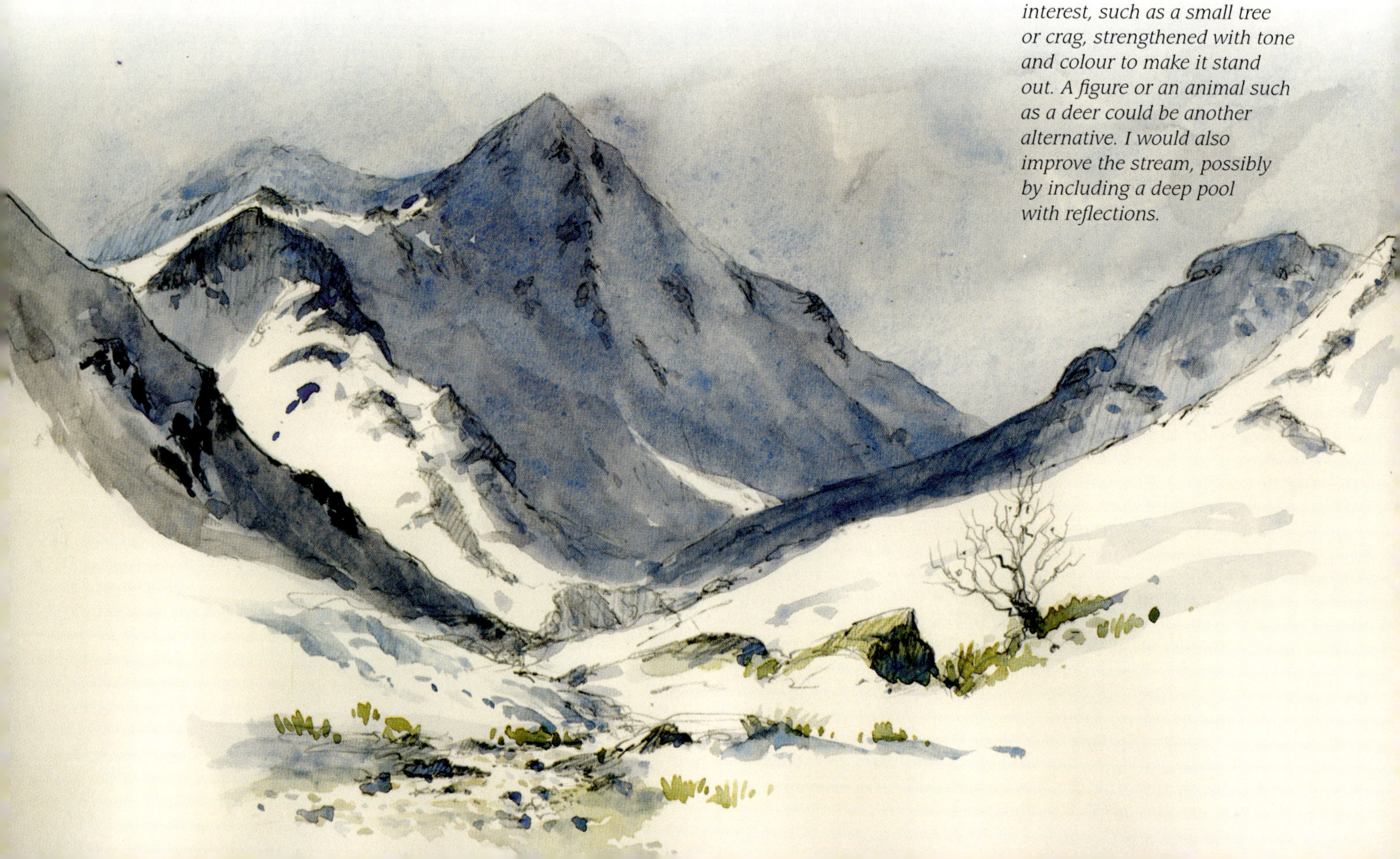

Ben Challium, Scotland

This watercolour sketch, done on the spot, shows a classic mountain composition viewed from the valley, with the peak in the distance and a stream leading into the composition. Part of the mountain is highlighted by sunshine on a ridge that leads upwards towards the top left, then turns back towards the summit. A foreground boulder adds interest here, but slightly altering the tree might help improve matters. If it was extended a little higher, it would break up the long diagonals coming down from the middle right-hand side. Nearly all diagonal slopes in the sketch meet at the foot of the mountain and this would be an excellent place to position a strong centre of interest, such as a small tree or crag, strengthened with tone and colour to make it stand out. A figure or an animal such as a deer could be another alternative. I would also improve the stream, possibly by including a deep pool with reflections.

Mountain perspective

Nowhere is the sense of space and distance more obvious than in the high mountains, as demonstrated in the scene shown below.

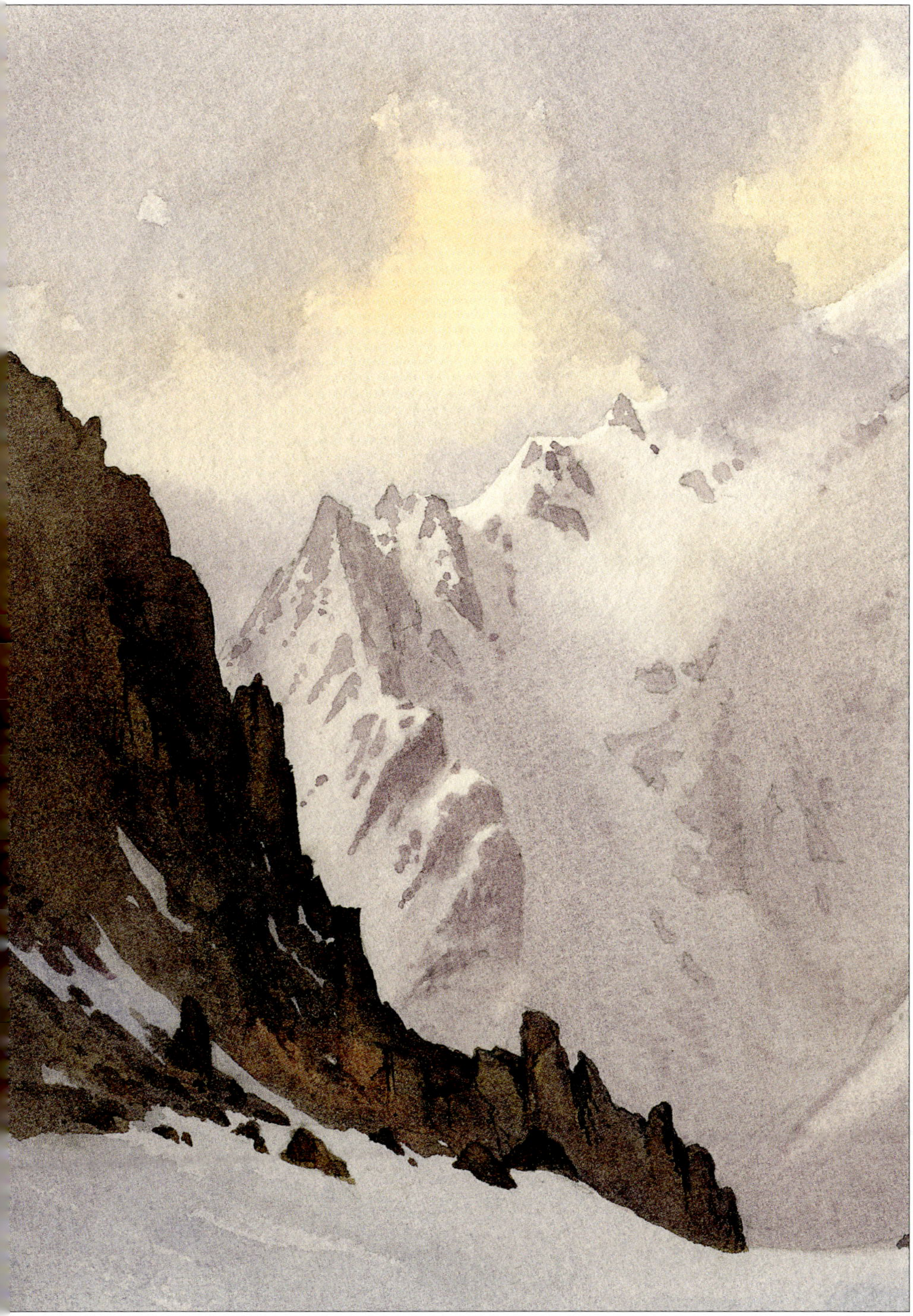

Aerial perspective

In this scene the distant crags and ridge appear to be much further away because of the lighter tones and lack of strong detail when compared with the foreground crags. I also dropped a splash of orange into the lower rocks while they were still wet. Warm colours like orange help to suggest that the feature is closer to the viewer.

Ways to suggest depth in a landscape

- Warm colours (red, orange, etc) in the foreground
- Cool colours (blues, greys, greens) in the distance
- Stronger, darker tones close to the viewer
- Lighter tones further away
- Stronger detail in the foreground
- Hardly any detail in the distance
- Larger objects (eg, trees, clouds, people) closer to the viewer
- Roads, tracks, streams and walls narrowing as they recede

Note: the colour temperature can vary considerably within a colour, such as green for example, which can be warm, cool or neutral.

High level perspective and composition

Although high-level ridges are for the fit and experienced mountain climbers, the lessons on these two pages are invaluable for all those who wish to paint mountains. In normal landscape painting, the height of the viewpoint often does not matter, but in the mountains it can be critical, as seen in these examples. Two of these three watercolours, depicting the Cuillin Ridge on Skye, one of the Western Isles of Scotland, show poor composition which detracts considerably from the finished result in numerous ways.

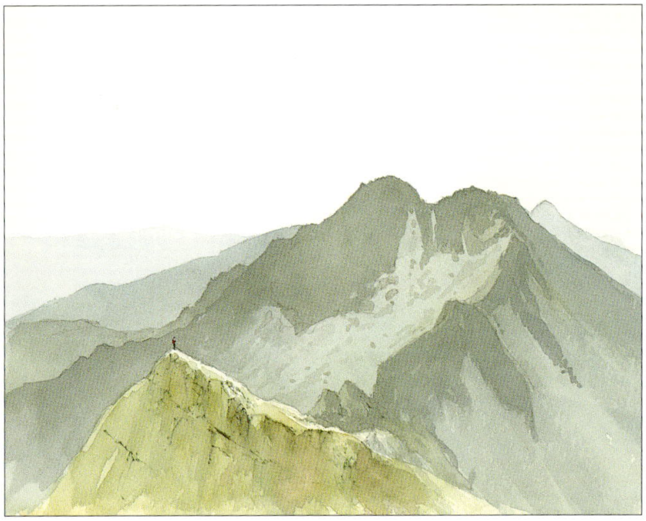

Cuillin Ridge 1

At high level, the height that the artist works from can be critical, as well as the angle. In this first view of the mountain Sgurr Thormaid, the focal point is too far to the left and quite low in the picture: not the ideal composition.

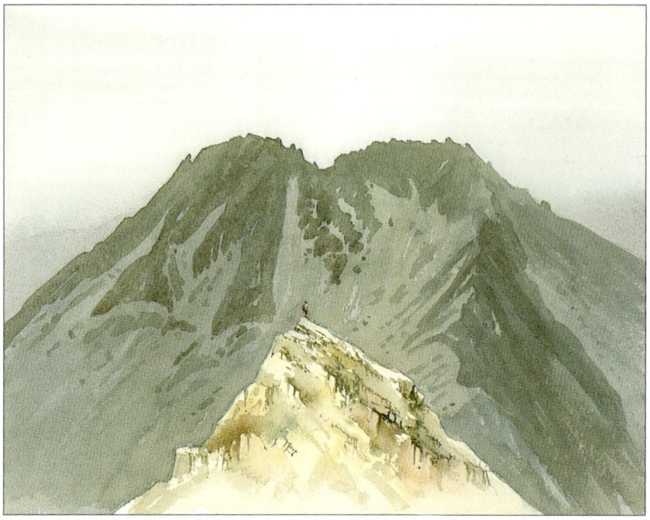

Cuillin Ridge 2

In this view I have moved further left along the ridge to bring the peak forming the focal point into the centre, but as well as being too central the absolute peak is directly below the notch in the distant twin summits. Coincidences like this should be avoided if possible. Although my lower viewpoint has increased the height of Sgurr Thormaid, the composition still needs adjustment.

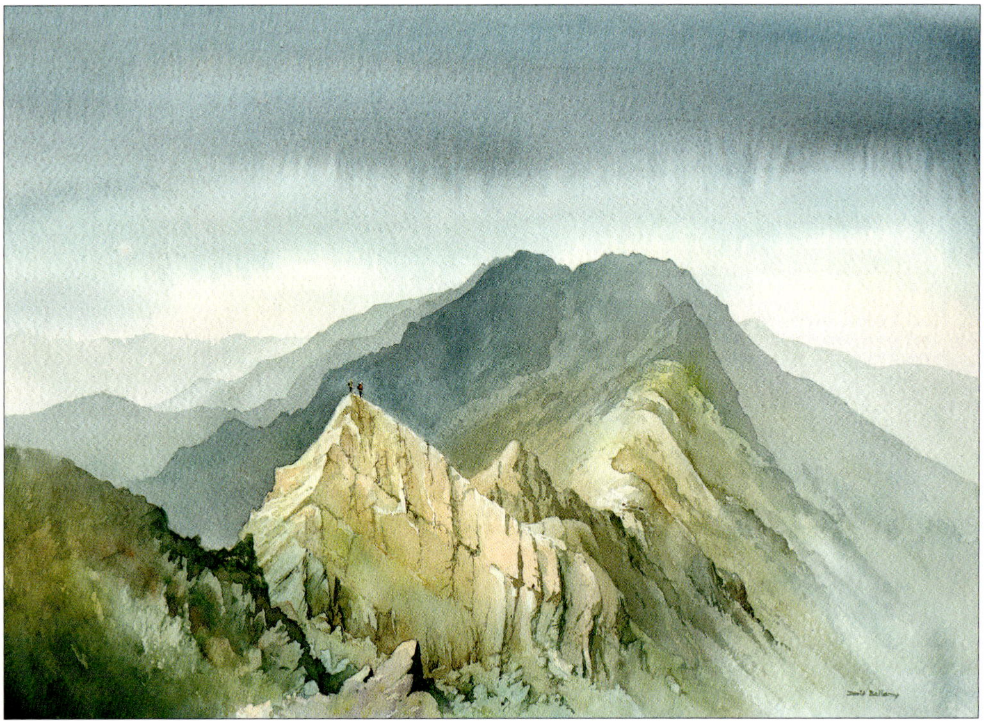

Cuillin Ridge 3

30.5 x 40.6cm (12 x 16in)

This is my final composition, which I feel works best. It shows the handsome line of the main Cuillin Ridge dipping and curving, with Sgurr Thormaid standing out warm-coloured against a cooler, duller background. Showing more of the peak has added to the drama of the situation, and I felt it was wise to give the climber a companion. Although lower than its companion peaks, Thormaid has a shape and ruggedness that make it a fine centre of interest, but of course all this would be to little avail if it were not for the strong light on the peak.

Using atmosphere to lose detail

Without atmosphere a painting of the mountains is lacking an important ingredient, but atmosphere can also be used to get rid of unwanted detail, so that you are killing two birds with one stone. Here we look at how storms and mist can be used to throw emphasis onto certain parts of the composition.

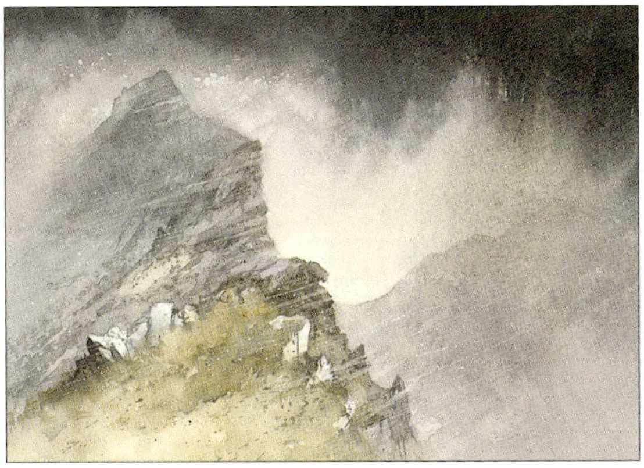

Stormy Ridge

To achieve the effect of a storm, it helps to have at least part of the sky dark and threatening. Here I have lost the hard edges as the ridge rises to the summit by running the wash into a damp surface. Scratches and stabs with a scalpel were used to suggest wind hurling flurries of snow. Practise this method first on a failed watercolour, as it is a difficult technique to rectify once the paper is scored.

The Obergabelhorn
22.8 x 30.5cm (9 x 12in)

The Obergabelhorn in Switzerland boasts a number of fine ridges with a shapely summit, but even so, you don't always want to include everything. Often these views work best when the mountain is partly hidden, but you can always invent your own cloud or mist. In this watercolour the closest ridge zigzags towards the summit, which is partly obscured, with a suggestion of further ridges beyond. If you compare the snow on the foreground ridge with that in the main amphitheatre beyond, you will see the former is white paper and the latter a slightly darker wash of light blue-grey, which was washed over most of the painting as the first application of colour. When this was dry, a medium blue-grey wash then outlined the far ridges leading up to the summit, taking the right-hand ridge only halfway up. Again, this was left to dry before a wash of clear water was brushed over the entire background, avoiding the white paper. This had the effect of softening the edges of the distant ridges, and while still wet a further wash of the same colour was floated on, to show the sky area, leaving highlights in places, including a lightish patch in the middle-right to make the ridge stand out a little more.

Once more I let the paper dry, then applied a medium blue-grey strip of darker colour directly behind the summit, softening off the upper part of this patch with clear water. After this I gradually worked my way towards the foreground with increasingly stronger tones. Mist will turn all the background into a monochrome, so it is only when we get closer to the foreground that colours begin to emerge.

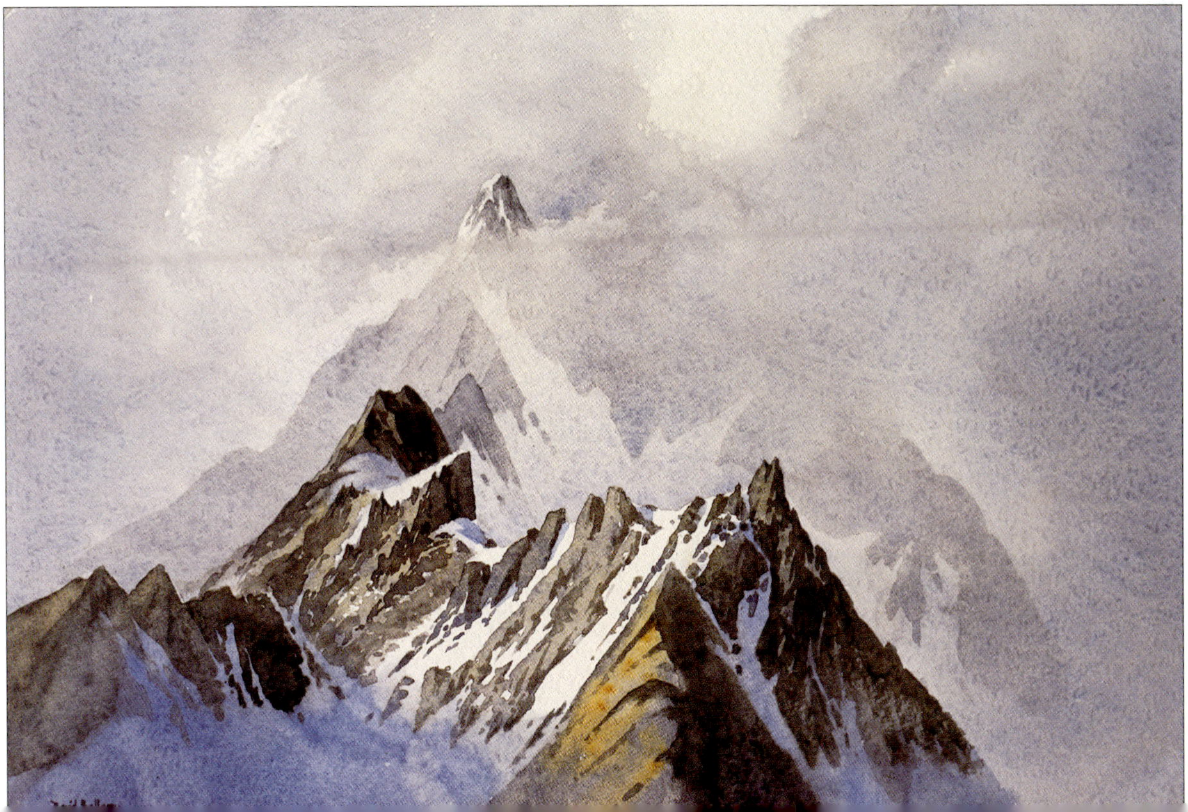

Rendering mountain slopes

The sides of mountains are so varied, covered in massed conifers in lower parts, cliffs, crags and boulder fields, scree, mixed bushes and scrub, gullies, gorges, ridges and of course snow slopes. We have covered examples of these elsewhere, but here I want to tackle that bane of all mountain painters: the bald, uninteresting rounded mountainside, and turn it into something more appealing.

Detail of Loch Pityoulish painting (shown opposite)

The numbering indicates the order of working.

1. A weak wash of French ultramarine and cadmium red over the whole mountainside, visible at this point.

6. Strongest tones applied again with French ultramarine and burnt umber.

2. This more level area catches the light, so I dropped some weak aureolin into the French ultramarine/cadmium red wash while it was still wet.

5. Weaker details as the features recede.

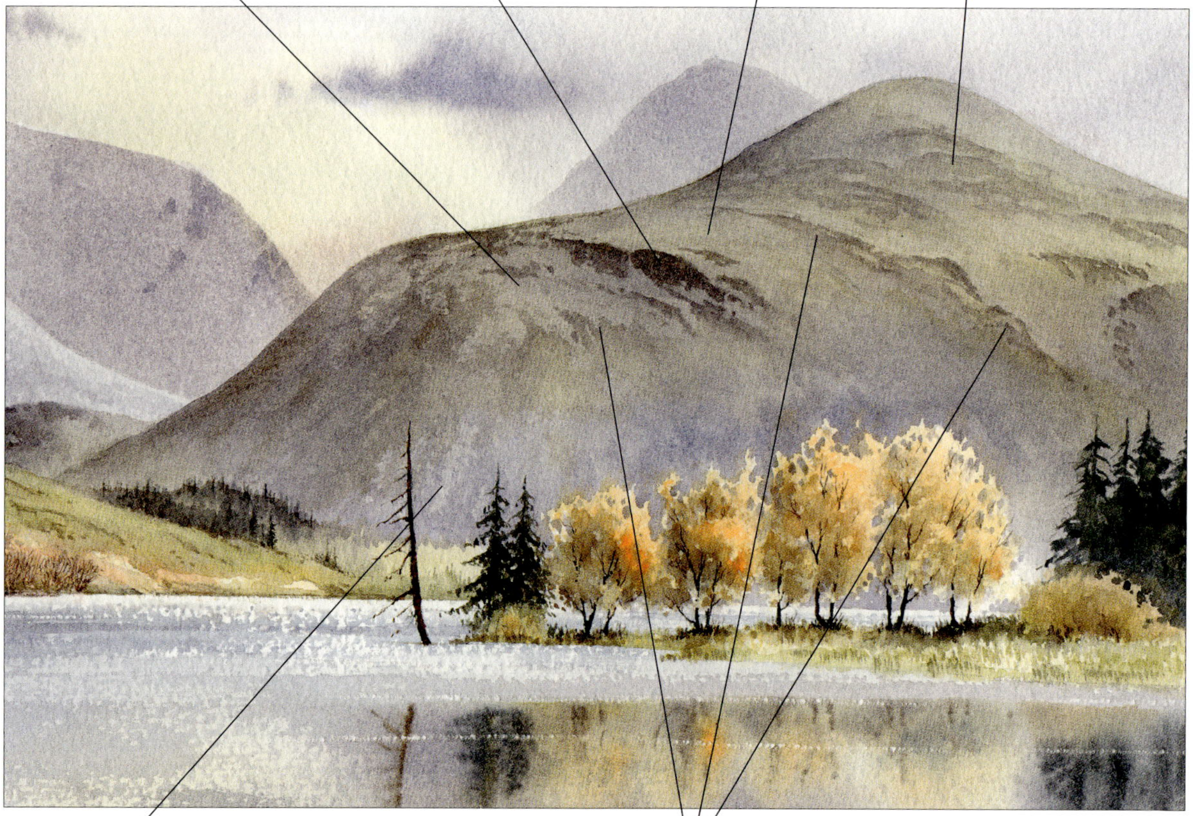

4. At this point I got rid of any excess water on the brush and used almost vertical strokes to create the dry brush effect.

3. Medium-toned applications of French ultramarine plus burnt umber to suggest rocks running down towards the trees, without any detail. This was done on a dry surface.

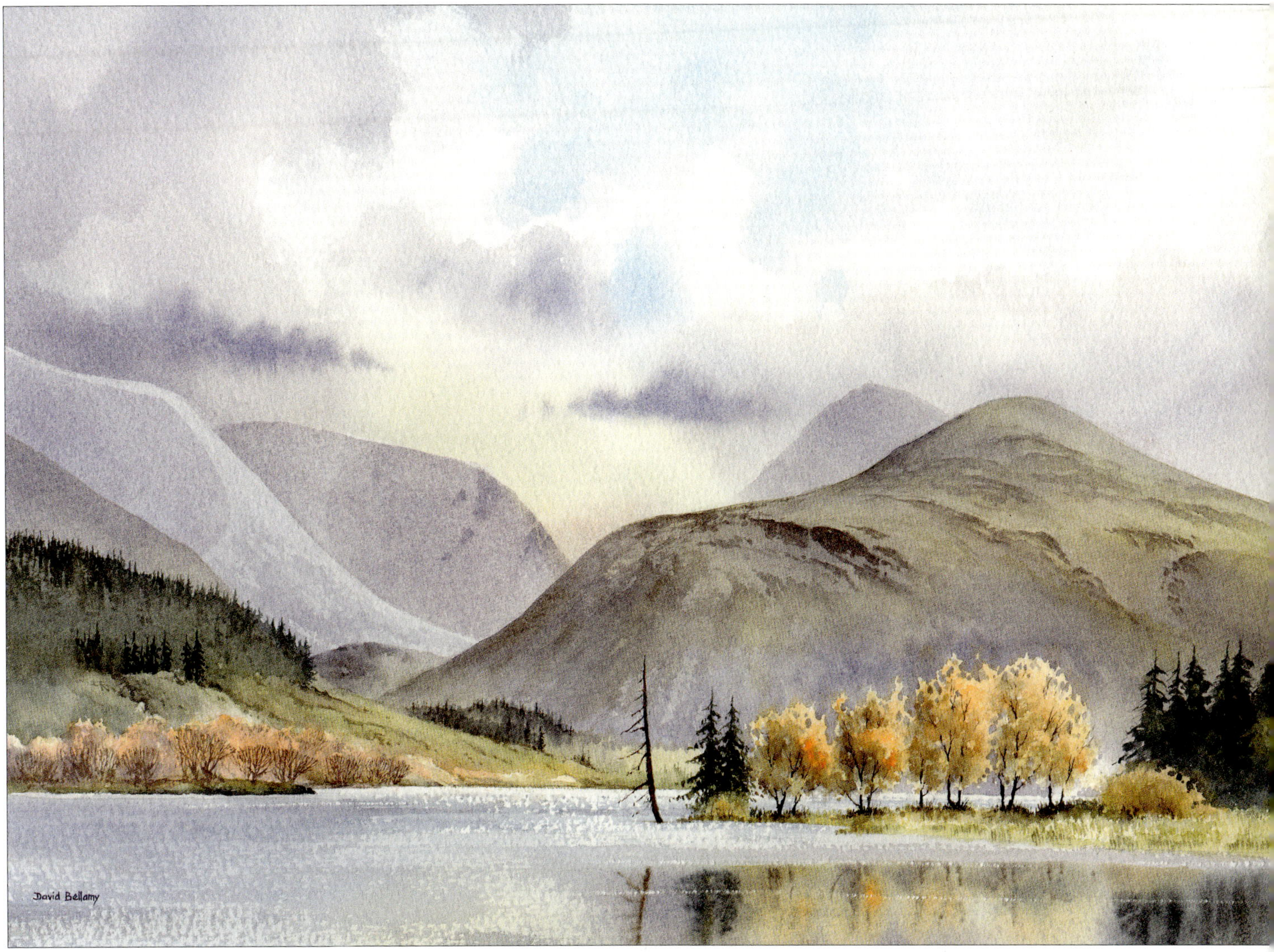

Loch Pityoulish

28 x 40.7cm (11 x 16in)

In this view of Loch Pityoulish in the Cairngorms in Scotland, the large bulk of the hillside rising directly on the far side of the loch is typical of this range of mountains – rounded and lacking in dramatic outlines. Creating interesting textures on such slopes is important, but should not be overdone as this passage needs to support the focal point – in this case the trees – rather than compete.

In this instance the matter was complicated by the birch trees being so much lighter than the background. I began by painting in the autumn colours in cadmium orange with some yellow ochre, leaving the detail and shadows until later. When this was dry, I brought down a mixture of French ultramarine and cadmium red over the hillside, stopping at the tops of the trees, at the same time defining their ragged edges. While the wash was wet, I dropped a hint of aureolin into the upper half and allowed it to dry. Then, with varying strengths of French ultramarine and burnt umber, I painted in the rock masses, making them less intense higher up where the mountain receded into the distance. The same mixture was then brought down over the lower slopes, mainly with downward strokes of the brush to suggest the direction of the slope. This is most evident where I have deliberately allowed the brush to become thirsty, thus creating a dry brush effect behind the dead pine in the centre. The lower area of the hillside needed to be fairly devoid of detail to avoid cluttering up the immediate background to the trees.

While the main lesson in this painting describes the mountain slopes, the techniques to achieve the surface of the lake are also of interest. I laid the dry brush application over what represents the further part of the water and softened the bottom band off with a wet brush so that there would be a lack of definition between the sparkling wind-rippled water and the smoother, sheltered surface. The latter was brushed in with a fluid wash of French ultramarine and cadmium red, and the reflected colour was dropped in wet into wet, though more subdued than the actual trees. Once this wash had dried, I scratched over the area with a scalpel using horizontal strokes.

Using figures to create a sense of scale

Figures can intrude in a painting, especially if not handled sensitively, and it is a good idea to ask yourself why you wish to include them, and where they will have most effect. If shown in the immediate foreground they become the main subject of the painting, with the mountain simply as a backdrop. Further back they give a much better sense of scale to the mountain. Two or three figures is usually enough – the only time I have painted a large group is when depicting a mountain rescue incident or army patrol. Are your figures to be shepherds, farmers, walkers, climbers, hunters or what? All these people dress for their particular pursuit and colour has an important influence in how they are seen.

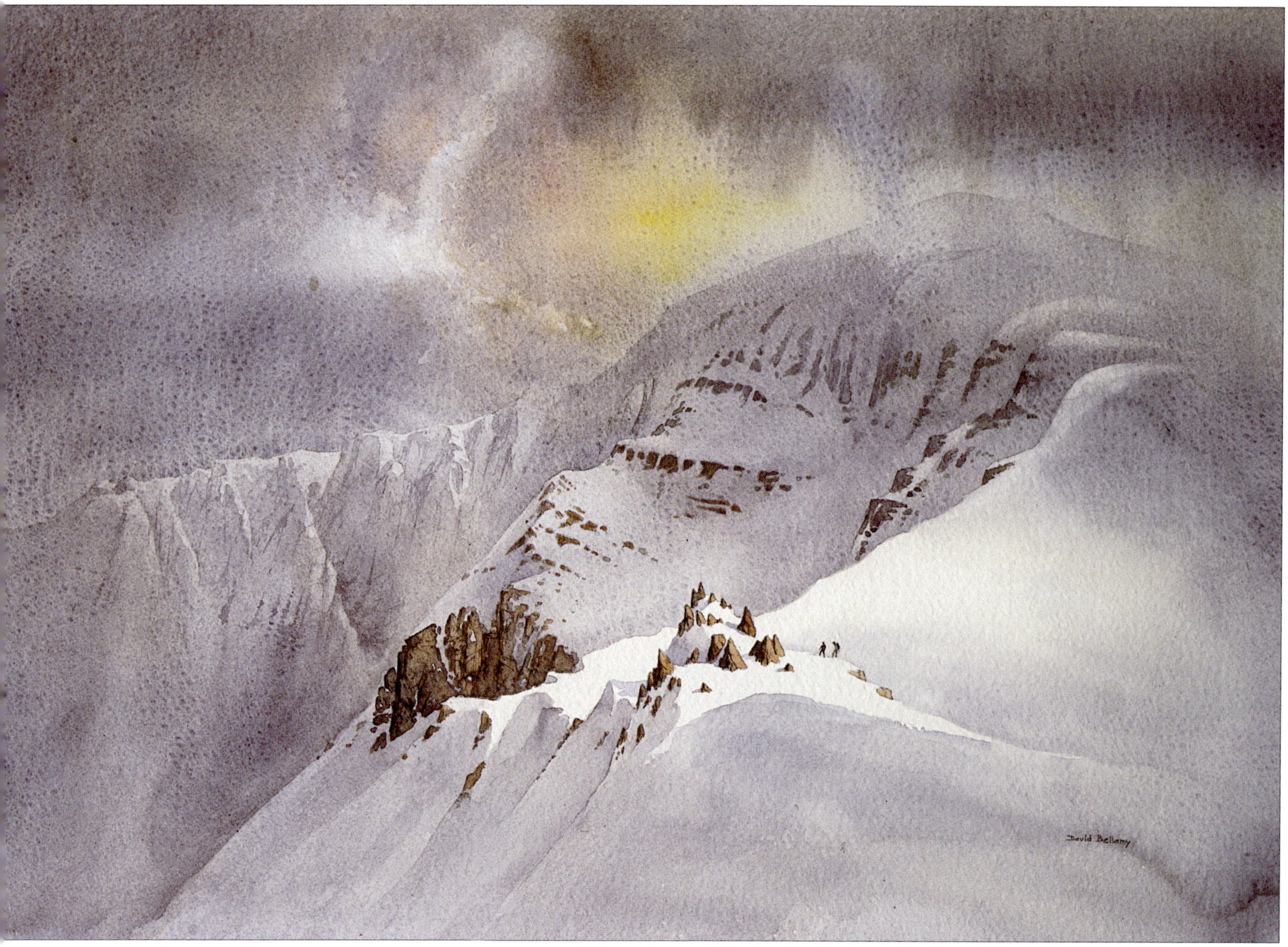

Mountain View With Figures
28 x 45.7cm (11 x 18in)

This painting shows the north face of Carnedd Dafydd, in Snowdonia, Wales. Without the tiny figures, this composition would lose its sense of scale, as well as the centre of interest. There is nothing else in this painting to give any idea of the size of the mountain – no trees, no houses, no cars, nothing that will give us a clue. By changing the size of figures in a mountain painting, you can effectively suggest a larger or smaller peak, but you need to place them in the middle distance to give a reasonably true sense of height.

Painting snow and ice

Snow can graphically bring out the stark delineations of rocks and crags, but depending on the light, can lose many less obvious features. Photographs of snow scenes can be extremely deceptive in anything approaching flat lighting, when all subtle tones can be completely lost. Sunshine on snow slopes can be harsh, so I wear neutral-tinted sunglasses. If your eyes are not comfortable with the light, it can drastically affect your tonal judgement.

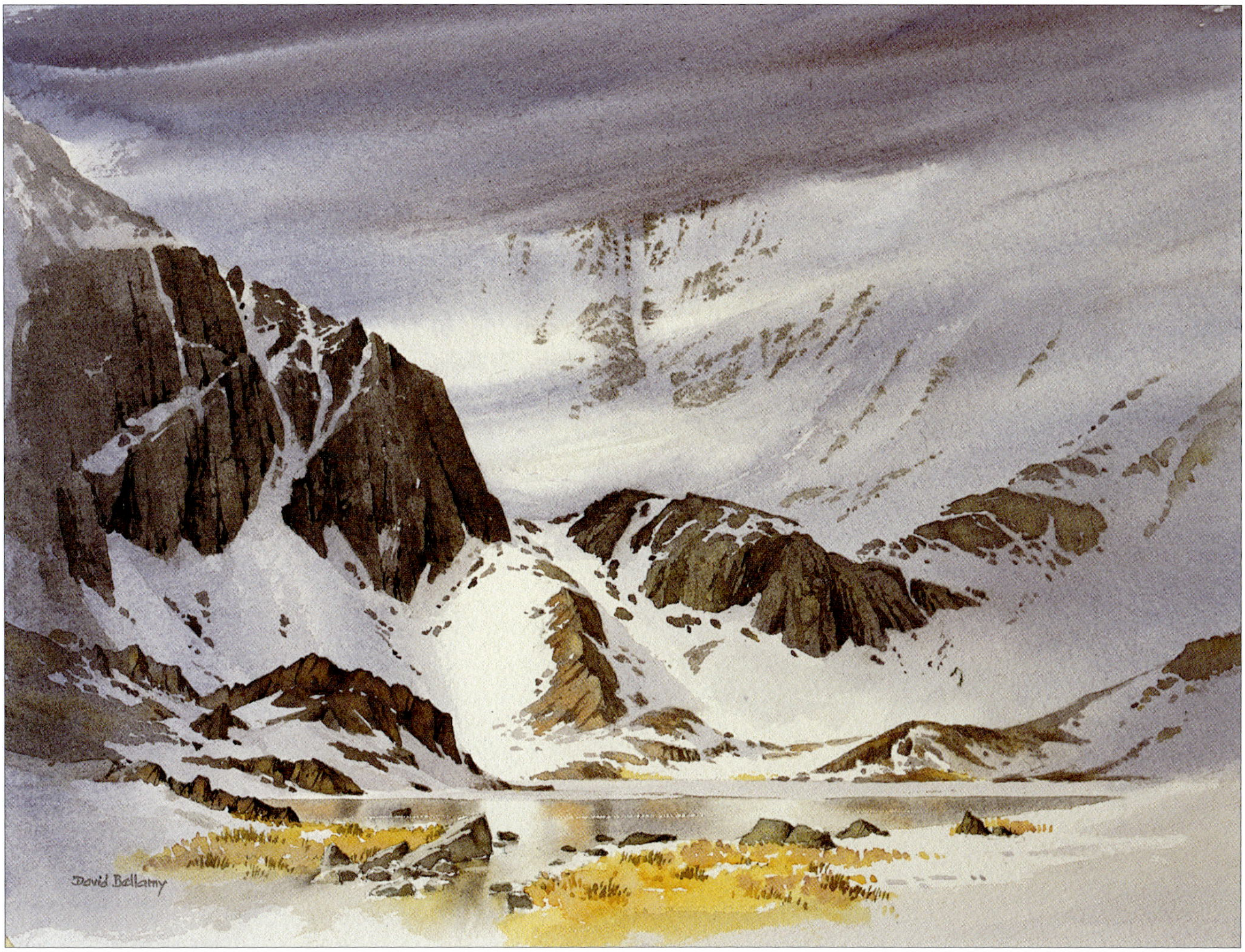

The Well of the Moon
22.8 x 30.5cm (9 x 12in)

One of the dangers in painting snow-covered mountains is in seeing only black and white. This is especially true on gloomy days, without sunlight to bring colours to life. Look hard for colours in rock. In this painting of Ffynnon Lloer – The Well of the Moon – in North Wales, the important rocks have had cadmium red dropped into their basic colour whilst still wet, warming them up considerably. Light red and yellow ochre are two other colours that are excellent for this purpose. The shadows are important in suggesting the snow slopes and providing relief from the contrast of white snow and dark rock. They were achieved with French ultramarine and cadmium red.

Note how snow lies in cracks and gullies and shows up the rocks and crags. The effect of strong winds blowing cloud streamers across the upper reaches has been achieved with horizontal brush strokes with a mop brush, and completed before the closer cliffs and crags were painted.

The ice on the tarn was achieved by the wet into wet technique. Firstly I floated clear water over the area, then after allowing it to begin drying, I dropped in the vague reflections with appropriate colours. To achieve the feeling of ice, avoid pin-sharp reflections and use downward strokes of the brush into a damp surface. If any colour drifts too far across, simply pull it out with a damp, clean brush.

Glaciers

Ice-falls on glaciers provide dramatic scenes, and it is in the crevasses and breaches in the ice that you will find the most vivid and exciting blues, greens, yellows and so on. As the ice formations are constantly changing, you are not bound to copy each shape faithfully, so there is considerable opportunity to arrange your composition to suit your needs.

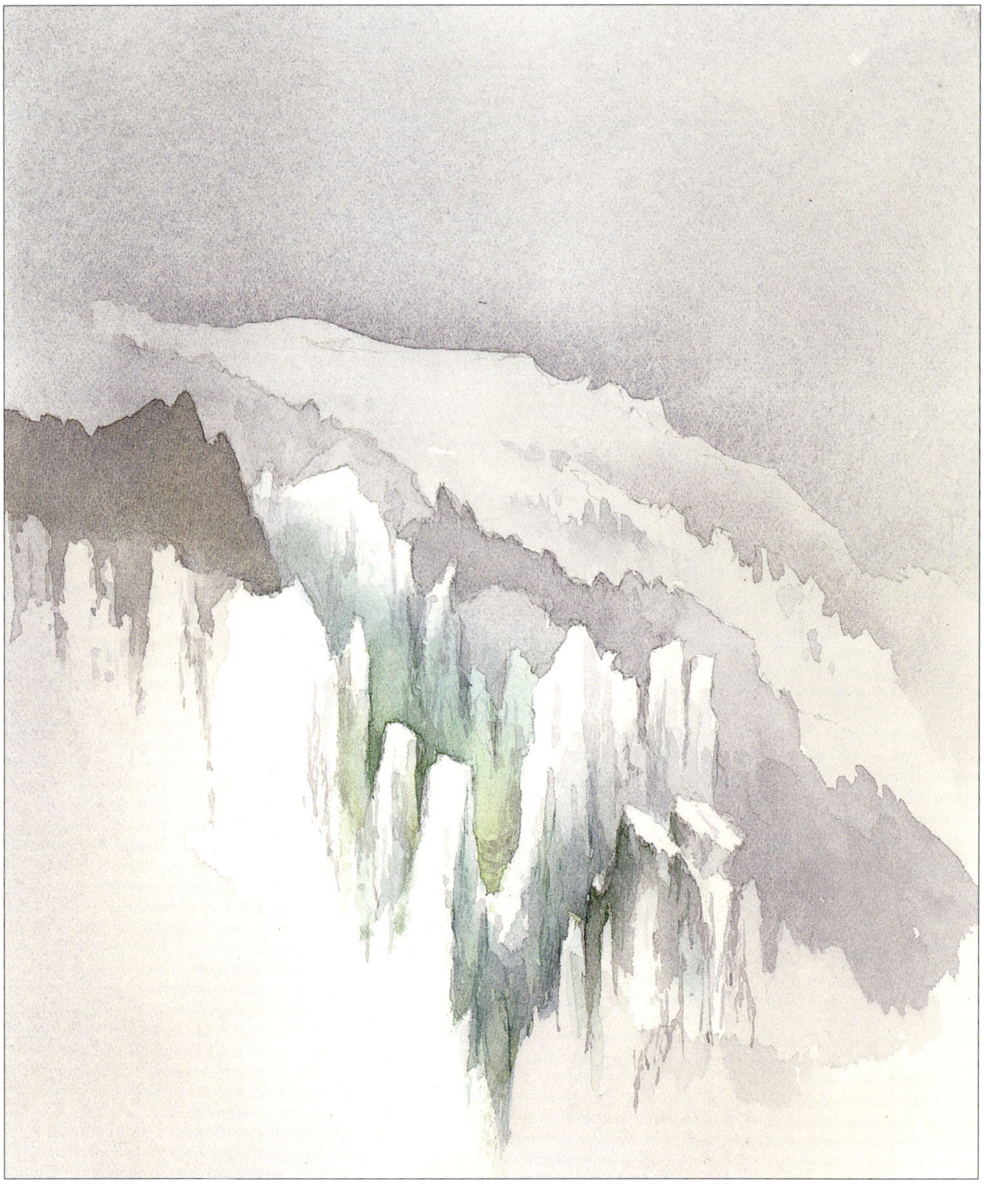

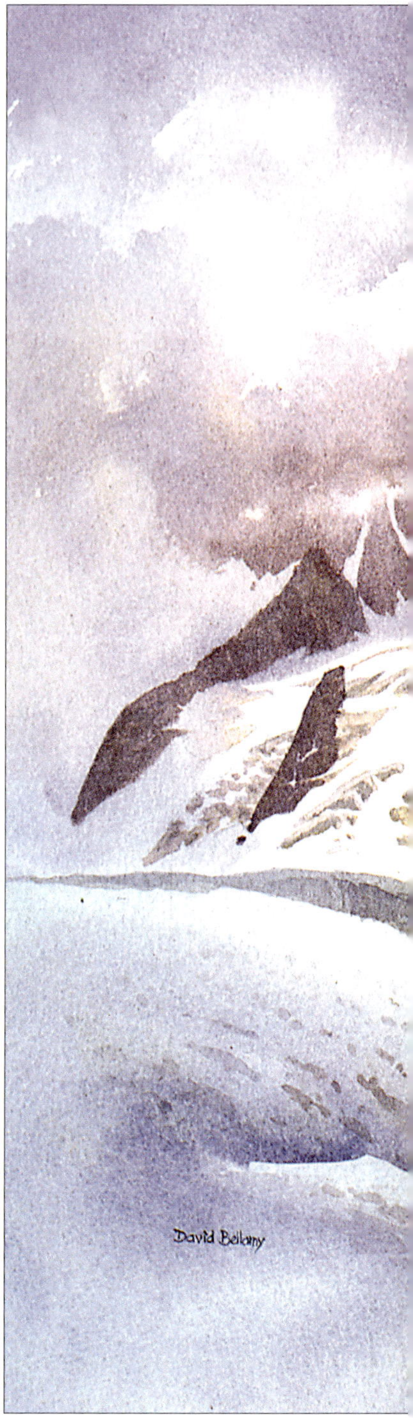

Glacier Study

This small colour study of the edge of the Russells Glacier in Greenland illustrates the varied tones and colours that can be seen in glaciers. The amount and strength of colour in ice can often be astonishing and it is worth moving around to see where it is most intense. These strong colours work well in supporting a focal point, and while a figure would be excellent to suggest scale, only a madman would climb amongst this array of unstable ice towers.

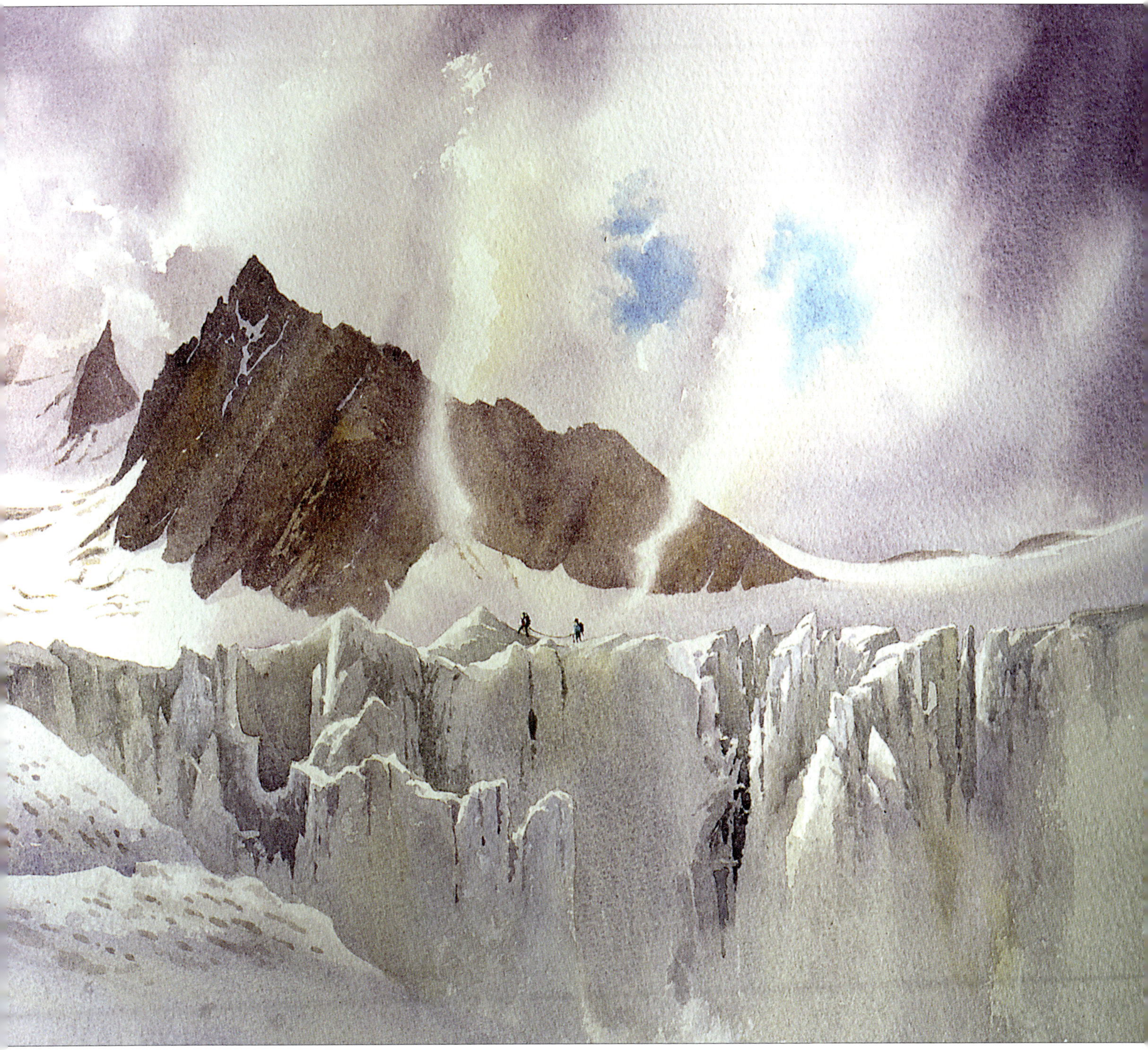

Bec Rouge and the Glacier du Tour

28 x 45.7cm (11 x 18in)

So intense was the sunlight on snow and ice in this scene from the French Alps, that I could not do without my glacier goggles – they are a neutral colour to avoid a colour cast which can seriously affect the finished result. Although I didn't put a lot of colour into the ice here, I did lay some cadmium yellow pale into the shadow areas of the crevasse walls in places. The tops of the ridges and seracs (ice columns) have been left as white paper. On the gentler slopes on the left are a series of hollows in the hard ice, although they look like footprints. I laid these on before slightly subduing them with a shadow over-laid with a wash of French ultramarine and cadmium red. The ice forms have been considerably simplified, especially in the immediate foreground, and the figures give some idea of the size of the chasm.

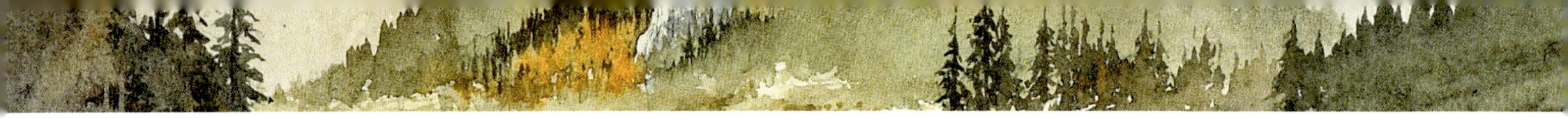

Mountains From the Valley

In this scene the mountain forms a distant backdrop, so it is important to avoid too much detail there. One of the main lessons here is that of rendering a series of ridges cloaked in massed conifers, together with the associated reflections in the lake.

Materials used

Saunders Waterford 640gsm (300lb) Not watercolour paper

Brushes: squirrel mop, 13mm (½in) flat, no. 7 round, 6mm (¼in) flat, no. 4, no. 10 and no. 8 round, no. 1 rigger and no. 1 round

Colours: cobalt blue, permanent alizarin crimson, cadmium red, yellow ochre, raw umber, new gamboge, cadmium orange, burnt umber

Paper tissue

Sponge

Scalpel

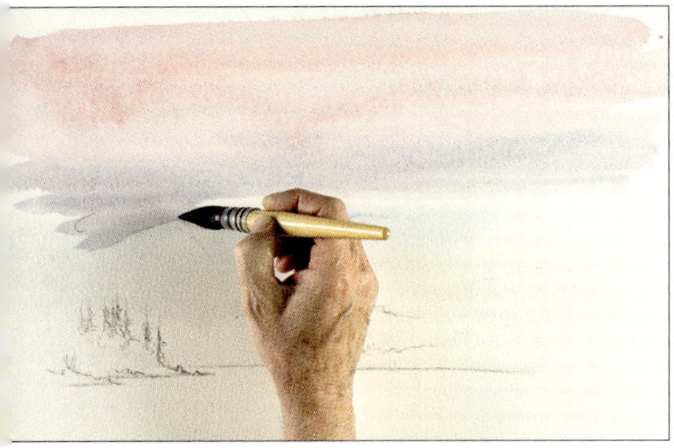

1 Draw the scene. Wet the sky and mountains with a squirrel mop and clean water and paint a pale wash of cobalt blue over the mountains. Allow to dry. Sweep a wash of alizarin crimson across the sky in horizontal strokes. Drop in a mix of cobalt blue and alizarin crimson at the bottom, working round the peaks to highlight the snow.

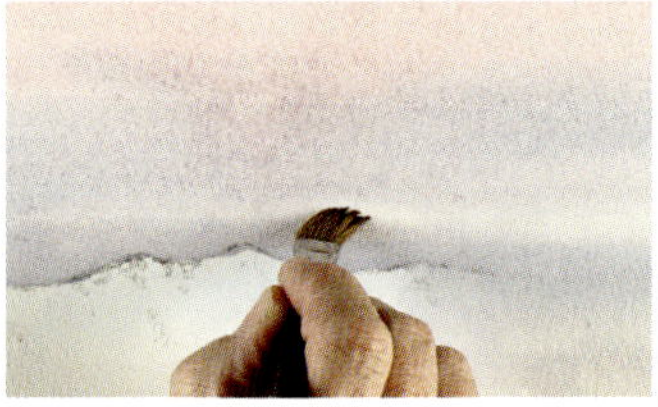

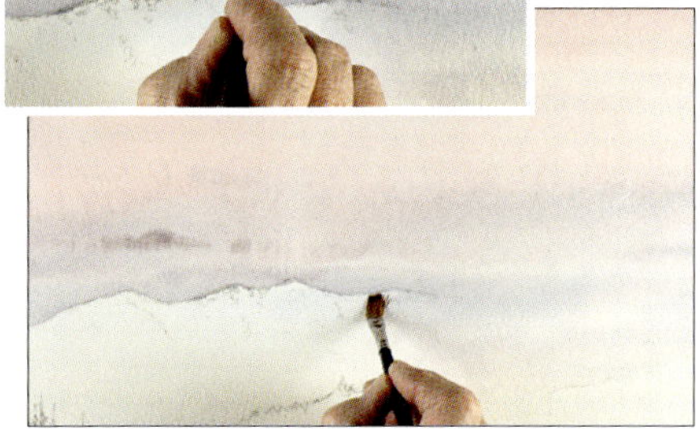

2 While this is wet, lift out some slivers of light with the 13mm (½in) flat brush, wetted and blotted on a paper tissue. Use the no. 7 brush and a mix of cadmium red and cobalt blue to drop in clouds wet into wet. Allow to dry. Use the 6mm (¼in) flat brush and clean water to soften the edge of the mountain to fade it into the cloud.

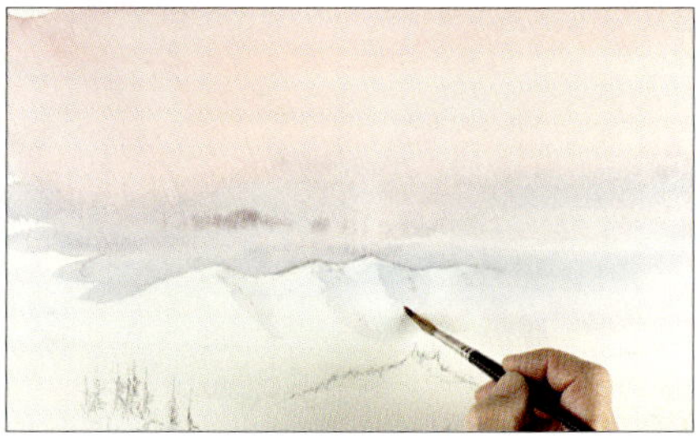

3 Create undulations in the distant peaks to highlight ridges running down the mountain, using the no. 7 brush and a weak wash of cobalt blue with a touch of alizarin crimson.

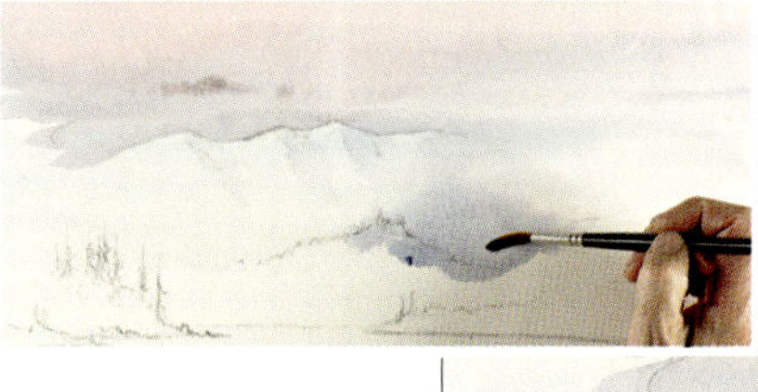

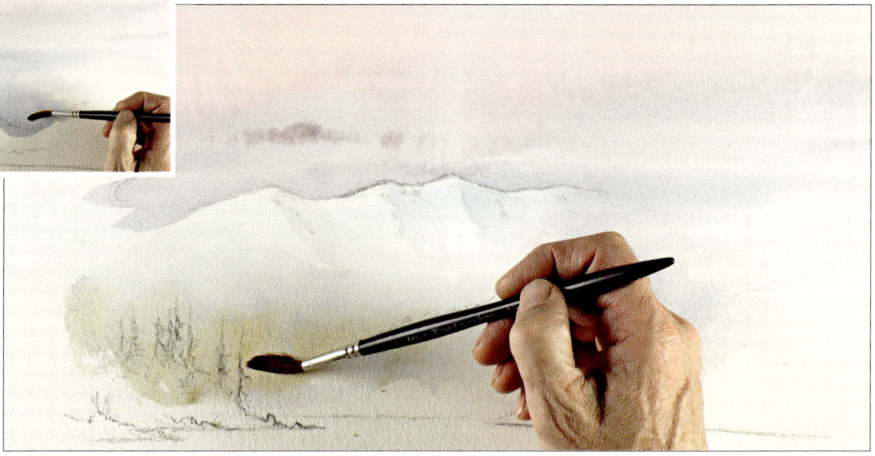

4 Run water over the right-hand side of the middle distance and drop in a stronger mix of cobalt blue and alizarin crimson. Soften the edges with clean water. Paint shadow on the left-hand side in the same way, then drop in yellow ochre as the mountain reaches the ground. Allow to dry.

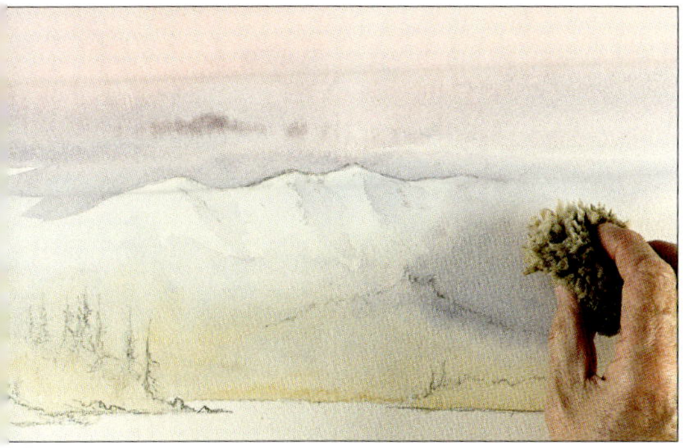

5 Get rid of any unwanted hard edges that have formed using a sponge and clean water to soften them. Allow to dry.

6 Use the no. 4 brush and a mix of cadmium red and cobalt blue to paint the details of crags sticking out of the snow on the mountain tops. Use a weaker mix and the brush on its side to create texture on the lower slopes.

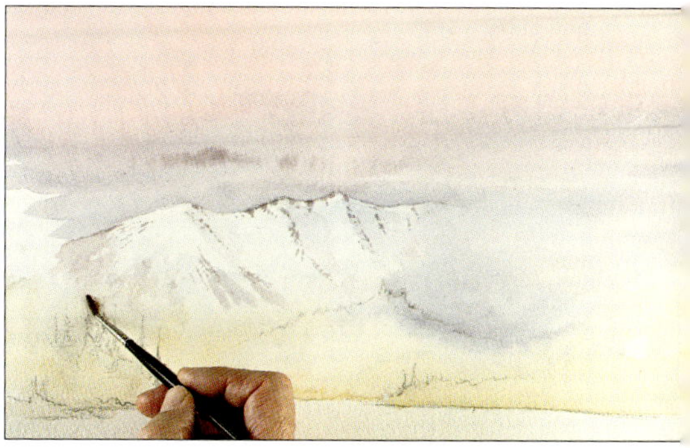

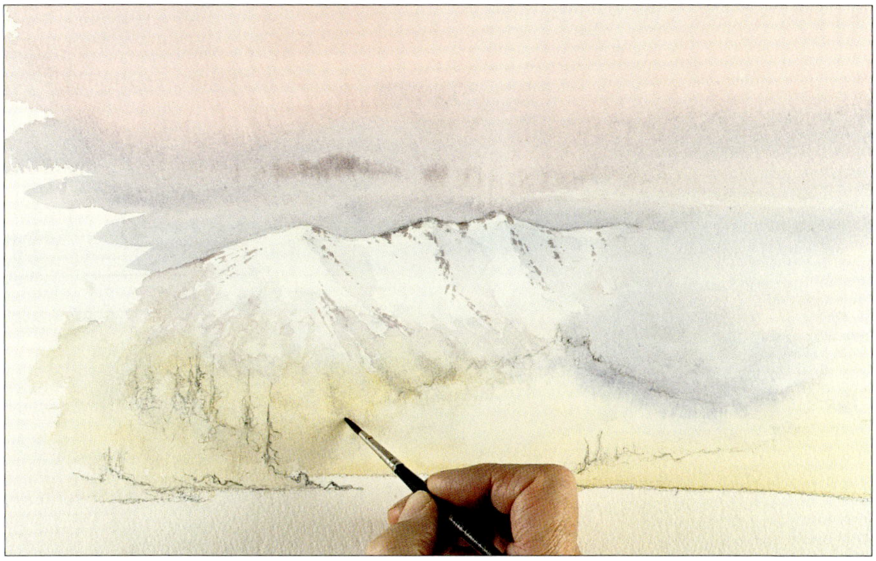

7 Dab in yellow ochre wet into wet. Wait until this is just damp, and paint in gullies with raw umber, cobalt blue and alizarin crimson. Here we are creating the illusion that the lower part of the mountain is much nearer to us. Soften off at the bottom with clean water.

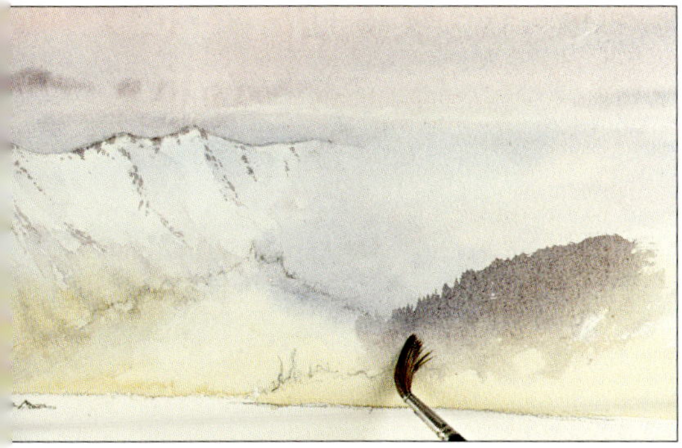

8 Create another ridge in the distance with a mix of cobalt blue and cadmium red, using the shape of the brush to suggest treetops. Soften at the bottom with clean water and allow to dry.

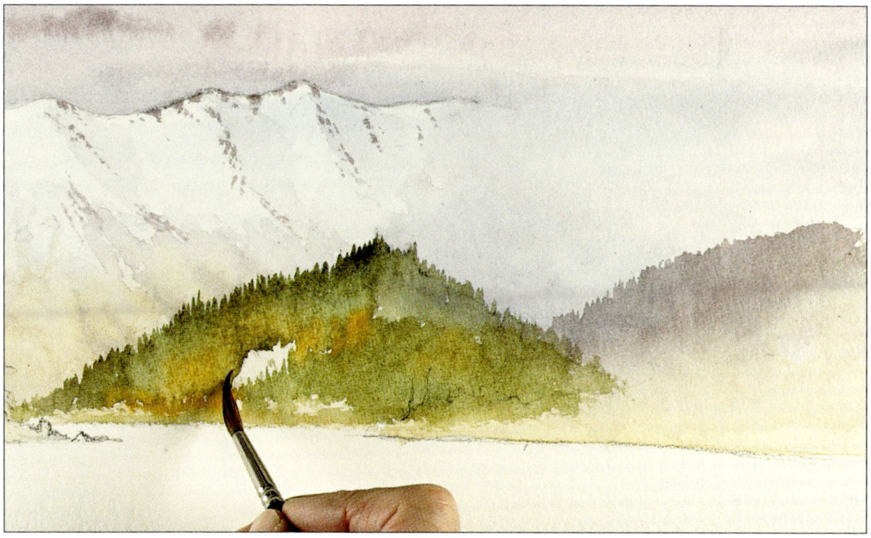

9 Use a no. 7 brush with a good point and a mix of cobalt blue and new gamboge to create massed conifers in the middle distance. Darken with raw umber in places and continue, then drop in cadmium orange to break the monotony and to suggest larches. Paint round the crag.

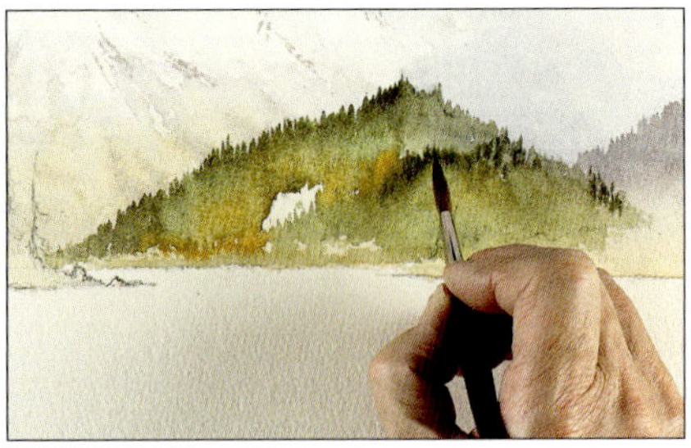

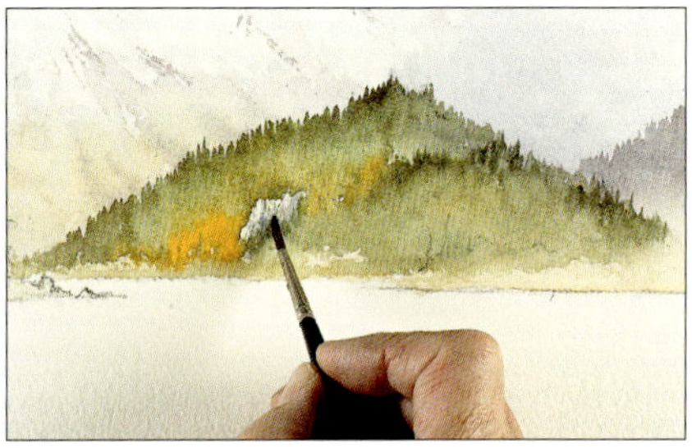

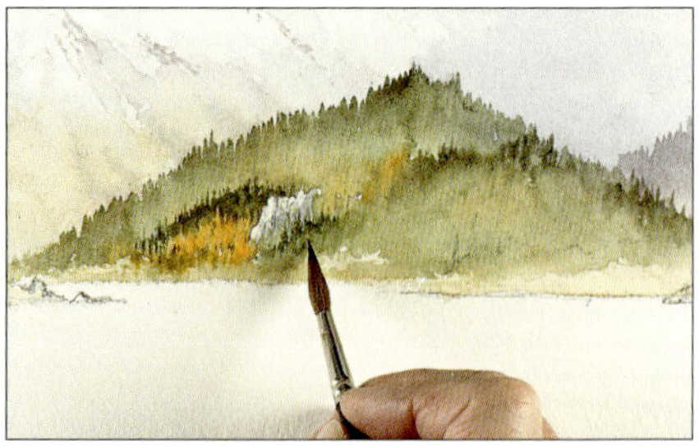

10 Mix cobalt blue and raw umber and paint a darker ridge of conifers.

11 Paint the fracture lines in the crag with the point of the brush and a mix of burnt umber and cobalt blue. Drop in more cadmium orange. Add shade to the lower part of the crag with the no. 4 brush and a mix of cobalt blue and burnt umber. Allow to dry.

12 Make the larches stand out by painting a dark mix of cobalt blue and raw umber behind them, then paint more dark trees beneath the crag, and soften them in with clean water.

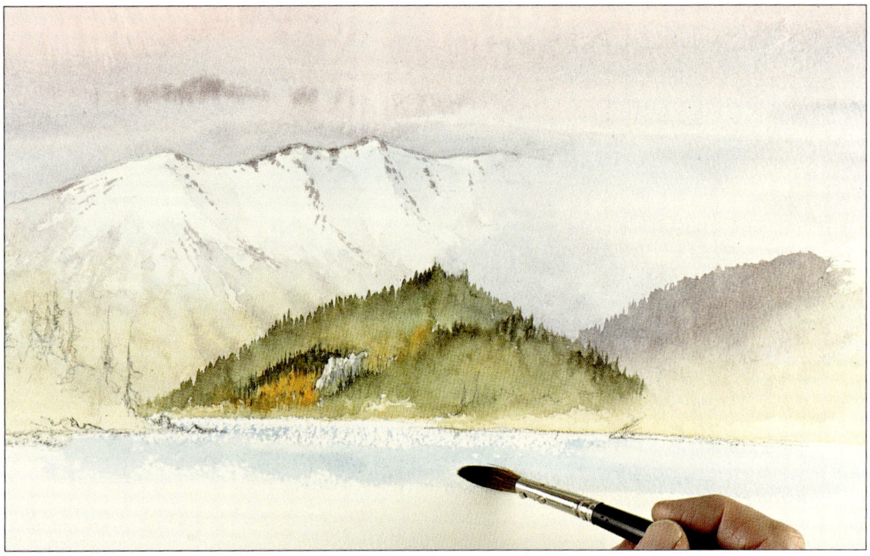

13 Use the no. 10 brush and the dry brush technique to paint cobalt blue over the water by the far shore. Soften this at the bottom to create a soft transition between the ruffled and the smooth water.

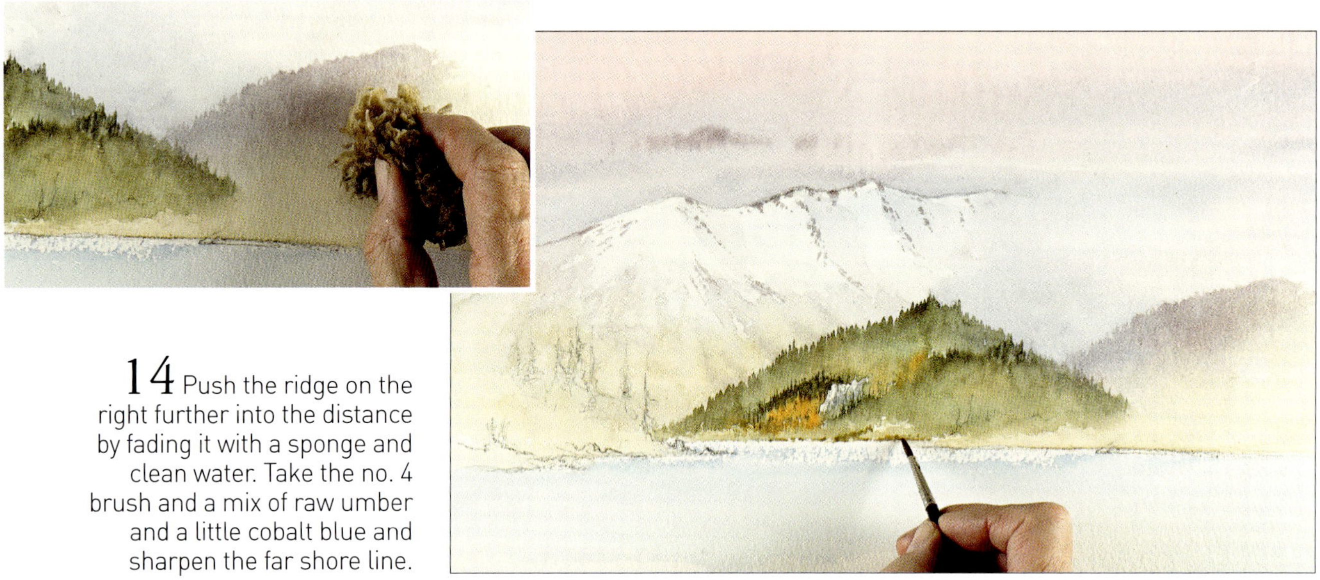

14 Push the ridge on the right further into the distance by fading it with a sponge and clean water. Take the no. 4 brush and a mix of raw umber and a little cobalt blue and sharpen the far shore line.

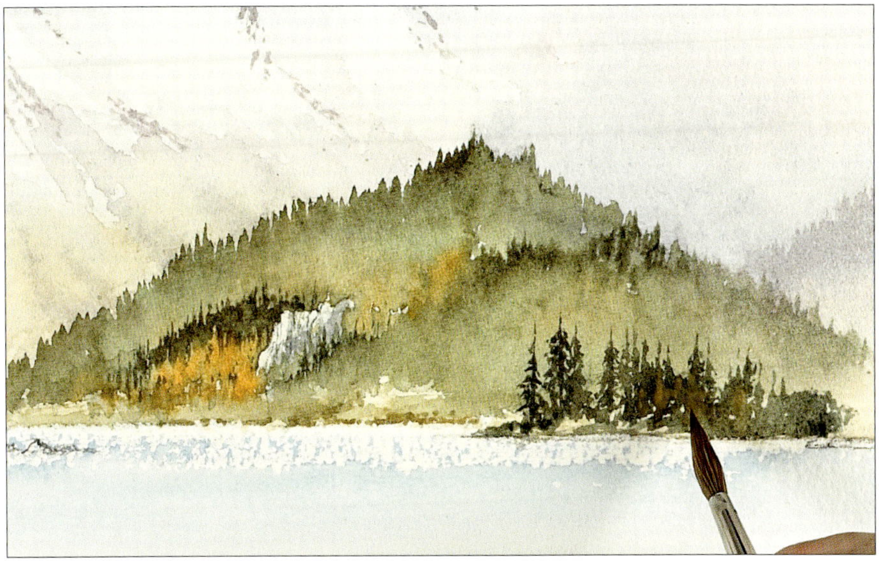

15 Paint trees with raw umber and cobalt blue, and drop in yellow ochre.

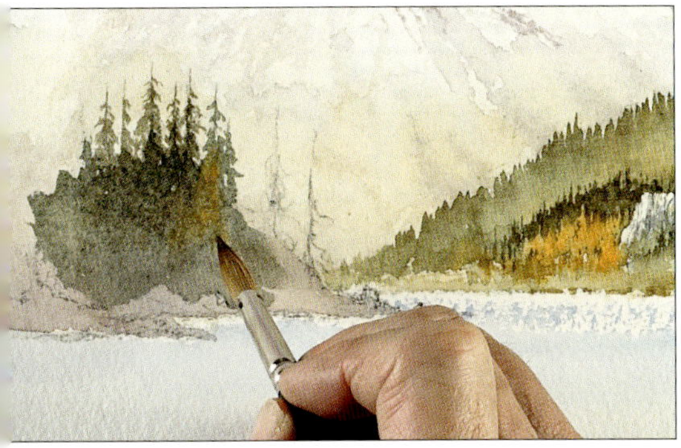

16 Paint the area on the left of the shore line with cadmium red and cobalt blue. Allow to dry. Use the point of the no. 8 round to paint conifers with raw umber and cobalt blue. Drop in yellow ochre.

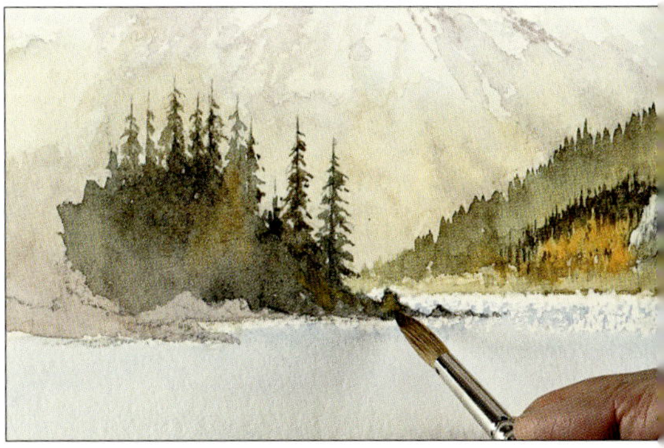

17 Paint rocks with the same mix, making them sharp and strong against the light background, then drop in cadmium orange while they are wet.

18 Use the no. 1 rigger with a mix of cobalt blue and burnt umber to paint the fracture lines on the rocks and to darken behind them. Change to the no. 4 round and paint a darker line of rocks with cobalt blue and raw umber, then drop in yellow ochre and allow to dry.

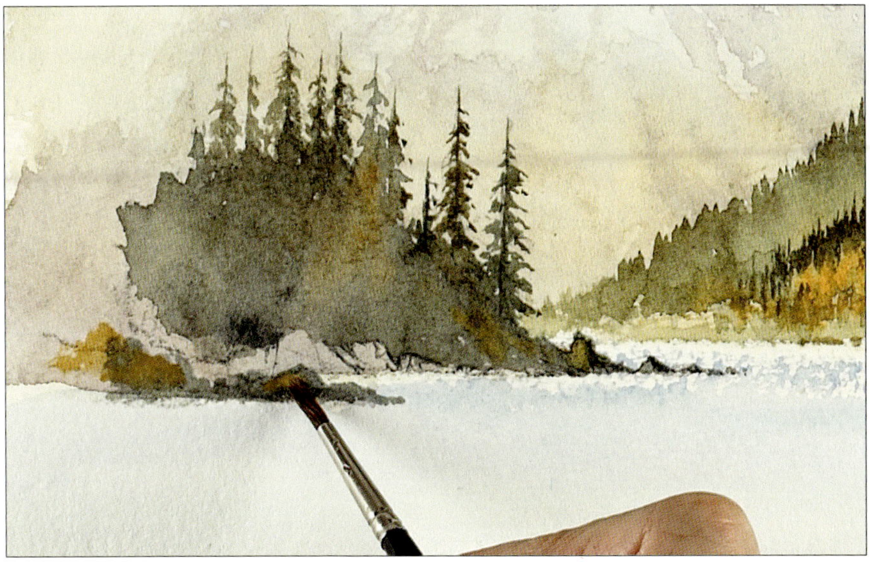

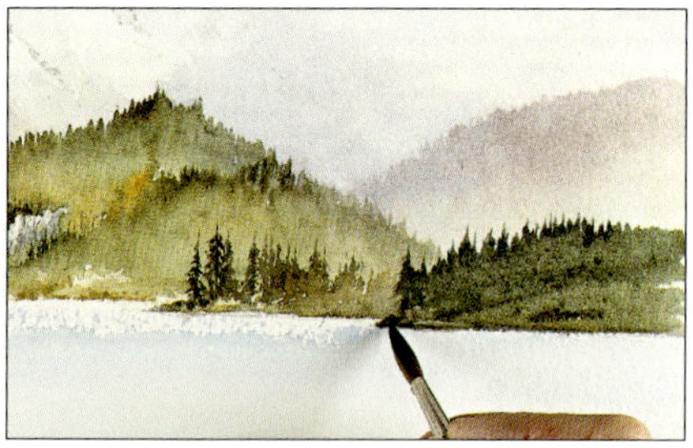

19 Use the no. 7 brush and raw umber with cobalt blue to paint trees on the right, then mix burnt umber and cobalt blue to paint rocks beneath the trees.

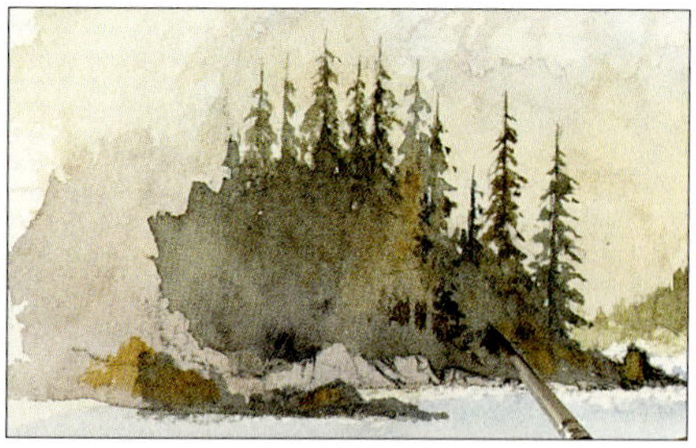

20 Change to the no. 1 round brush and do some negative painting in the trees on the left with cobalt blue and burnt umber. Hint at tree trunks. This is the focal point so needs to draw the eye.

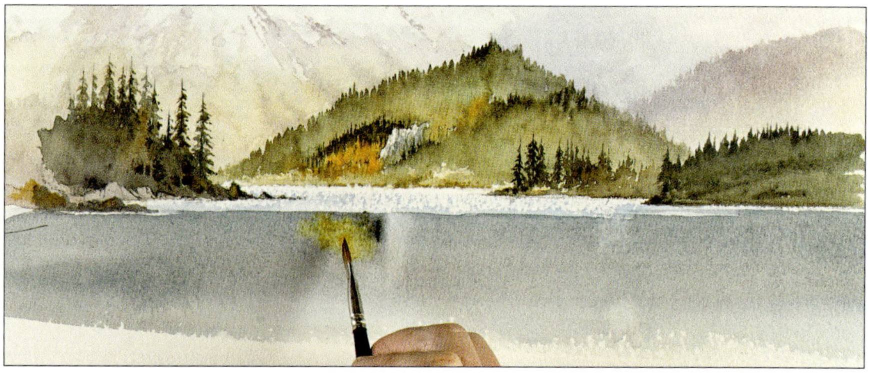

21 Wash cobalt blue and burnt umber across the lake with the squirrel mop. Lift out a little of the colour with the 6mm (¼in) flat brush, to suggest a reflection of the crag. Drop in raw umber and cobalt blue reflections, then cadmium orange with the no. 7 round brush.

22 Paint tree reflections while the area is wet with cobalt blue and raw umber. Vary the mix to suit the trees that are being reflected. Paint some of the green in the orange reflection.

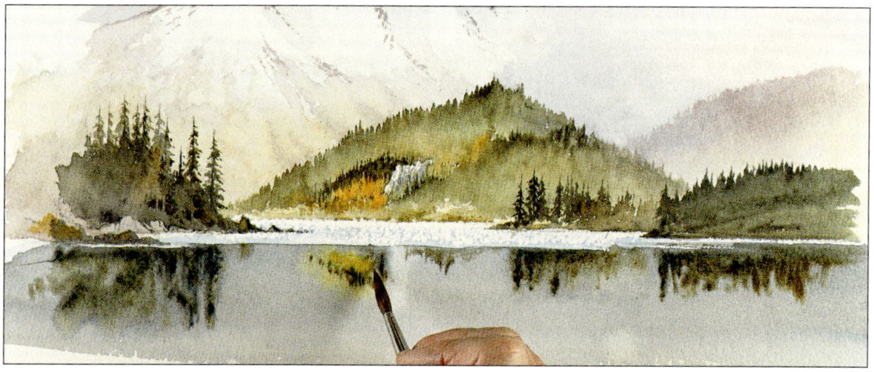

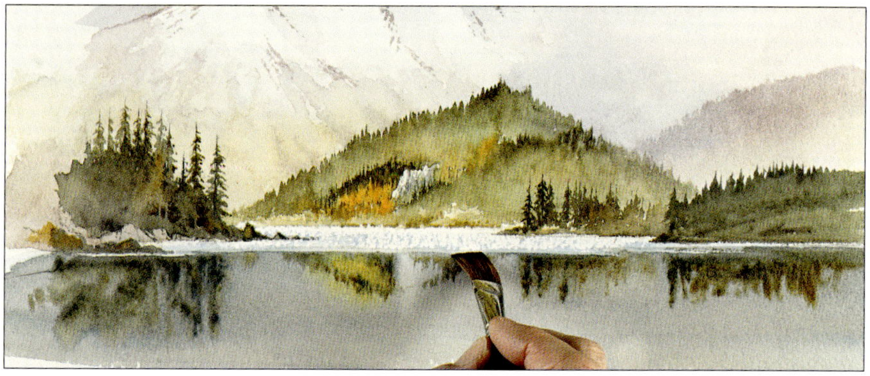

23 Soften the transition between the smooth and the ruffled water with the 13mm (½in) flat brush and clean water.

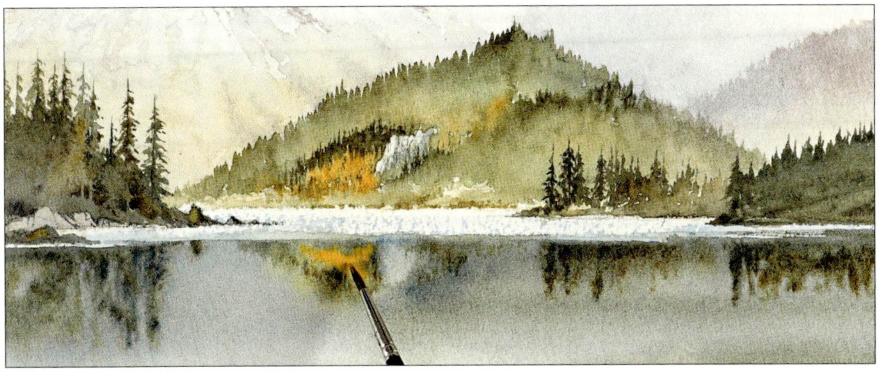

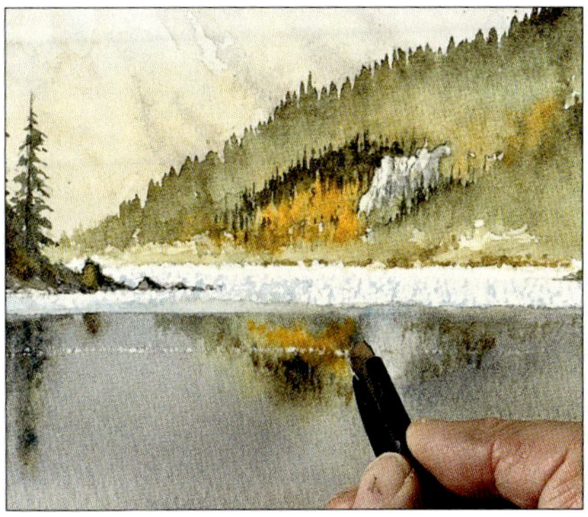

24 Continue working on the reflections while the area is wet. Paint a reflection of the green hill with the no. 7 brush and cobalt blue with raw umber, then intensify the reflection of the larches with the no. 4 brush and cadmium orange. Allow to dry.

25 Scratch out ripples across the reflections using a scalpel.

The finished painting.

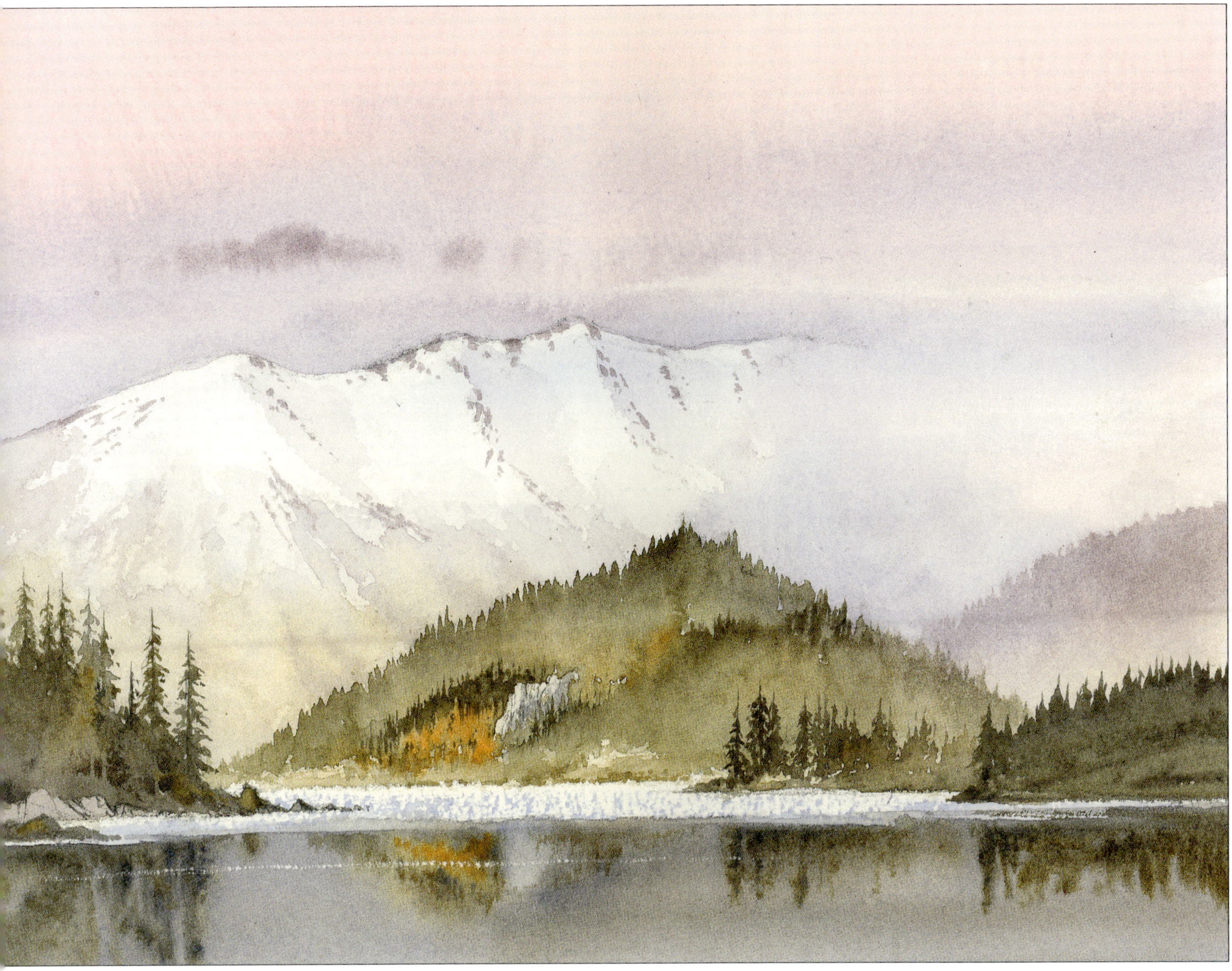

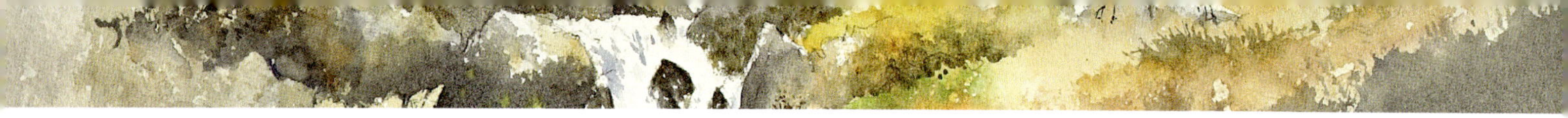

Mountain Cascade

The combination of rocks and tumbling water provides a fascinating centre of interest, and in this demonstration the strength of this centre of interest is accentuated by strong detail and tonal contrasts, bright colours, a lead-in and a backdrop that gives further emphasis to the falls.

Materials used

Saunders Waterford 640gsm (300lb) Rough watercolour paper

Brushes: squirrel mop, no. 12, no. 10, no. 7 and no. 4 round, no. 1 rigger and 6mm (¼in) flat

Colours: Naples yellow, French ultramarine, burnt umber, raw umber, yellow ochre, burnt sienna, cadmium yellow pale, cadmium red, perylene maroon, viridian

Water spray

Scrap paper

Sponge

Scalpel

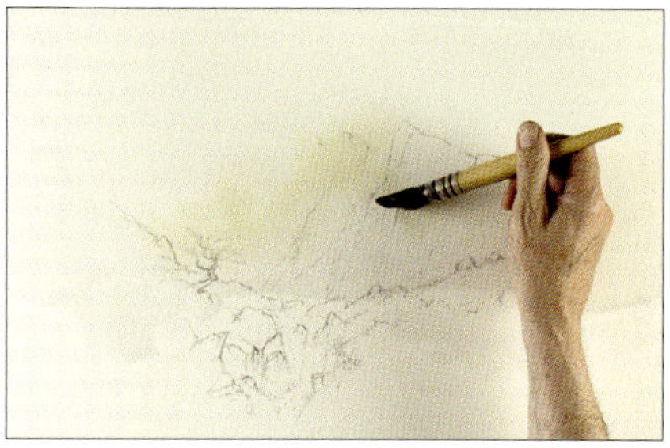

1 Draw the scene. Apply water to the sky and mountains using the squirrel mop, then drop in a little Naples yellow.

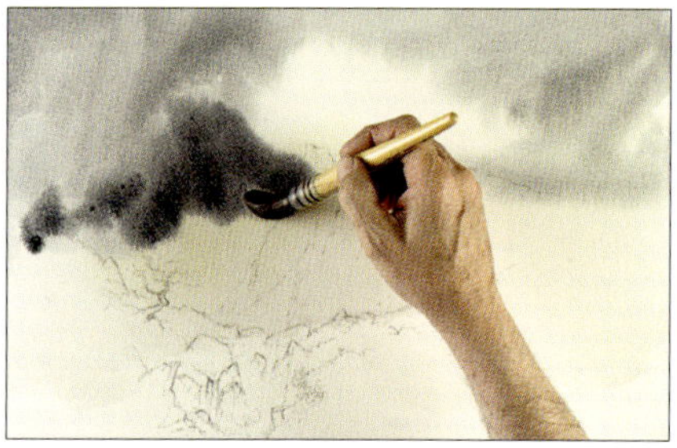

2 Paint the dark cloudy areas of the sky with ultramarine and burnt umber, and put in the rising peak on the left with a stronger mix of the same colours, all while the paper is wet.

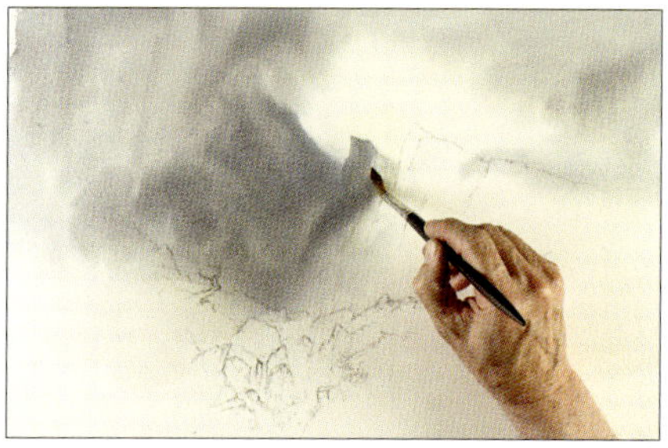

3 Define the edge of the peak by lifting out colour with a clean, damp, no. 12 brush. Paint the next peak with a no. 10 round and the same mix, and drop in raw umber wet into wet. Allow to dry.

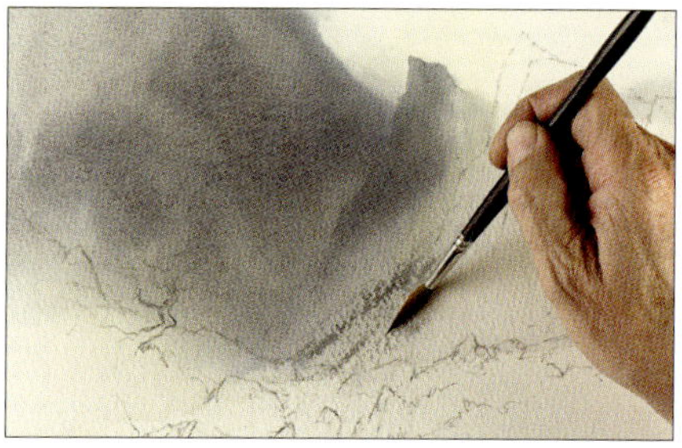

4 Use the no. 7 brush fairly dry, on its side, with a mix of burnt umber and ultramarine to create the scree coming down the mountain with the dry brush technique. Allow to dry.

5 Paint the middle peak, creating a strong, hard edge and using the point of the brush and the same mix to create structure. Add a little raw umber and water as you come forwards.

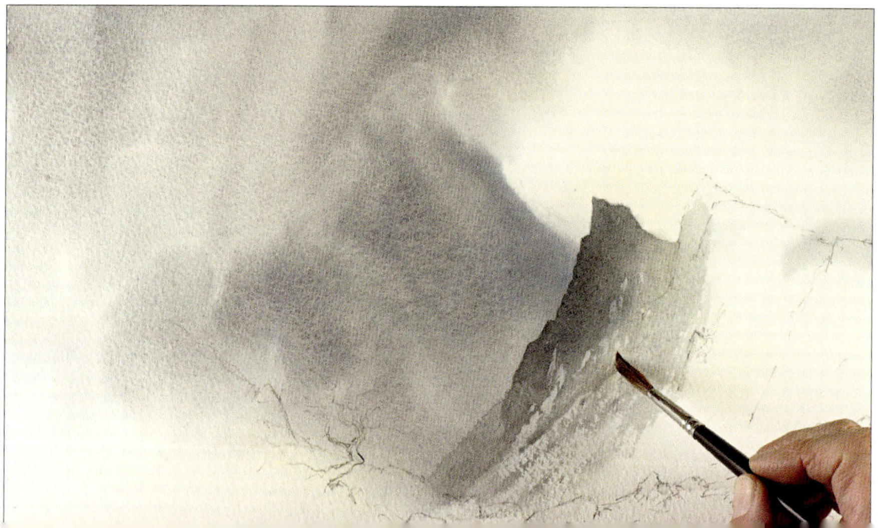

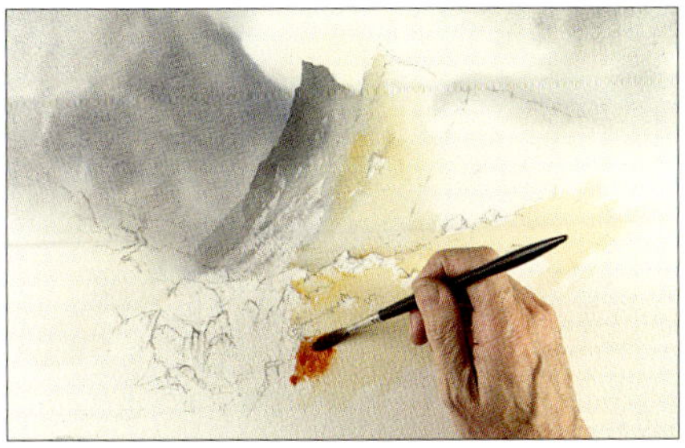

6 Bring in yellow ochre further forwards, and drop in a little burnt sienna to suggest warm-coloured earth to lift the scene.

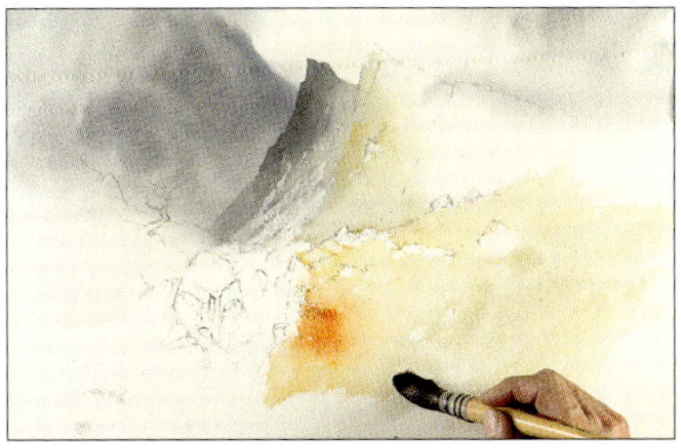

7 Use the squirrel mop to extend the yellow ochre wash across the right-hand foreground.

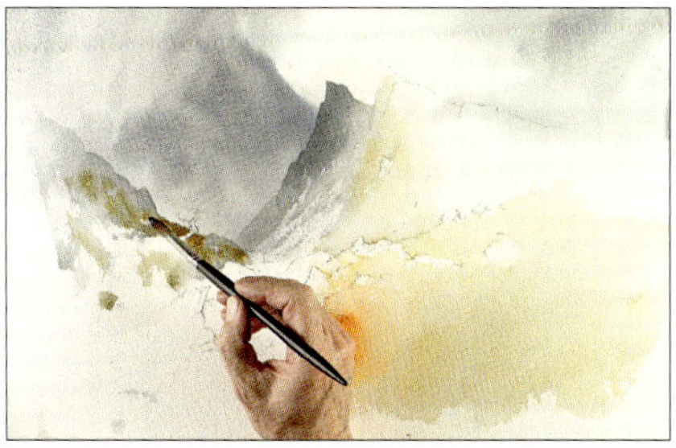

8 Change to the no. 10 round brush to paint the sloping crags on the left, working negatively around the trunk of the thorn bush. Drop in raw umber wet into wet.

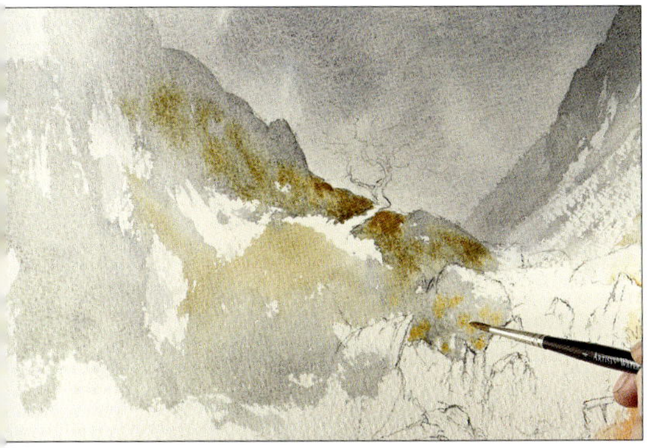

9 Use the brush on its side to create a textural finish for the rock with raw umber and a touch of ultramarine, then change to the no. 4 brush and drop in yellow ochre.

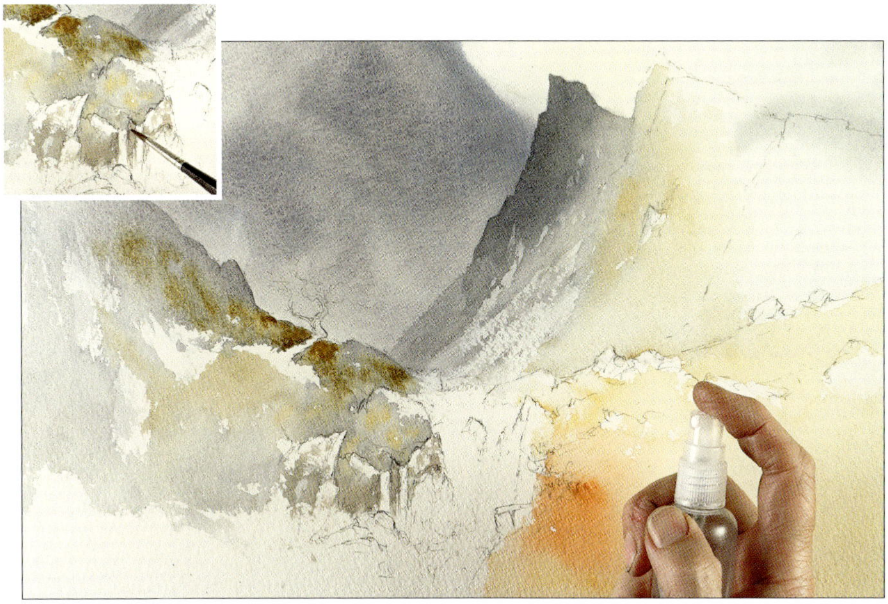

10 Paint the rock beside the cascade with a mix of raw umber and ultramarine. Spray the rocky area around the cascade with water to create textural effects. Allow to dry.

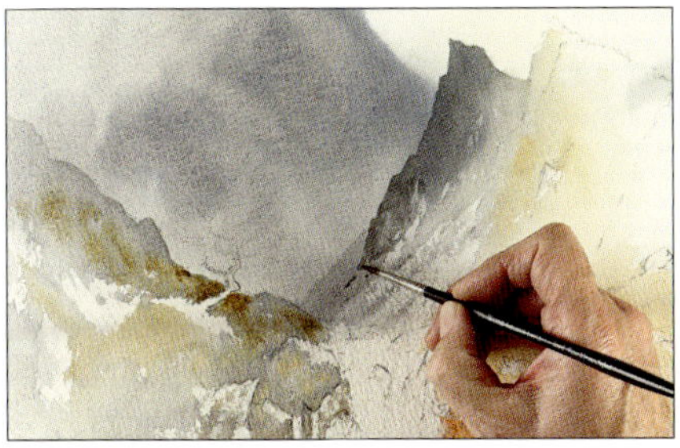

11 Tidy and strengthen the edge of the middle peak with the no. 4 brush, using a mix of ultramarine and burnt umber.

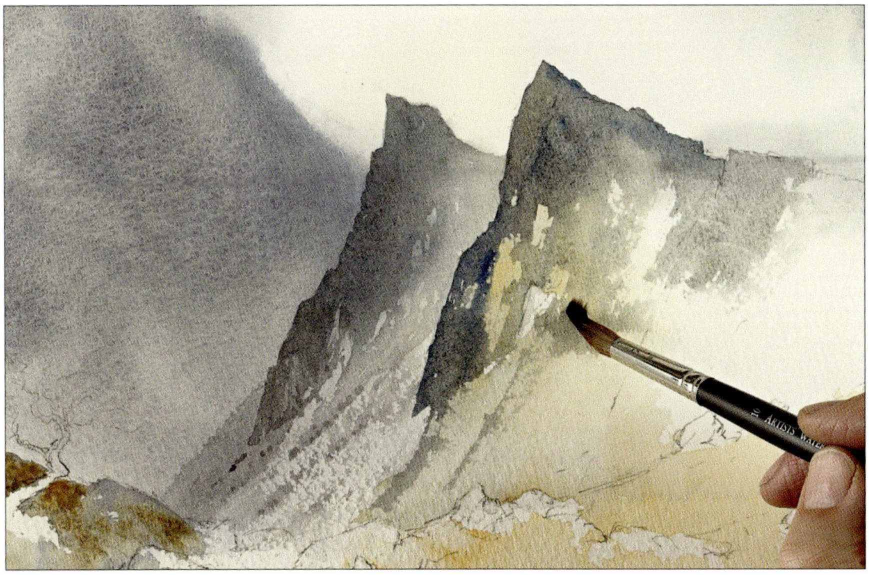

12 Change to the no. 7 brush to paint more of the mountain.

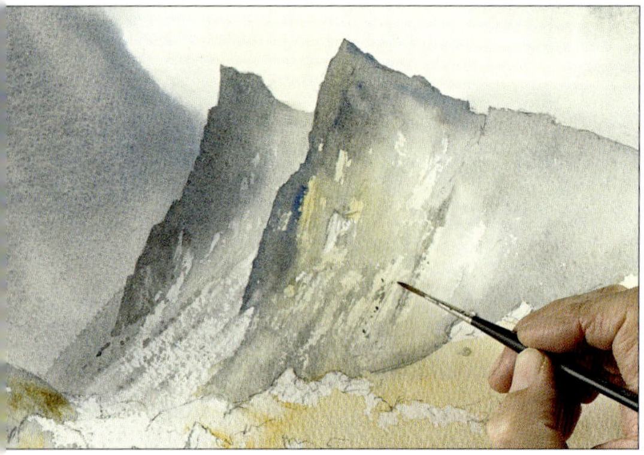

13 Use the no. 1 rigger and a mix of ultramarine and burnt sienna to paint fracture lines on the mountain. Allow to dry.

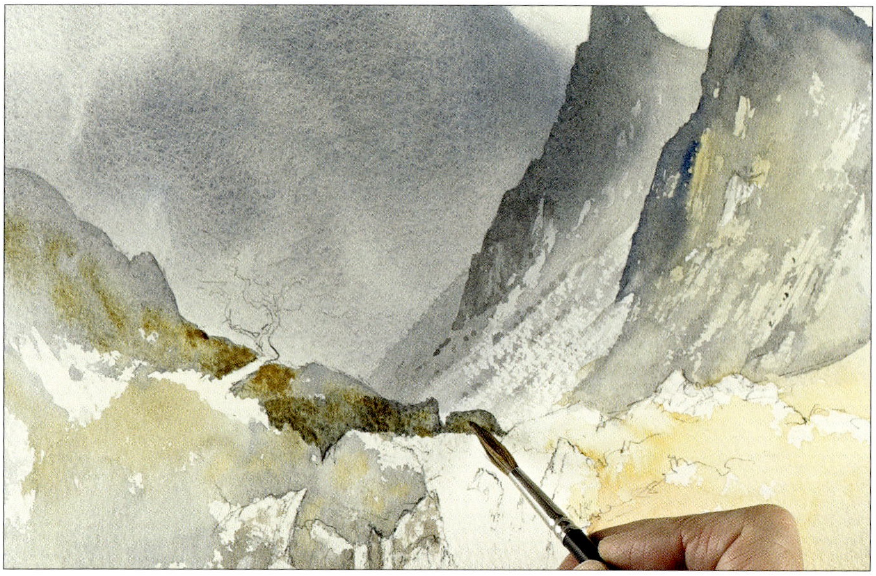

14 Paint the boulders above the cascade with the no. 7 brush and the same mix, then drop in yellow ochre wet into wet.

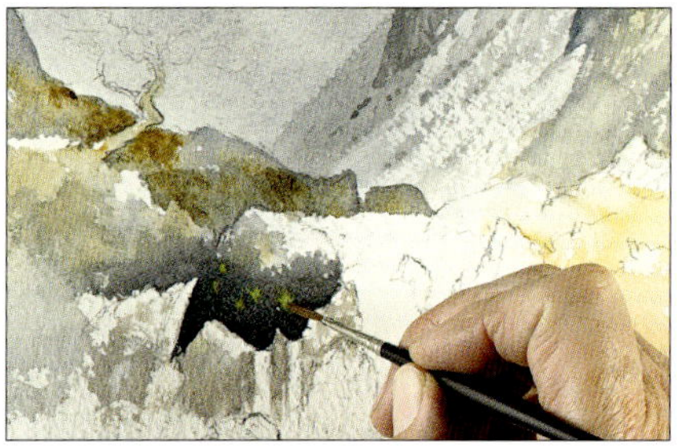

15 Strengthen the boulder with ultramarine and burnt umber, then paint the trunk of the thorn bush with raw umber. Spray this area again to create speckles. Use the no. 1 rigger and cadmium yellow pale to paint dots of lichen on the boulder.

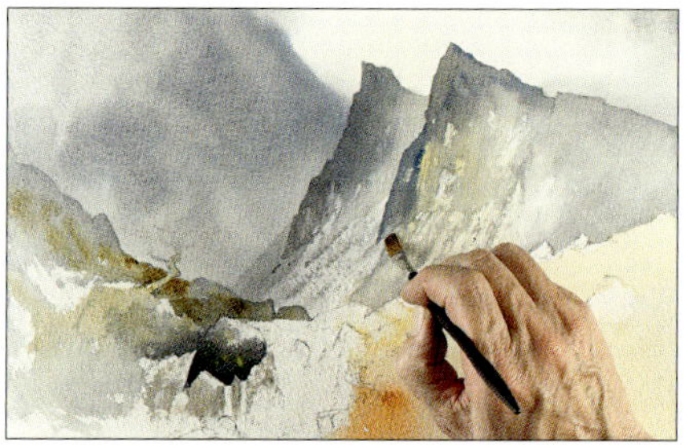

16 Soften some of the hard edges of the peaks with the 6mm (¼in) flat brush and clean water.

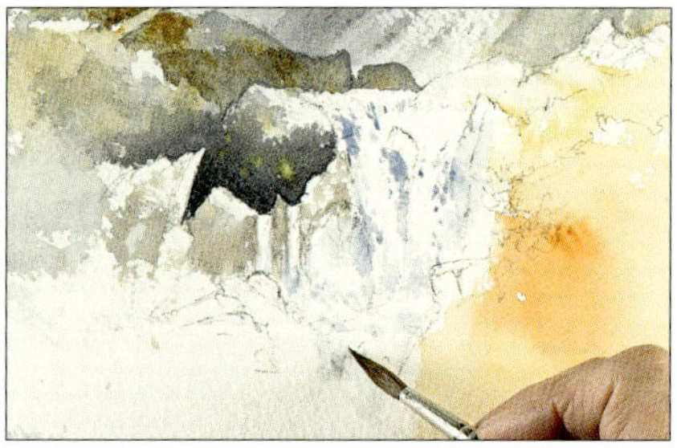

17 Paint the shaded areas of the waterfall using the no. 7 brush and ultramarine. Leave some of the paper white, especially where the water is aerated lower down.

18 Use the tip of the no. 7 brush to paint the sharp rocky edges on the left-hand side of the scene with burnt umber and ultramarine. Drop in yellow ochre.

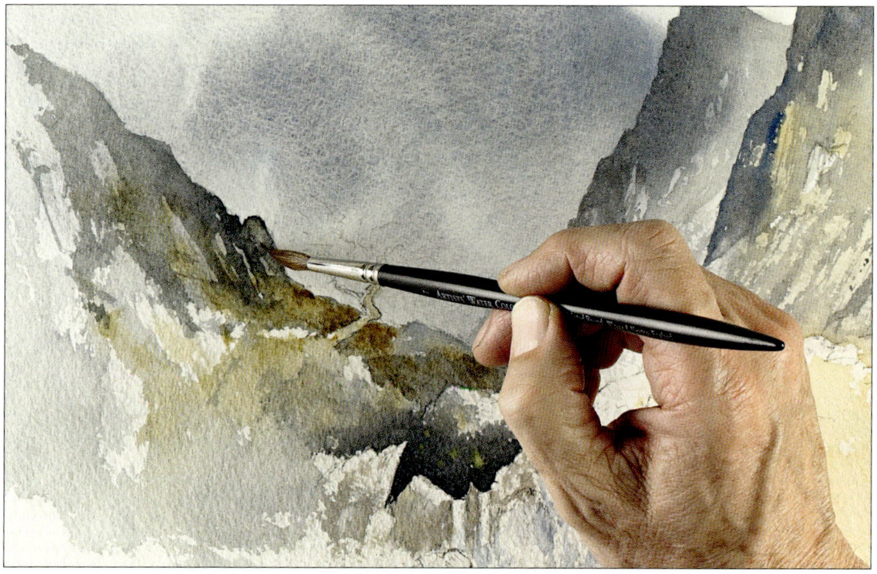

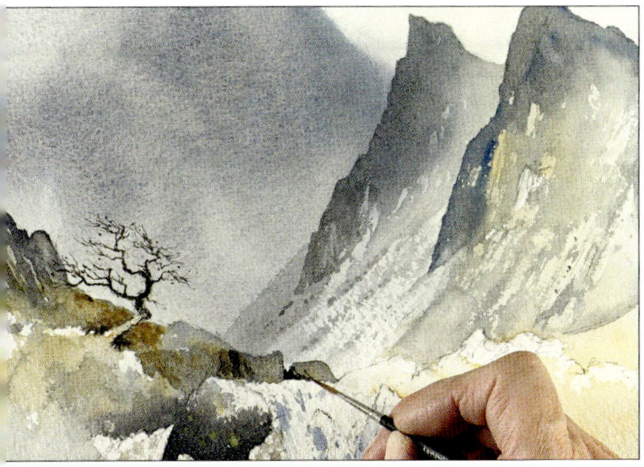

19 Use the no. 1 rigger and ultramarine and burnt umber to paint the thorn bush. Allow to dry. Reinforce the darker area behind the trunk with negative painting, then paint shadows and streaks in the rock with the same brush and mix.

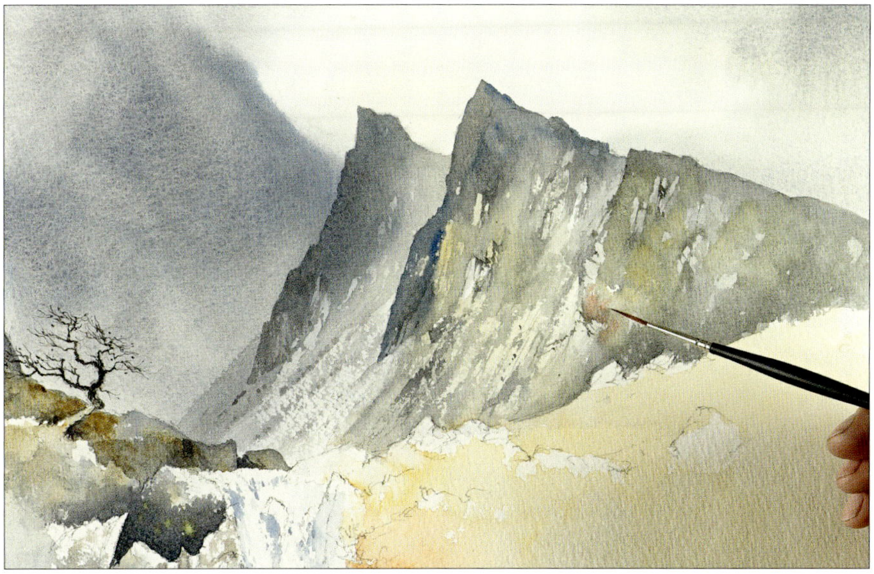

20 Use the point of the rigger to suggest fractures in the mountainside as it slopes into the corrie – the shape sculpted out by a glacier – and other features of the rock face. Soften in places with clean water and use the rigger almost dry and on its side to create texture. Drop yellow ochre, then cadmium red into the wet wash.

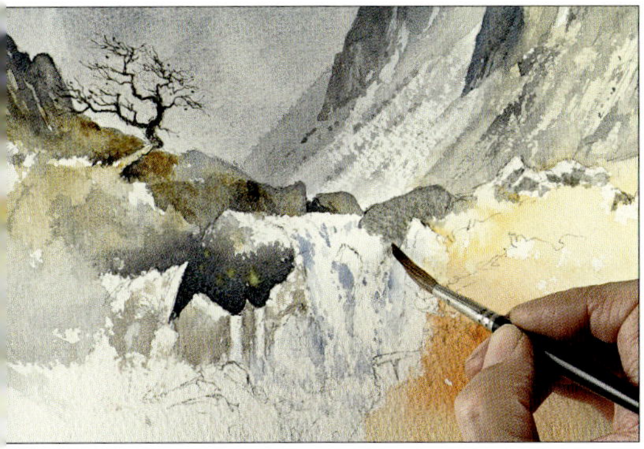

21 Paint rocks near the white water with the no. 7 brush and burnt umber and ultramarine.

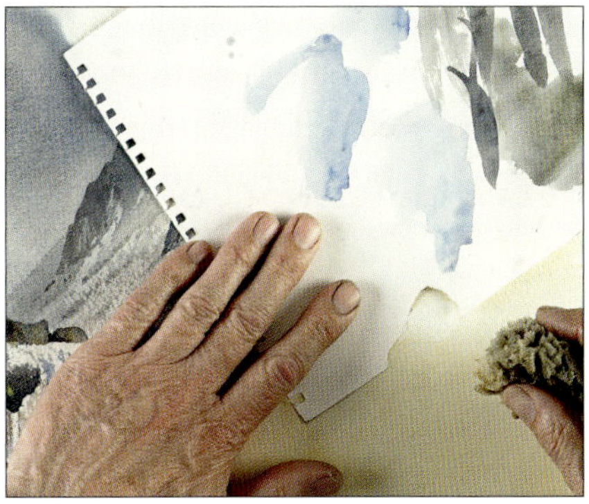

22 Make a stencil by tearing a piece of scrap paper and use it with a sponge to lift out colour from the yellow ochre area on the right to create a new rock.

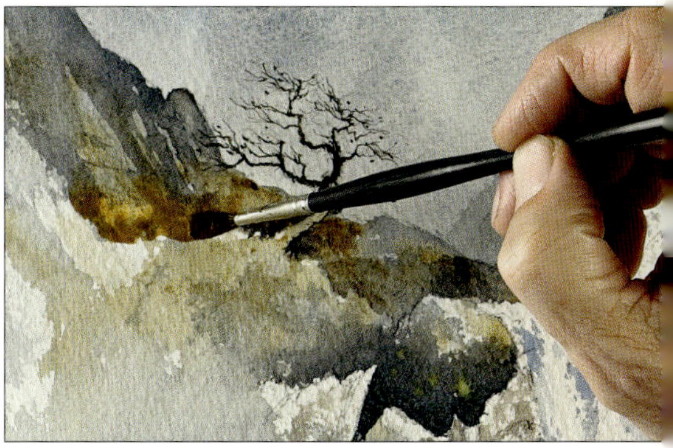

23 Paint raw umber on the rocks around the waterfall and thorn bush with the no. 4 brush.

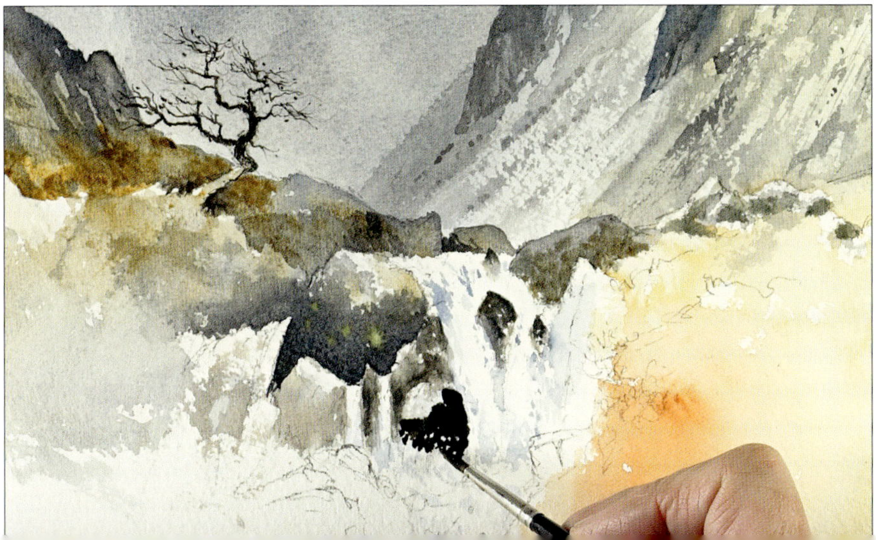

24 Paint rocks in and around the cascade with ultramarine and burnt umber, leaving speckles of white to suggest water bubbling up.

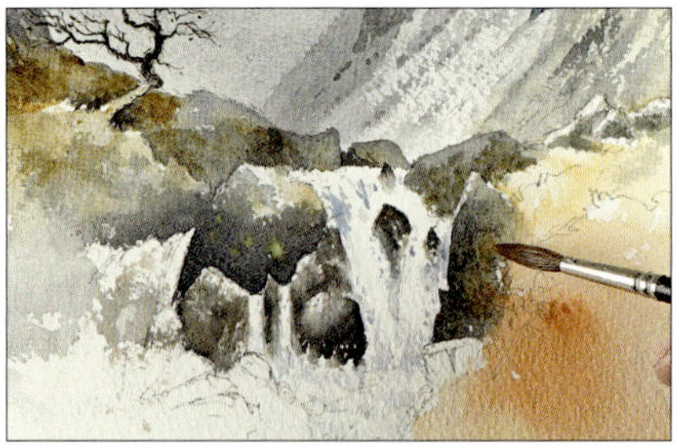

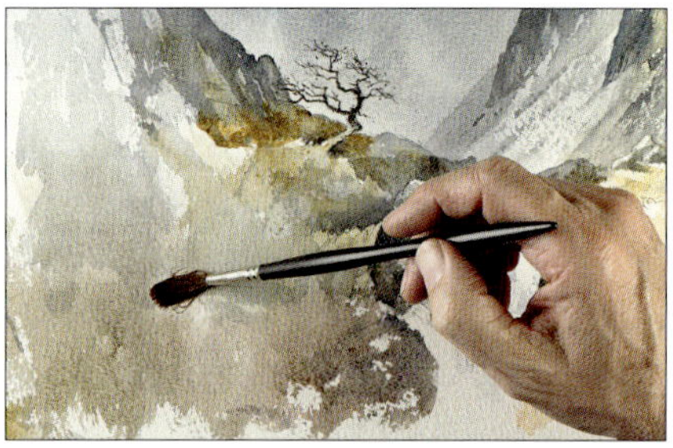

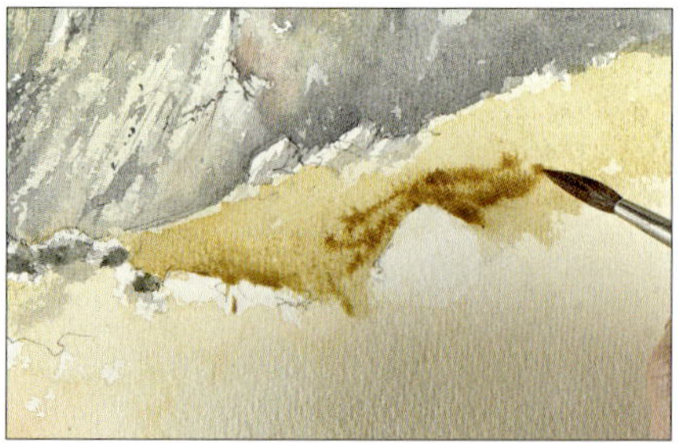

25 Paint the rock to the right of the cascade with the no. 7 brush and burnt umber and ultramarine, then drop in yellow ochre.

26 Fill in the area to the left of the cascade with a wash of raw umber, then paint perylene maroon and ultramarine just below this, and raw umber at the bottom left of the scene.

27 Apply a wash of yellow ochre and then raw umber around the stencilled rock.

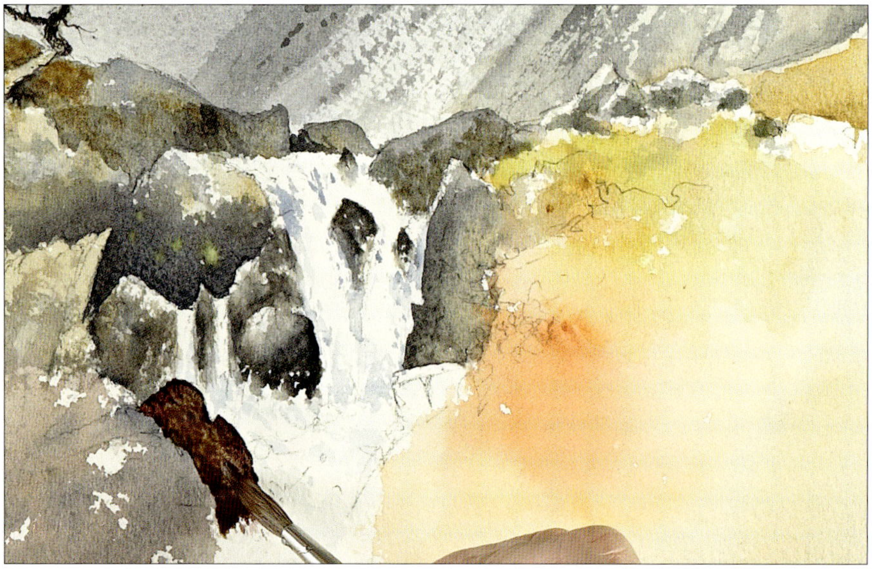

28 Wash in more raw umber and then cadmium yellow pale to create brightness to the right of the cascade, which is the focal point. Paint a rock with perylene maroon, and drop in yellow ochre.

29 Use a very pale mix of perylene maroon and ultramarine to paint the rocks on the right, leaving white highlights at the top, then drop in yellow ochre.

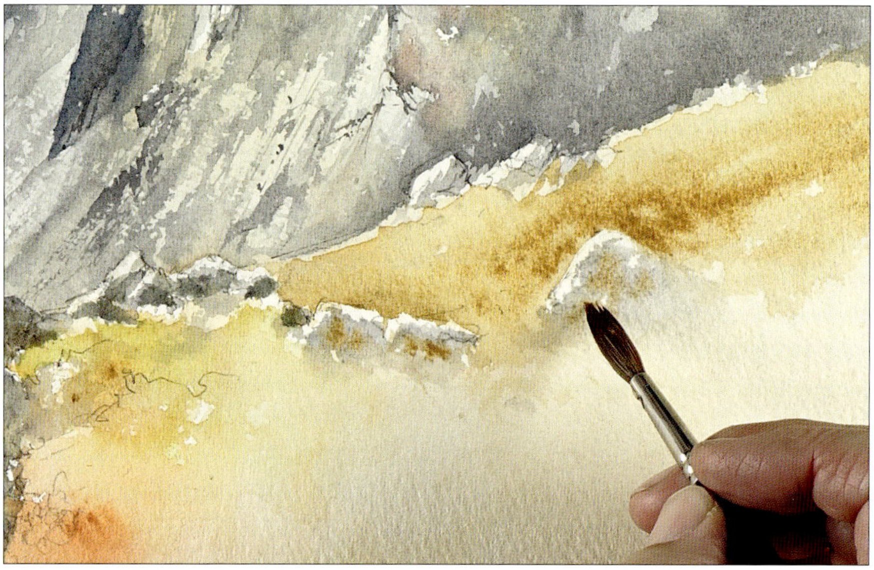

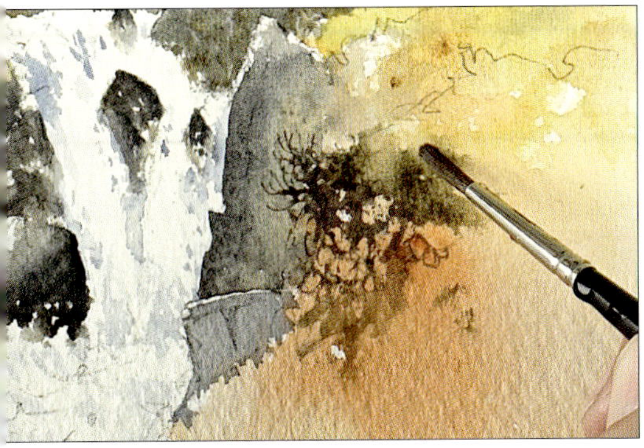

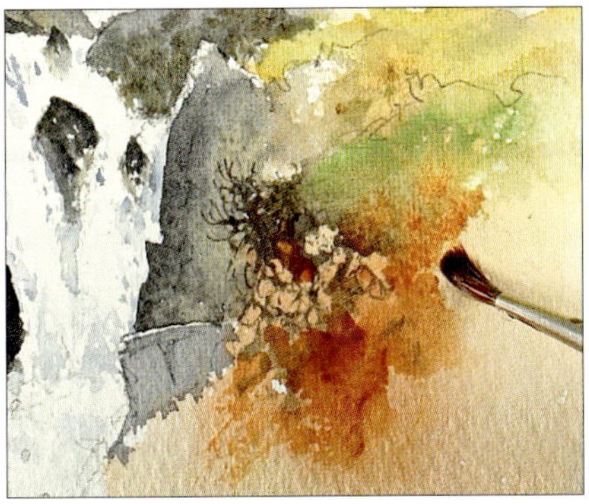

31 Mix viridian with cadmium yellow pale and drop in green around the thorn bush, then burnt sienna to imply undergrowth.

30 Paint the heather to the right of the cascade with the no. 1 rigger and burnt umber and ultramarine, then add tone with the no. 4 brush.

32 Paint rock shapes with burnt umber and ultramarine, then use the no. 1 rigger to create the effect of heather around the rocks.

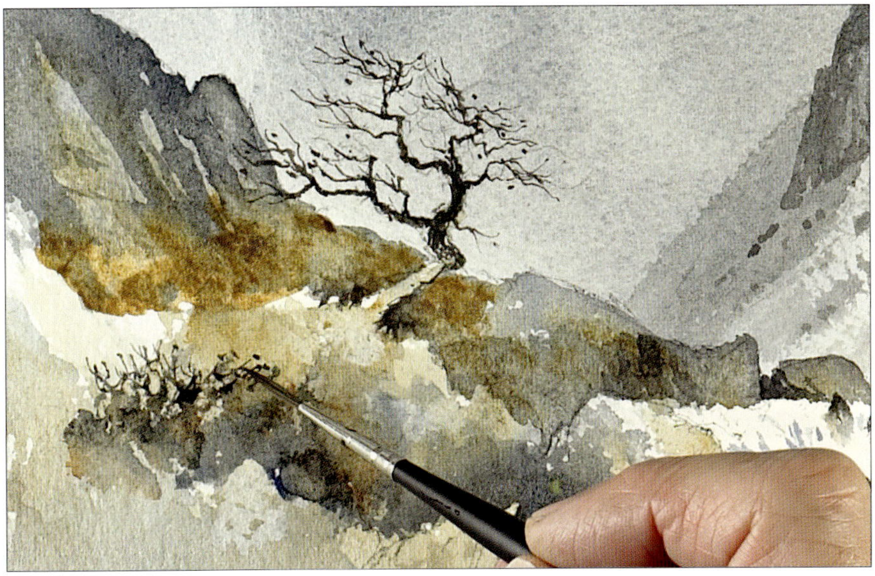

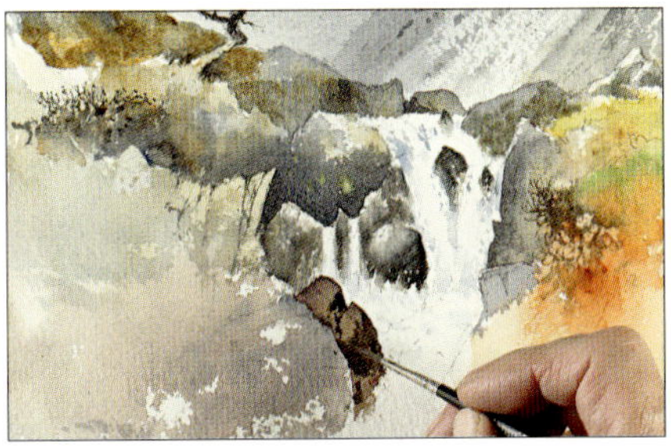

33 Create fracture lines and other rock details with the same brush and mix.

34 Add shadow to the side of the grey rock beside the cascade with ultramarine and burnt umber.

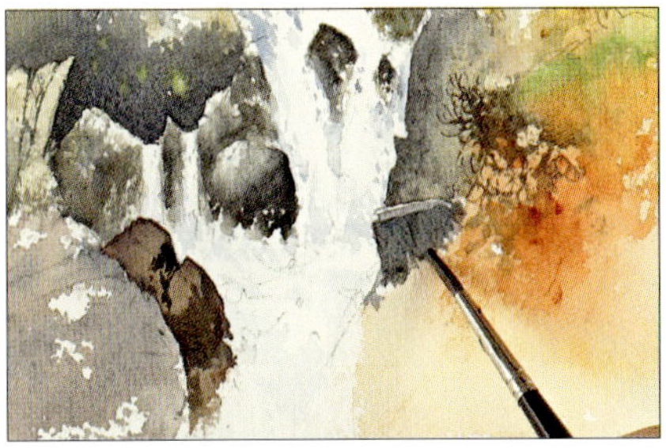

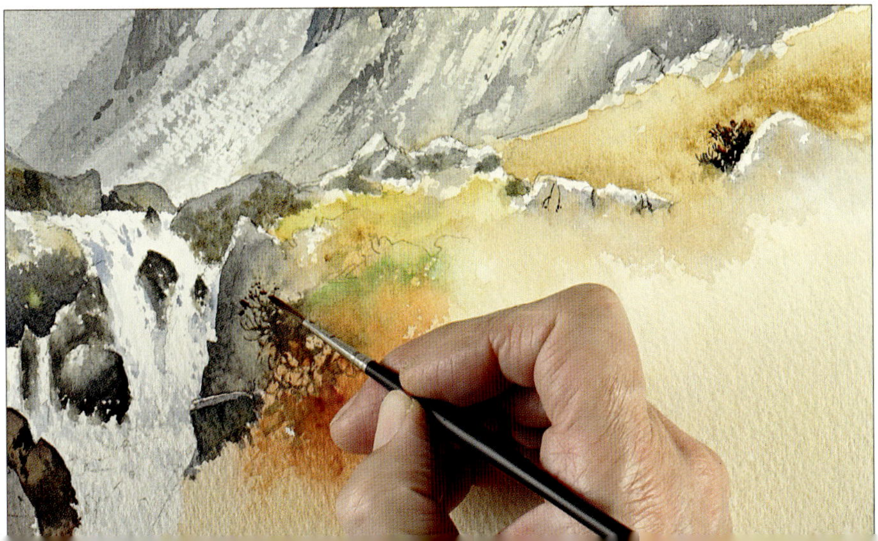

35 Still using the no. 1 rigger and the same mix, paint the heather to the left of the white rock that was stencilled, then drop in perylene maroon to this and the heather beside the cascade.

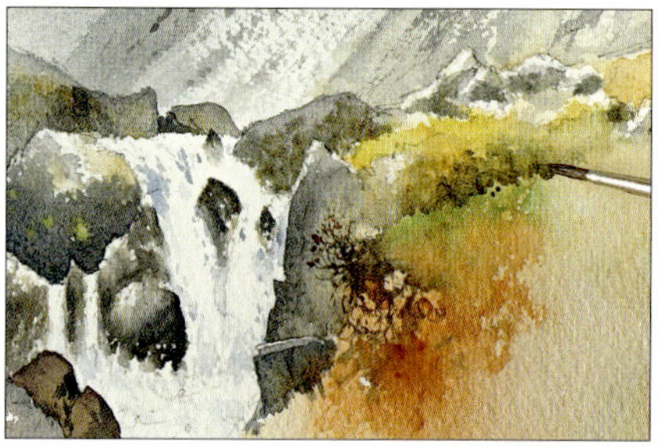

36 Use the no. 4 brush and a mix of raw umber and ultramarine to paint a darker area behind the bright green grass to highlight it.

37 Change to the no. 1 rigger to paint grasses beneath the right-hand rocks with the same mix, then with the no. 4 brush, paint yellow ochre below the grasses and drop in perylene maroon.

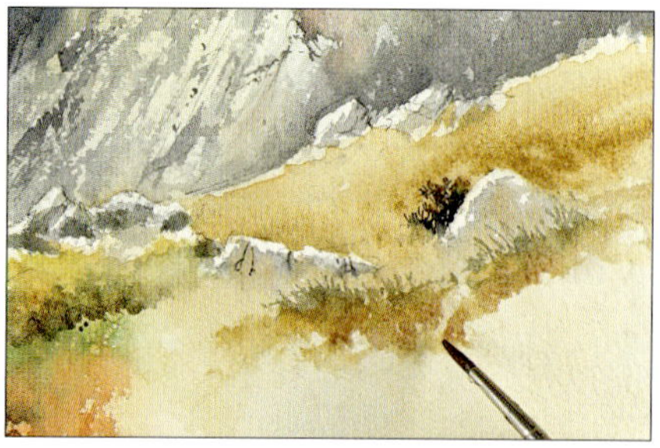

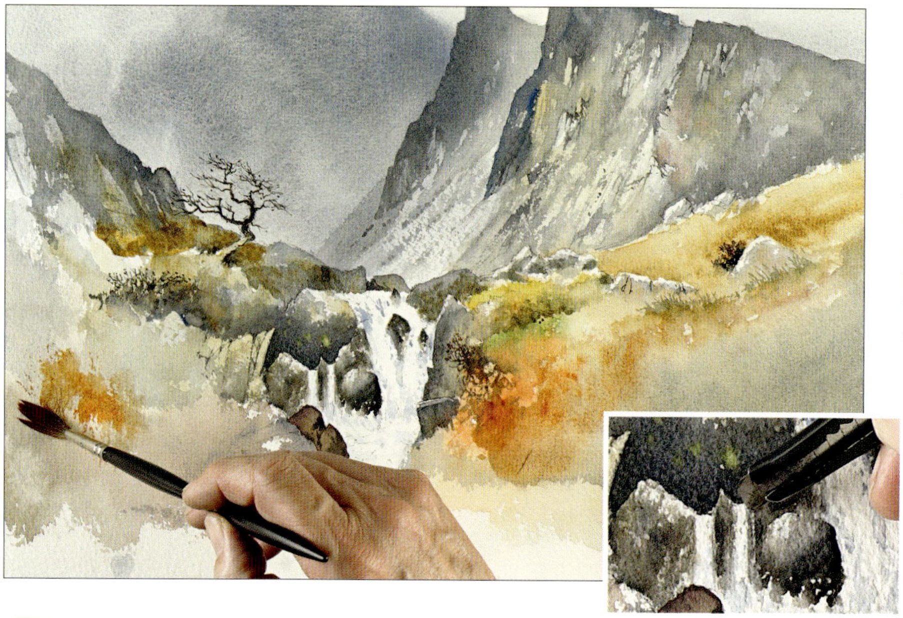

38 Wet the painting at the bottom and use the no. 7 brush and burnt umber and ultramarine to grey the lower part of the right-hand side. Drop in burnt sienna wet into wet, and paint some on the left-hand side to balance it. Paint more of the burnt umber and ultramarine mix to subdue any areas that are too light, and allow to dry. Use the scalpel blade to scratch out drips of water against the dark rock.

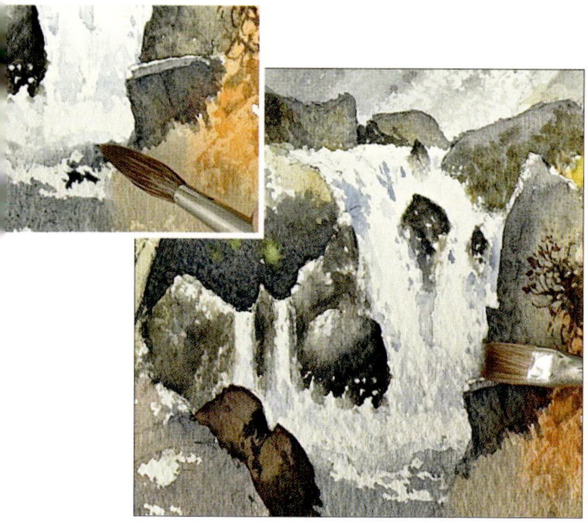

39 Paint a little ultramarine and burnt umber at the bottom of the waterfall with the no. 7 brush, then use the 6mm (¼in) flat brush with clean water to soften the rock to the right, creating the effect of misty spray.

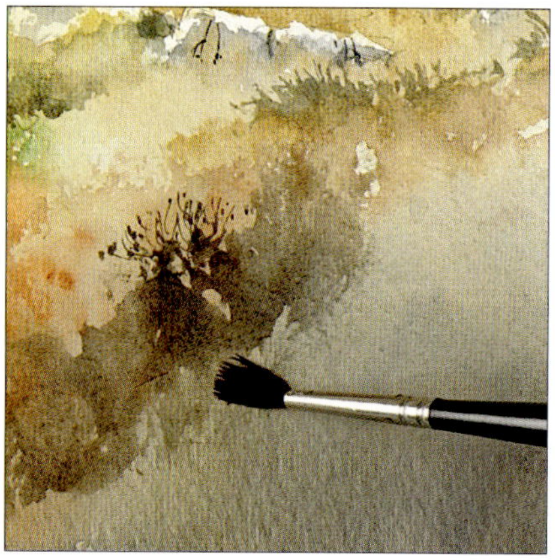

40 Paint heather on the right with the no. 1 rigger and ultramarine and burnt umber, then use the no. 4 brush to add tone around it.

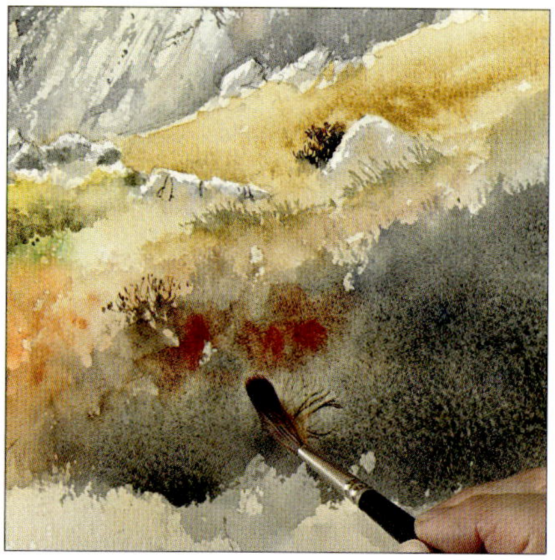

41 Darken the bottom right-hand side of the painting with the no. 7 brush and a bluer mix of the same colours, then drop in perylene maroon.

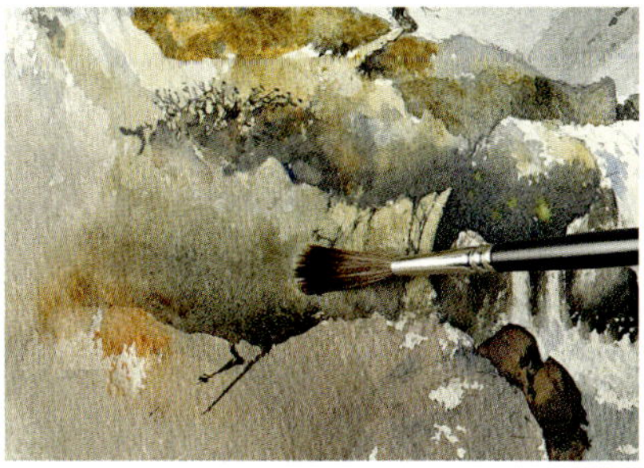

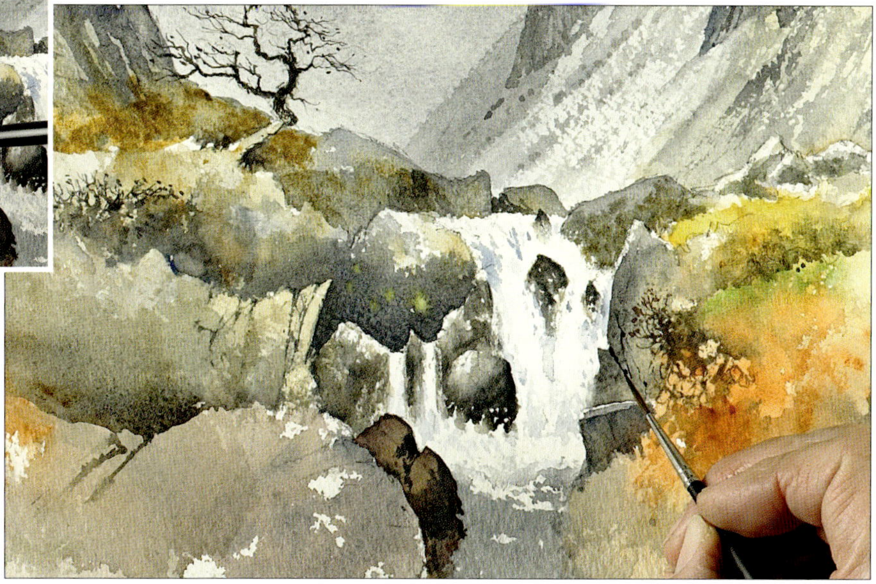

42 Use the no. 7 brush and ultramarine and burnt umber to suggest rock shapes on the left of the painting. Change to the no. 1 rigger to add fractures to various rocks.

The finished painting.

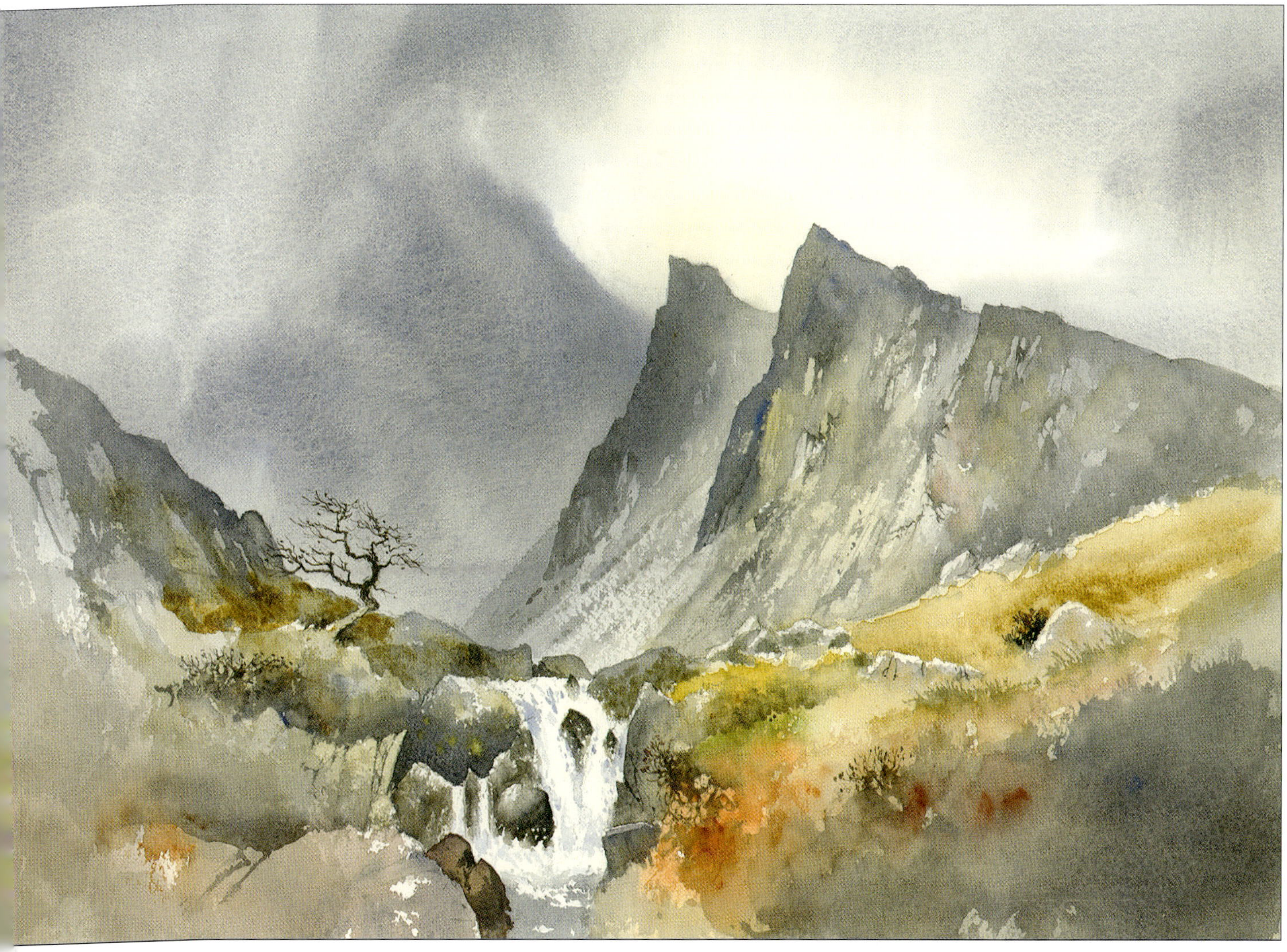

Index

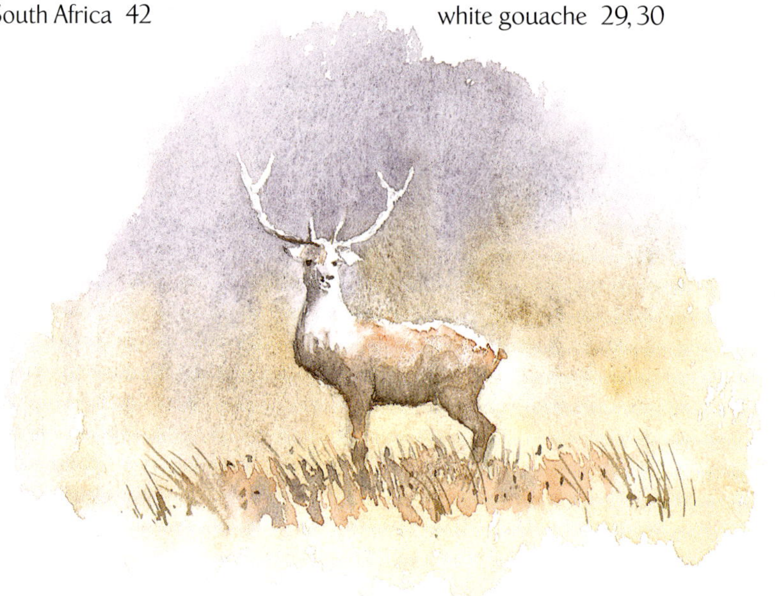